Halving hunger: it can be done

Lead authors
Pedro Sanchez, Coordinator
M.S. Swaminathan, Coordinator
Philip Dobie
Nalan Yuksel

UN Millennium Project
Task Force on Hunger
2005

EARTHSCAN
London • Sterling, Va.

Millennium Project

First published by Earthscan in the UK and USA in 2005

Reprinted 2005

ISBN: 1844072207 paperback

For a full list of publications please contact:

Earthscan
8–12 Camden High Street
London, NW1 0JH, UK
Tel: +44 (0)20 7387 8558
Fax: +44 (0)20 7387 8998
Email: earthinfo@earthscan.co.uk
Web: www.earthscan.co.uk
22883 Quicksilver Drive, Sterling, VA 20166-2012, USA

Earthscan is an imprint of James and James (Science Publishers) Ltd and publishes in association with the International Institute for Environment and Development

A catalogue record for this book is available from the British Library

Library of Congress Cataloging-in-Publication Data

A catalog record has been requested

This publication should be cited as: UN Millennium Project 2005. *Halving Hunger: It Can Be Done.* Task Force on Hunger.

Photos: Front cover Christopher Dowswell/UNDP; back cover, top to bottom, Christopher Dowswell/UNDP, Pedro Cote/UNDP, Giacomo Pirozzi/Panos Pictures, Liba Taylor/Panos Pictures, Jørgen Schytte/UNDP, UN Photo Library, Giacomo Pirozzi/UNICEF, Curt Carnemark/World Bank, Pedro Cote/UN, Franck Charton/UNICEF, Paul Chesley/Getty Images, Ray Witlin/World Bank, Pete Turner/Getty Images.

This book was edited, designed, and produced by Communications Development Inc., Washington, D.C., and its UK design partner, Grundy & Northedge.

The Millennium Project was commissioned by the UN Secretary-General and supported by the UN Development Group, which is chaired by the Administrator of the United Nations Development Programme. The report is an independent publication that reflects the views of the members of the Task Force on Hunger, who contributed in their personal capacity. This publication does not necessarily reflect the views of the United Nations, the United Nations Development Programme, or their Member States.

Printed in Malta by Gutenberg Press on elemental chlorine-free paper

Foreword

The world has an unprecedented opportunity to improve the lives of billions of people by adopting practical approaches to meeting the Millennium Development Goals. At the request of UN Secretary-General Kofi Annan, the UN Millennium Project has identified practical strategies to eradicate poverty by scaling up investments in infrastructure and human capital while promoting gender equality and environmental sustainability. These strategies are described in the UN Millennium Project's report *Investing in Development: A Practical Plan to Achieve the Millennium Development Goals,* which was coauthored by the coordinators of the UN Millennium Project task forces.

The task forces have identified the interventions and policy measures needed to achieve each of the Goals. In *Halving Hunger: It Can Be Done,* the Task Force on Hunger underscores that the goal to reduce hunger by half by 2015 is achievable with proven, effective, targeted interventions—a message that is shared in *Investing in Development. Halving Hunger* calls for concrete steps to reduce hunger across the world through actions in several key areas, including investments to improve the agricultural production of food-insecure farmers, improvements in the nutritional status of the chronically hungry and vulnerable, investments in productive safety nets, promotion of rural markets and off-farm employment to increase the incomes of the hungry, and restoration and conservation of natural resources essential for food security.

These specific investments require political actions by local and national governments and international development partners, and the report identifies and describes these actions in thoughtful detail. The report also urges an urgent focus on "hunger hotspots" around the world, places where a significant proportion of children suffer from chronic undernutrition.

This report has been prepared by a group of leading experts who contributed in their personal capacity and generously volunteered their time and great expertise to this important task. I am very grateful for their thorough and skilled efforts, and I know that the avenues of action they have outlined in this report will make an important contribution to achieving the Millennium Development Goals. I strongly recommend this report to all who are interested in halving hunger by 2015, a goal that certainly should be embraced, and achieved, around the world.

Jeffrey D. Sachs
New York
January 17, 2005

Contents

Figures

Maps

Tables

Task force members

Task force coordinators

Pedro A. Sanchez, Director of Tropical Agriculture, The Earth Institute at Columbia University, New York, N.Y., United States (2002 World Food Prize laureate)

M.S. Swaminathan, UNESCO Chair of Ecotechnology and President, M. S. Swaminathan Research Foundation, Chennai, India (1989 World Food Prize laureate)

Task force members

Abenaa Akuamoa-Boateng, Head of Nutrition Ashanti Region, Ministry of Health, Kumasi, Ghana

Tom Arnold, Chief Executive, Concern Worldwide, Dublin, Ireland

Richard Beahrs, President and Chief Operating Officer (retired), Court TV, New York, United States

David Beckmann, President, Bread for the World and Bread for the World Institute, Washington, D.C., United States

Bo Bengtsson, Professor Emeritus, Department of Crop Science, Swedish University of Agricultural Sciences, Uppsala, Sweden

Roland Bunch, Program Coordinator, Sustainable Agriculture and Rural Livelihoods, World Neighbors, Palo Alto, United States

Kevin Cleaver, Director, Agriculture and Rural Development Department, World Bank, Washington, D.C., United States

William Dar, Director General, International Crops Research Institute for the Semiarid Tropics, Patancheru, India

Glenn Denning, Director, Millennium Development Goals Technical Support Centre, Associate Director of Tropical Agriculture, The Earth Institute at Columbia University, Nairobi, Kenya

Philip Dobie, Director, Drylands Development Centre, United Nations Development Programme, Nairobi, Kenya

Don S. Doering, Senior Associate, Winrock International, Washington, D.C., United States

Christopher Dowswell, Special Assistant to the President, Sasakawa Global 2000, Mexico City, Mexico

Hans Eenhoorn, Senior Vice President (retired), Unilever, Rotterdam, The Netherlands

Joan Holmes, President, The Hunger Project, New York, United States

Robert Horsch, Vice President, Product and Technology Cooperation, Monsanto Company, St. Louis, United States

Bashir Jama, Regional Coordinator for East and Central Africa, World Agroforestry Centre, Nairobi, Kenya

Monty P. Jones, Executive Secretary, Forum for Agricultural Research in Africa, Accra, Ghana (2004 World Food Prize laureate)

Freddie Kwesiga, Regional Coordinator for Southern Africa, World Agroforestry Centre, Harare, Zimbabwe

Peter Matlon, Director, Africa Regional Program, Rockefeller Foundation, Nairobi, Kenya

Njabulo Nduli, Deputy Director-General for Agricultural Production and Resources Management, Department of Agriculture, Pretoria, South Africa

Johnson Nkuuhe, Member of Parliament, Kampala, Uganda

Timothy Reeves, Director General (retired), International Maize and Wheat Improvement Center, Geelong, Australia

Sara J. Scherr, Director of Ecosystem Services and Director of Ecoagriculture Partners, Forest Trends, Washington, D.C., United States

Meera Shekar, Senior Nutrition Specialist, World Bank, Washington, D.C., United States

Kostas Stamoulis, Chief, Agricultural Sector in the Economic Development Service, Food and Agriculture Organization of the United Nations, Rome, Italy

Joachim von Braun, Director General, International Food Policy Research Institute, Washington, D.C., United States

Florence Wambugu, Director, Africa Harvest Biotech Foundation International, Nairobi, Kenya

Patrick Webb, Chief of Nutrition, Policy, Strategy and Program Support Division, United Nations World Food Programme, Rome, Italy

Lars Wiersholm, Senior Vice President (retired), Yara International, Norway

Task force manager

Lisa Dreier, Program Manager, Tropical Agriculture Program, The Earth Institute at Columbia University, New York, United States

Task force associates

Individuals who have made major analytic contributions to the work of the task force:

Akin Adesina, Associate Director, Food Security, The Rockefeller Foundation, Nairobi, Kenya

Chandrika Bahadur, Policy Advisor, UN Millennium Project, New York, United States

Alex de Sherbinin, Senior Staff Associate, Center for International Earth Science Information Network, New York, United States

Rafael Flor, Research Coordinator, Tropical Agriculture Program, The Earth Institute at Columbia University, New York, United States

Lawrence Haddad, Director, Institute for Development Studies, Brighton, United Kingdom

Nwanze Okidegbe, Rural Strategy Advisor, World Bank, Washington, D.C., United States

Cheryl Palm, Senior Research Scientist, Tropical Agriculture Program, Earth Institute at Columbia University, New York, United States

Manohar Sharma, Research Fellow, Food Consumption and Nutrition, International Food Policy Research Institute, Washington, D.C., United States

Adam Storeygard, Staff Associate, Center for International Earth Science Information Network, New York, United States

Nalan Yuksel, Policy Advisor, Canadian International Development Agency, Ottawa, Canada

Preface

This report sets out priority interventions for the world to address immediately to halve hunger by 2015. It builds on the many previous attempts to eliminate world hunger that resulted in cutting the proportion of hungry people in the world from 33 percent to 18 percent in the past 40 years. Yet 852 million people still go to bed hungry every night. Most current plans share the view that it is feasible to rapidly reduce hunger. What is needed now is to translate recommendations into action on a scale commensurate with the problem. What is needed are business plans created at the country level that, in addition to identifying the recommended interventions, outline how they will be implemented, where the priority areas of intervention are, which organizations should implement them, how much the interventions are going to cost, and what the benefits will be. This report provides guidelines for poor countries to develop such plans.

On July 5, 2004, the UN Secretary-General addressed heads of African states and senior members of the international community at a presidential-level seminar on hunger in Addis Ababa, Ethiopia. Deploring "one of the most serious problems on earth—the plague of hunger," he stated, "Hunger is a complex crisis. To solve it, we must address the interconnected challenges of agriculture; healthcare; nutrition; adverse and unfair market conditions; weak infrastructure; and environmental degradation." He called for a "uniquely African Green Revolution in the twenty-first century" to spearhead the fight against hunger.

This report sets out actions that respond to the Secretary-General's call for concerted action to reduce hunger—in Africa and throughout the world. It differs from other global initiatives in its response to the Millennium Development Goals and its interdependence with the recommendations of the nine other task forces addressing the other Goals. The interventions recommended here are based on scientifically sound, proven, and effective approaches, policies, and technologies, as well as on the expert judgment of the task force members.

The Task Force on Hunger was charged with being conceptually right, analytically strong, and politically bold. The independence of the task force, with all members acting in their personal capacity and asked to "leave their institutional baggage at the door," was coupled with a secretariat that produced analysis and experience based on country case studies and extensive dialogue with stakeholders. The task force's seven main recommendations, and the interventions embedded in each of them, may challenge the status quo and make some practitioners uneasy. But the time has come for major changes, both in attitudes and resources, to reach the hunger Goal.

The work of the task force was supported by many individuals and institutions who generously contributed their expertise, financial resources, or in-kind support. To all of them, we are very grateful.

Our conclusion is that hunger can be halved by 2015 and eventually eradicated from our planet—with the deliberate and timely implementation of the recommendations in this report. It can be done.

Pedro A. Sanchez and M.S. Swaminathan
Coordinators, Task Force on Hunger, New York and Chennai
January 17, 2005

The Task Force on Hunger's methodology

The Task Force held intensive discussions at meetings in New York (October 2002), Nairobi and Lilongwe (March 2003), Des Moines (October 2003), Delhi and Chennai (February 2004), Kampala (April 2004), Addis Ababa (July 2004), and Bellagio (September 2004). In between meetings, members and associates engaged in extensive email dialogues that helped shape the task force's thinking and conclusions. Several contentious issues were exhaustively discussed until a consensus emerged. These issues included the relative importance of agricultural versus nutritional interventions, development versus food aid, mineral versus organic fertilizers, plant biotechnology versus conventional breeding approaches—and others. Field studies were conducted in Western Kenya; Southern Malawi; Tigray, Ethiopia; and Rajasthan, Chennai, and Pondicherry in India. The fieldwork enabled members and associates to develop a common framework around hunger issues, and to discuss it with farmers, community members, national government leaders, and institutions working in the field. Regional consultations were held with South Asian stakeholders in Delhi (February 2004) and with African stakeholders in Kampala (April 2004) to provide a "reality check" for the emerging recommendations. A special consultation on three key issues (soil health, markets, and reinventing extension) was held at the World Bank in June 2004.

The task force commissioned 15 papers dealing with a variety of issues, many of them through the International Food Policy Research Institute (see appendix 2 for a complete listing). The papers provided the analytical basis for our recommendations, but we also relied on our expert judgment when conclusive data were not available. The task force also undertook original research on hunger hotspots, in close collaboration with associates and with the Center for International Earth Science Information Network at Columbia University and the M.S. Swaminathan Research Foundation in Chennai, India. This research and the task force's emerging recommendations were presented in a background paper in January 2003 and in an interim report in December 2003.

Together with other task forces, advisory work in pilot countries was conducted in Ghana, Kenya, and Ethiopia through the newly established Millennium Development Goals Technical Support Centre in Nairobi, as well as in Uganda, a pilot country specific to our task force. These studies sharpened our analysis through interactions with government officials, donors, and the national nongovernmental organization community.

Task force members presented work in progress and solicited feedback through a wide array of invited presentations. In Europe these included presentations at the Food and Agriculture Organization, the International Fund for Agricultural Development, the United Nations World Food Programme (Rome); Trinity College and the United Nations World Food Programme Senior Management Conference (Dublin); the Agricultural University and the Ministry of Development Cooperation (Norway); and the OECD Donor Assistance Committee (Stockholm, Paris). In India, the National Food Summit, Delhi. In Africa, the Consultative Group on International Agricultural Research Annual General Meeting, held at the United Nations Environment Programme, Nairobi; various working sessions with the New Partnership for Africa's Development (Johannesburg); several meetings of the Ethiopia Food Security Coalition, Addis Ababa; the Forum for Agricultural Research in Africa, Dakar; the Economic Commission for Africa, Addis Ababa; and the 2020 Conference on Food Security in Africa, in Kampala. In Canada, the Canadian International Development Agency, the International Development Research Centre, and Guelph University. In the United States, the International Center for Research on Women; the World Bank 2003 Rural Week and other meetings; the United States Agency for International Development, the U.S. Congress Senate Agriculture and Foreign Relations Committees and House of Representatives Human Rights and Congressional Human Rights Caucus; the United Nations Development Programme, UN Economic and Social Council; the UN Commission on Sustainable Development; the UN Standing Committee on Nutrition; the American Society of Agronomy, World Food Prize Symposia 2002, 2003, and 2004; the Council on Foreign Relations; New York Academy of Sciences; New State of the Planet Conference and Mailman School of Public Health, Columbia University; the Marine Biological Laboratory, Woods Hole, Mass.; Kansas State University; Crop Science Society of America; University of Florida; International Food Policy Research Institute; University of Missouri; World Agricultural Forum; Cornell University; and Ohio State University. In Mexico, the Monterrey Bridge Coalition, and the Consultative Group on International Agricultural Research 2004 Annual General Meeting in Mexico City.

A focal point of the task force's constituency-building was the presidential-level seminar on "Innovative Approaches to Meeting the Hunger Millennium

Development Goal in Africa," cohosted by the government of Ethiopia and the Task Force on Hunger on July 5, 2004, in Addis Ababa. At that meeting, which drew seven heads of state and more than 550 policymakers, UN Secretary-General Kofi Annan called for the launch of a "Uniquely African Green Revolution in the Twenty-first Century."

Acknowledgments

The Task Force on Hunger is indebted to the many individuals, institutions, and communities that contributed to its work.

Jeffrey Sachs provided bold leadership for the UN Millennium Project. He and the staff of the Project Secretariat, particularly John McArthur and Chandrika Bahadur, contributed tremendously to our work.

Many institutions generously hosted or co-organized task force meetings, events, or study tours in Africa, India, Europe, and the United States: the Earth Institute at Columbia University, the International Food Policy Research Institute, the International Livestock Research Institute, the UN Millennium Project, the New Economic Partnership for Africa's Development, the Rockefeller Foundation, the M.S. Swaminathan Foundation, the World Agroforestry Centre, the World Bank, the World Food Prize Foundation, and the United Nations World Food Programme in India, Ethiopia, and Italy.

The task force drew from the research and expertise of many institutions engaged in hunger-related issues. It also commissioned research papers to augment the knowledge base, with thanks to all the authors who contributed. At the International Food Policy Research Institute: Stuart Gillespie, Suneetha Kadiyala, Joseph M. Hunt, Natalia Caldes, Akhter Ahmed, Ruth Meinzen-Dick, Monica di Gregorio, Lawrence Haddad, Joanne Gaskell, Manohar Sharma. At the M.S. Swaminathan Research Foundation: Swarna S. Vepa, Lavanya Ravikanth Anneboina, Ruchita Manghnani. At Bread for the World: David Beckmann and Emily Byers. At the International Research Institute for Climate Prediction: James W. Hansen, Maxx Dilley, Lisa Goddard, Esther Ebrahimian, Polly Ericksen. The Center for International Earth Science Information Network prepared all the GIS-based maps for this report, together with Rafael Flor of the Earth Institute, and conducted spatially based statistical analysis by Alex de Sherbinin, Marc Levy, Adam Storeygard, Deborah Balk.

At the International Center for Research on Women: Kavita Sethuraman and Kathy Kurz. At the World Bank: Kevin Cleaver, Andrew Goodland, Meera Shekar. At Columbia University: Jeffrey D. Sachs, Daniel Hillel. In addition, we thank Sara Scherr, lead author of the task force's background paper, Don Doering, lead author of the task force's interim report, and Philip Dobie and Nalan Yuksel, lead authors of the final report, for their extraordinary hard work. Lisa Dreier and Rafael Flor served as contributing authors to the final report, together with many members of the task force.

The task force is grateful to its donors and funding partners, whose support allowed our group to undertake broad participation and stakeholder engagement. Agencies that generously supported the Task Force on Hunger are the United Nations Millennium Project Trust Fund, the United Nations Development Programme, the Canadian International Development Agency, the U.K. Department for International Development, the Earth Institute at Columbia University, Development Cooperation Ireland, the Rockefeller Foundation, the Swedish International Development Association, the World Bank, and the United Nations World Food Programme.

The task force extends deep appreciation to those who provided incisive reviews of this report, particularly Professors Per Pinstrup-Andersen and Christopher Barrett of Cornell University, as well as the Food and Agriculture Organization, the United Nations World Food Programme, the World Bank, the UN Standing Committee on Nutrition, the U.K. Department for International Development, and many others. They contributed much to the final quality of this report.

Last, we thank the communities in hungry regions visited by the task force. They inspired us with their tenacity, innovations, and hope. We dedicate this work to them.

Abbreviations

CGIAR	Consultative Group on International Agricultural Research
EU	European Union
FAO	United Nations Food and Agriculture Organization
GDP	gross domestic product
HIV/AIDS	human immunodeficiency virus/acquired immune deficiency syndrome
IMF	International Monetary Fund
NGO	nongovernmental organization
OECD	Organisation for Economic Co-operation and Development
PRSP	Poverty Reduction Strategy Paper
USAID	United States Agency for International Development
USAID/MOST	United States Agency for International Development Micronutrient Program
WHO	World Health Organization

goals

Millennium Development Goals

Goal 1 **Eradicate extreme poverty and hunger**	**Target 1.** Halve, between 1990 and 2015, the proportion of people whose income is less than $1 a day **Target 2.** Halve, between 1990 and 2015, the proportion of people who suffer from hunger
Goal 2 **Achieve universal primary education**	**Target 3.** Ensure that, by 2015, children everywhere, boys and girls alike, will be able to complete a full course of primary schooling
Goal 3 **Promote gender equality and empower women**	**Target 4.** Eliminate gender disparity in primary and secondary education, preferably by 2005, and in all levels of education no later than 2015
Goal 4 **Reduce child mortality**	**Target 5.** Reduce by two-thirds, between 1990 and 2015, the under-five mortality rate
Goal 5 **Improve maternal health**	**Target 6.** Reduce by three-quarters, between 1990 and 2015, the maternal mortality ratio
Goal 6 **Combat HIV/AIDS, malaria, and other diseases**	**Target 7.** Have halted by 2015 and begun to reverse the spread of HIV/AIDS **Target 8.** Have halted by 2015 and begun to reverse the incidence of malaria and other major diseases

Goal 7

Ensure environmental sustainability

Target 9.

Integrate the principles of sustainable development into country policies and programs and reverse the loss of environmental resources

Target 10.

Halve, by 2015, the proportion of people without sustainable access to safe drinking water and basic sanitation

Target 11.

Have achieved by 2020 a significant improvement in the lives of at least 100 million slum dwellers

Goal 8

Develop a global partnership for development

Target 12.

Develop further an open, rule-based, predictable, nondiscriminatory trading and financial system (includes a commitment to good governance, development, and poverty reduction—both nationally and internationally)

Target 13.

Address the special needs of the Least Developed Countries (includes tariff- and quota-free access for Least Developed Countries' exports, enhanced program of debt relief for heavily indebted poor countries [HIPCs] and cancellation of official bilateral debt, and more generous official development assistance for countries committed to poverty reduction)

Target 14.

Address the special needs of landlocked developing countries and small island developing states (through the Program of Action for the Sustainable Development of Small Island Developing States and 22nd General Assembly provisions)

Target 15.

Deal comprehensively with the debt problems of developing countries through national and international measures in order to make debt sustainable in the long term

Target 16.

In cooperation with developing countries, develop and implement strategies for decent and productive work for youth

Target 17.

In cooperation with pharmaceutical companies, provide access to affordable essential drugs in developing countries

Target 18.

In cooperation with the private sector, make available the benefits of new technologies, especially information and communications technologies

Executive summary

Over the past 20 years, the proportion of the world's people who are hungry has declined from one-fifth to one-sixth, and the absolute number of hungry people has fallen slightly. But 852 million people are still chronically or acutely malnourished. Most of them are in Asia, particularly India (221 million) and China (142 million). Sub-Saharan Africa has 204 million hungry and is the only region of the world where the prevalence of both general undernourishment and children's underweight status are increasing. If current trends continue, this region will not only fail to achieve the hunger Goal, but it is likely to suffer from increasing numbers of hungry people. That is why this report emphasizes the needs of Sub-Saharan Africa while addressing global hunger.

Hunger continues to be a global tragedy. It requires a concerted and persistent worldwide effort to eliminate it. The Task Force on Hunger is convinced that hunger can be halved by 2015. Indeed, the task force will not be satisfied with the mere attainment of that goal. It sees reaching the hunger Goal as a milestone in the global effort to eliminate hunger.

Setting the stage

Hunger is both a cause and an effect of poverty—it holds back economic growth and limits progress in reducing poverty. The negative economic impact of hunger is dramatic, with annual losses of at least 6–10 percent in forgone GDP due to losses in labor productivity. Economic growth alone is insufficient for eliminating hunger because so many hungry people live in deep "poverty traps," beyond the reach of markets. Poor and hungry people often face social and political exclusion, unable to demand their rights. They have little access to education, health services, and safe drinking water.

The challenge of halving hunger is thus closely linked with that of achieving the other Millennium Development Goals (see Goals on p. xxiv). Reducing

Reducing hunger should be a major part of poverty reduction strategies

hunger will speed progress toward other Goals, and vice versa. Political action to reduce hunger should address hunger, poverty, and disease simultaneously. It is particularly important that reducing hunger should be a major part of poverty reduction strategies, since little progress in reducing poverty is likely as long as large numbers of people suffer from malnutrition.

Kinds of hunger

Hunger occurs in three different forms: acute, chronic, and hidden. Most people with access to television have seen haunting images of the starvation that typically occurs during famines and disasters. But those suffering from such acute hunger represent only a small part—roughly 10 percent—of the world's hungry. Most of the hungry, approximately 90 percent, are chronically undernourished. Chronic undernourishment is caused by a constant or recurrent lack of access to food of sufficient quality and quantity, good healthcare, and necessary caring practices. It results in underweight and stunted children—as well as high child mortality brought about by associated diseases. Hidden hunger, caused by a lack of essential micronutrients (vitamins and minerals), afflicts more than 2 billion, even when they consume adequate amounts of calories and protein. The world has demonstrated its generosity in helping the victims of acute hunger. Unfortunately chronic and hidden forms of hunger are not as dramatic, and receive much less global attention and support.

Causes of hunger

People go hungry despite an abundant world food supply, because they cannot obtain food of sufficient quantity or quality to meet their nutritional requirements. There are many reasons for this to be so. In analyses by the task force and other researchers, the following factors emerged as strongly correlated with high levels of underweight preschool children in developing countries: poverty, low food production, mothers' lack of education, poor water, sanitation and health facilities, and climatic shocks. Research has found that women's education was associated with 43 percent of the reduction in child malnutrition between 1970 and 1995, followed by increases in agricultural production (26 percent), and improvements in the health environment (19 percent) and in women's status relative to men (12 percent).

Adequate nutrition begins at the household level, where gender discrimination, traditional practices, and inadequate nutrition awareness can limit the food intake of women and children. For example, the best nourishment for small children is exclusive breastfeeding for the first six months, then breastfeeding plus complementary foods through their first two years. Yet women may not be able to produce breastmilk of sufficient quality and quantity when they themselves are malnourished. In some parts of the world, intrahousehold inequalities may result in women and girls eating last, finishing what remains after the men and boys have eaten.

Poverty is a major cause of hunger

Many women, besides having limited education, become mothers at a young age, have improper birth spacing, and lack awareness of or access to basic nutrition and child nurturing. Undernourished, they often become anemic when they are pregnant due to lack of iron in their diet. This increases the risk of low birthweight in their babies, perpetuating a vicious circle of malnourishment over generations. Good health, coupled with safe water and good sanitation, is vital for maintaining adequate nutrition. Common infectious diseases prevent people from absorbing and utilizing food properly, and parasites often compete for much that is eaten.

The interaction works both ways. Malnutrition and hunger are the number one risk factor for illness worldwide. The interactive threats of hunger and HIV/AIDS in parts of the world are leading to complex humanitarian crises, whereby people affected by AIDS are unable to grow food or work for a living. Moreover, malnourishment weakens the immune system and strength of those affected by HIV/AIDS, making them succumb more quickly to the disease. Similarly, nearly 57 percent of malaria deaths are attributable to malnutrition.

Poverty is a major cause of hunger. Despite the increases in food production brought about by the Green Revolution and the associated declines in food prices, many poor people still cannot afford to buy enough food of sufficient quality in the market place. Their poverty is often associated with macro and micronutrient deficiencies—typically due to limited diets based on basic starchy foods, with little in the way of animal products, vegetables, and fruits, which tend to be more expensive. Ways of improving economic access to sufficient food and to a balanced diet remains a major challenge.

Despite gains in the yields of major food crops, low food production persists in rural areas, especially where agriculture is rainfed. Paradoxically, a high percentage of the world's hungry people are either farmers or others who earn their living in rural areas. The worst affected rural areas are those most remote from markets—or where food production is risky due to economic, environmental, climatic, or other shocks. Poor access to markets means that many farmers are unable to diversify from staple food crops into higher value commodities or add value to their output through processing enterprises. Because of indebtedness, poor grain storage, and the urgent need for cash, many small farmers are forced to sell their crop for a low price after harvest, only later to buy grain in the market at a higher price to feed their families until the next harvest.

Who are the hungry?

The hungry are the poor and the vulnerable. Many of these households are unable to obtain enough food to feed the family. While accurate data are difficult to find, estimates indicate that the majority of hungry people live in rural areas. The task force believes that about half of the hungry are smallholder

Roughly half of the hungry are in smallholder farm households

farming households unable either to grow or to buy enough food to meet the family's requirements.

Adequate employment opportunities to boost the purchasing power of the poor are seldom available off the farm in poor rural areas. We estimate that roughly two-tenths of the hungry are landless rural people. A smaller group, perhaps one-tenth of the hungry, are pastoralists, fisherfolk, and people who depend on forests for their livelihoods. For them, the conservation of their environment is vital to their nutrition. The remaining share of the hungry, around two-tenths, live in urban areas. Hunger spurs many to leave stagnant and isolated rural economies, migrating to cities where they swell the ranks of the urban poor, many of whom also go hungry, especially when they first arrive.

Where are the hungry?

Maps of hunger commonly show which countries have high levels, but not where the concentrations are within a country. As an attempt to show the variation within a country, the task force focused on subnational units (states, provinces, or districts) to identify hunger hotspots. Hunger hotspots are defined as subnational units where the prevalence of underweight children under age five is greater than or equal to 20 percent. Of the 605 subnational units (provinces, states, or districts) analyzed, the task force identified 313 hunger hotspots, where chronic hunger is most persistent and severe. By identifying areas with these high percentages of underweight children, hotspots reveal levels of malnutrition defined by the World Health Organization (WHO) and by the Task Force on Hunger as "high" and "very high."

- Of 366 subnational units analyzed in Africa, 229 were found to have a prevalence of underweight children under age five of 20 percent or higher. These hunger hotspots contain about 28 million preschool children who are underweight—around 88 percent of Africa's underweight children under age five.
- Of 172 subnational units analyzed in Asia, 76 are considered hunger hotspots. These contain approximately 78 million preschool children who are underweight, or around 95 percent of Asia's underweight children under age five.
- In Latin America and the Caribbean, only 106 subnational units were identified due to limited data; of these, only 8 met the definition as hotspots. These 8 units contain about 400,000 preschool children who are underweight—or around 17 percent of the hungry children in this region.
- Globally, the 313 hunger hotspots identified contain around 107 million preschool children who are underweight—roughly 79 percent of the world's 134 million.

Hungry people are highly vulnerable to crises and hazards they cannot control

This analysis, when supplemented by additional data, can help identify the priority regions for targeting interventions to end hunger. Poor countries are encouraged to refine the analysis with up-to-date data and to define their own hunger hotspots.

Some 71 countries (of 152 countries that have had at least one nutrition survey since 1990) have insufficient data or no data at all for judging their progress in reducing hunger. This high number is alarming. If governments are committed to the hunger Goal, collecting and monitoring reliable data to measure their progress toward this goal should be a priority. Much more investment is needed to collect both national and subnational data. It is also important to begin to standardize sampling units for population density and size.

Vulnerability

Hungry people are highly vulnerable to crises and hazards they cannot control. The crises may be caused by such natural disasters as major droughts or floods or such manmade disasters as war. The hazards include insecure rights to land and other natural resources, lack of improved agricultural technology, inability to store produce after harvest, variations in the weather, widespread environmental degradation, poor health, food shortages, and lack of income-earning opportunities. These elements of vulnerability are the starting point for five of the seven recommendations by the task force. Three key factors—gender inequality, HIV/AIDS, and climate change—exacerbate vulnerability in hungry countries.

Due to existing social inequalities, women are often disproportionately vulnerable to hunger. They produce 60–80 percent of the food in most developing countries and more than 80 percent of the food in Africa. Yet they own only 1 percent of the land and receive only 7 percent of agricultural extension time and resources. While they are responsible for the bulk of agricultural production and most of the household economy, they continue to be bypassed by most agricultural programs. They should be empowered and supported in their multiple roles as food producers, household nutrition managers, marketers and others. Gender equality is not simply socially desirable—it is a central pillar in the fight against hunger.

HIV/AIDS is increasing the vulnerability of millions of chronically hungry households. The interactions of drought, hunger, and AIDS should be better understood by decisionmakers. Agriculture, health, and other sectors should recognize their joint roles and take action together to combat the complex humanitarian crises triggered by HIV/AIDS, applying this report's recommendations in AIDS-affected areas.

The poor and food-insecure are the most vulnerable to the effects of climatic shocks, such as droughts and floods. Climate change is also expected to

The Task Force on Hunger recommends political action at all levels of society

disrupt ecosystems and the production of food on a devastating scale in the years ahead.

The seven recommendations

The UN Millennium Project focuses on the simple but powerful concept of making the Millennium Development Goals the centerpiece of national poverty reduction strategies supported by international processes. This requires focusing on the Goals as policy targets, with poor countries developing a coherent plan to achieve all the Goals by 2015 and rich countries supporting these plans through policy assistance and financial backing.

The task force is not proposing yet another stand-alone strategy for fighting hunger. Instead, we set forth a plan that forms part of a larger effort to address all the Millennium Development Goals simultaneously. Our report complements the UN Millennium Project recommendations in its report *Investing in Development: A Practical Plan to Achieve the Millennium Development Goals* (UN Millennium Project 2005) as well as the reports of the project's nine other task forces. National governments can incorporate these multiple approaches into Millennium Development Goals-based poverty reduction strategies—strategies that too often underemphasize agriculture and nutrition.

Within the UN Millennium Project's framework for achieving the Millennium Development Goals, the task force calls for simultaneous action in seven priority areas (figure 1).

Global-level interventions

Recommendation one: move from political commitment to action

Political commitments to end hunger, made repeatedly, have not been translated into effective action. All member countries of the United Nations committed to halving world hunger at the World Food Summits of 1996 and 2002, at the Millennium Summit of 2000, at the 2002 World Summit on Sustainable Development, and at the 2002 Monterrey Summit on Development Finance. The Task Force on Hunger recommends taking the next step: political action at all levels of society. The recommended interventions in this domain include:

1. Advocate political action to meet intergovernmental agreements to end hunger.
2. Strengthen the contribution of donor countries and developing-country governments to activities that combat hunger.
3. Improve global public awareness of hunger issues and strengthen advocacy organizations committed to ending hunger.
4. Strengthen developing country organizations that deal with hunger alleviation.

Figure 1
Task force recommendations at the global, national, and community scale

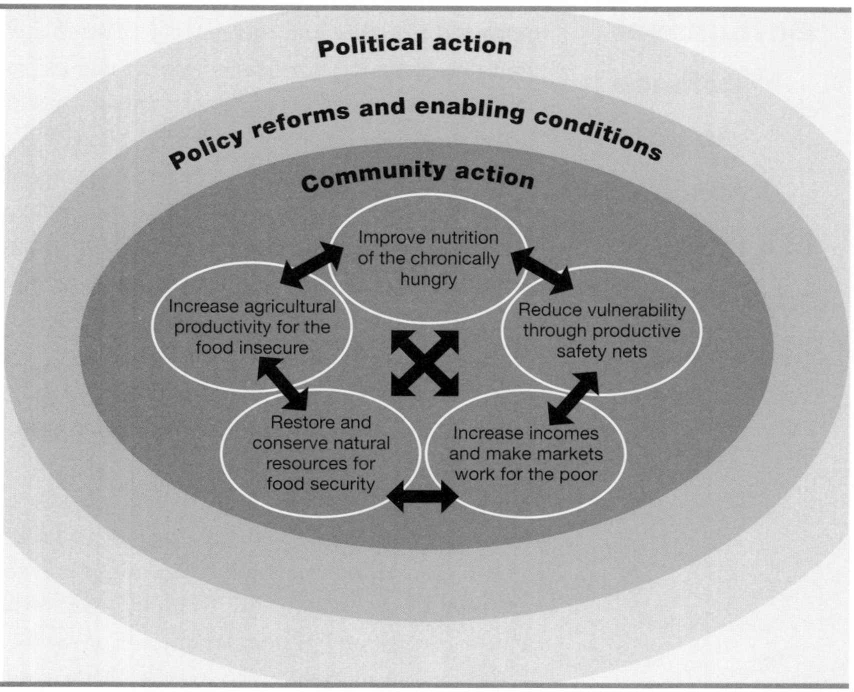

5. Improve monitoring and evaluation processes and practices and ensure accountability among those responsible for implementing antihunger programs.

The key message for political leaders is that halving world hunger is well within our means. What has been lacking is action to implement and scale up known solutions. Kofi Annan, Secretary-General of the United Nations, reinforced this message in July 2004 when he called for a "uniquely African Green Revolution in the twenty-first century." It would capitalize on existing knowledge to transform the region's agriculture, nutrition, and markets—using the pro-poor, pro-women, and pro-environment interventions embedded in this report. Variations of the approach, with greater emphasis on nutrition and markets, apply to parts of Asia and Latin America.

National governments need to be held accountable for the funding and implementation of national programs to address hunger. Establishing measurable indicators of progress and reporting them publicly can help strengthen governance and accountability.

If the hunger Goal is to be met, developed country governments must increase and improve their official development assistance, especially for agriculture and nutrition, and increase attention to capacity building. It is also imperative that they reform their agricultural and trade policies. But despite the need for such reforms, many of the poorest farmers in the developing world are likely to benefit more from the development of domestic and regional markets, at least in the short term. Developing country governments should thus

Government policies in poor countries can make or break efforts to end hunger

improve the quality and increase the scale of their national hunger reduction programs, targeting hotspots where the majority of the hungry live. Brazil and China are two good examples of increased political commitment to address hunger problems in their countries. Success is greatest when governments work in partnership with nongovernmental organizations (NGOs), the private sector, and local communities to bring about change.

Data from the Food and Agriculture Organization (FAO) show that highly food-insecure countries tend to spend two to three times as much on defense as on agriculture—and that the already low levels of investment in agriculture are declining. This combination of declining investment in agriculture and rising military expenditures is extremely worrying—and a sorry indicator of the real priorities of governments and donor agencies, despite their stated commitments.

Building public awareness of hunger and the issues that surround it can provide political leaders with the mandate and support they need to take action. Antihunger coalitions can articulate arguments for action that are compelling both morally and practically. To build broad public support, it is necessary to create a groundswell of popular opinion at the local level.

Strengthening public advocacy is also necessary in developing countries. Local NGOs can act as facilitators, assisting food-insecure groups in voicing their concerns to government. The strengthening and networking of local community and advocacy groups over the past decade is one of the most promising developments in the struggle against hunger.

Key ingredients in working toward the Millennium Development Goals will be accurate data collection and benchmarks to monitor progress. Developing relevant and robust monitoring and evaluation processes and practices is challenging, not least because of the difficulty of reaching agreement on sound and uniform methodologies.

National-level interventions

Recommendation two: reform policies and create an enabling environment

Government policies in poor countries can make or break efforts to end hunger. Good governance, including the rule of law, lack of corruption, and respect for human rights, is essential for promoting food security. Policies conducive to ending hunger and poverty need to be put in place at all levels, from the local to the national. The policy reform process needs to be undertaken in partnership with all stakeholders, including civil society and the private sector. The Task Force on Hunger proposes the following interventions:

1. Promote an integrated policy approach to hunger reduction.
2. Restore budgetary priority to the agricultural and rural sectors.
3. Build developing country capacity to achieve the hunger Goal.

Women's well-being, empowerment, and education are the driving factors in reducing children's malnutrition

4. Link nutritional and agricultural interventions.
5. Increase poor people's access to land and other productive resources.
6. Empower women and girls.
7. Strengthen agricultural and nutrition research.
8. Remove internal and regional barriers to agricultural trade.
9. Increase the effectiveness of donor agencies' hunger-related programming.
10. Create vibrant partnerships to ensure effective policy implementation.

Poor countries need to adopt a multisectoral approach to the reduction of hunger, since action in any one domain is unlikely to be effective by itself. National poverty reduction strategy processes and Poverty Reduction Strategy Papers (PRSPs), where they exist, offer the best opportunities for such an approach. The task force recommends that every low-income country integrate the Millennium Development Goals into its poverty reduction strategy or equivalent national planning process.

The task force recommends that African governments invest at least 10 percent of their national budget specifically in agriculture, in addition to making necessary investments in rural energy, infrastructure, health, education, and conservation of natural resources important for food security.

Building local capacity should be the central goal of both national government and donor-funded activities. One possible example of capacity building could be the creation of a corps of paraprofessional extension workers in agriculture, nutrition, and health, residing in villages identified as hunger hotspots.

Linking nutritional and agricultural interventions, so often implemented separately, would also create more effective hunger-reduction programs. Increasing poor people's access to productive resources is essential for their food security. Clearly assigned and enforceable rights to own, inherit, and trade land must be established, particularly for women. Innovative tenure arrangements, such as community property rights, can also be effective.

Women's well-being, empowerment, and education are the driving factors in reducing children's malnutrition. Political leaders at all levels should work with community groups to empower women through legal, policy, and institutional reforms. Women and girls need better access to such services as credit, healthcare, and education. It is important to develop and introduce technology and farm implements designed for rural women that will ease their workload, such as water harvesting technologies, trees for firewood grown close to home, and implements that minimize tillage.

Agricultural research has been a major driver of hunger reduction. The task force recommends doubling investments in national research to at least 2 percent of agricultural GDP by 2010. We also recommend that donors increase funding to the Consultative Group on International Agricultural Research (CGIAR) to $1 billion by 2010.

Making mineral fertilizers available at affordable prices and using them efficiently remain major challenges

The international community has an important role in removing trade barriers, to allow poor farmers access to developed country agricultural markets. Developing countries could also do more to promote cross-border trade at the regional level.

Donor agencies also have to increase the effectiveness of hunger-related programs. Shared country-level coordination mechanisms, agreements on common monitoring procedures, and systems for sharing results and knowledge are some of the modest steps that could make a difference.

Community-level interventions

Recommendation three: increase the agricultural productivity of food-insecure farmers

Small-scale farming families represent about half the hungry worldwide and probably three-quarters of the hungry in Africa. Raising the productivity of their crops, trees, and livestock is a major priority in the fight against hunger. It is also vital to enhance and sustain the productivity of forests and fisheries, which provide the livelihoods of significant proportions of hungry people. The interventions recommended in this domain are:

1. Improve soil health.
2. Improve and expand small-scale water management.
3. Improve access to better seeds and planting materials.
4. Diversify on-farm enterprises with high-value products.
5. Establish effective extension services.

Restoring health to the soil is often the first entry point for increasing agricultural productivity, especially in Africa. This can be done by applying appropriate combinations of mineral and organic fertilizers, using green manures to improve soil fertility, planting fertilizer trees, returning crop residues to the soil, and using improved methods of soil erosion control and water conservation.

Making mineral fertilizers available at affordable prices and using them efficiently remain major challenges. The task force believes that in critical situations, targeted subsidy programs should be carefully designed to supply both mineral and organic fertilizers to highly food-insecure farmers. Tamper-proof "smart cards," redeemable at private agrodealers, are a promising way of administering targeted subsidies and avoiding the inefficiencies of past subsidy programs. These programs require a long-term commitment to ensure economic growth, but should include a sunset clause so that the subsidies are gradually phased out over a given number of years, say 5–10 years, depending on the local conditions.

In the dry subhumid and semiarid tropics and subtropics, improving water availability can be just as important as improving soil fertility, if not more so. Various water harvesting and small-scale irrigation techniques can trans-

Adequate nutrition lies at the heart of the fight against hunger

form crop and livestock production in these zones. Water-related interventions depend heavily on developing the social capital to manage them at community level; solutions that rely on technology alone are unlikely to succeed.

Genetically superior crops, tree varieties, and improved animal breeds can greatly increase the productivity of small farms. The task force supports both conventional breeding and transgenic research with appropriate biosafety measures. Tolerance of such stresses as drought, salinity, poor soil fertility, pests, and diseases will benefit farmers in the more marginal areas. Early maturing varieties are especially useful in drought-prone areas. There has recently been some exciting progress in developing dual-purpose food/feed crops that enable farmers to diversify into livestock production without jeopardizing their short-term food security.

After farmers attain food security, they can begin to diversify their farming systems toward the production of high-value products. Livestock, farm trees, aquaculture, and vegetables are attractive options for small-scale farmers to diversify their diets and sources of income—and for improving the stability and sustainability of their farming enterprise. Increases in milk production, for example, can reduce malnutrition in both rural and urban settings. Recent growth in the smallholder timber sector suggests that smallholders could emerge as major timber suppliers of the twenty-first century.

Breathing new life into the moribund extension services of many developing countries is vital if the benefits of new knowledge and improved technology are to reach farmers. Despite the many shortcomings of conventional extension services, there are good extension practices and practitioners to help others learn. The task force recommends that every village in a hunger hotspot have extension workers trained in agriculture, together with counterparts in health. One of the most impressive track records is that of farmer field schools in Southeast Asia. This approach is now being developed for use in areas other than integrated pest management, such as soil and water conservation and livestock production.

Recommendation four: improve nutrition for the chronically hungry and vulnerable

Adequate nutrition lies at the heart of the fight against hunger. A targeted life-cycle approach is recommended to reduce the prevalence of underweight children, reduce stunting, and ensure adequate micronutrients for those suffering from vitamin and mineral deficiencies. Particular attention should go to children under the age of two and to supplemental feeding for pregnant and lactating mothers. The five interventions recommended in this domain are:

1. Promote mother and infant nutrition.
2. Reduce malnutrition among children under five years of age.
3. Reduce malnutrition among school-age children and adolescents.
4. Reduce vitamin and mineral deficiencies.

All feeding programs should be sourced, where possible, from locally produced foods rather than imported food aid

5. Reduce the prevalence of infectious diseases that contribute to malnutrition.

As the primary care providers for children and families, women are particularly important in improving nutrition for vulnerable groups. Ensuring universal access to reproductive health services is essential for improving the nutritional status of pregnant women and their children, particularly through the proper spacing of births. Increasing women's income and their control over family assets is also known to improve the nutritional status of their children. To promote community awareness and action in this field, the task force recommends improving both formal networks of paraprofessional nutrition extension workers and informal self-help and mother-to-mother groups of nutrition and health volunteers at the village level.

To break the intergenerational cycle of malnutrition, the task force recommends direct actions focused on supplemental feeding for underweight pregnant and nursing mothers. Exclusive breastfeeding up to six months of age is the best way of ensuring optimum nutrition for babies. Systems need to be put in place to raise awareness of this. But the risk of transmitting HIV through breast milk complicates the decisions women must make to ensure good nutrition for their babies. To reduce malnutrition among malnourished children under five, the task force recommends providing fortified or blended complementary foods, as well as therapeutic care for all seriously malnourished children and women, especially in remote rural areas.

The task force recommends that all feeding programs be sourced, where possible, from locally produced foods rather than imported food aid. These foods can be fortified with micronutrients as needed. School feeding programs can generate synergies with learning, attracting and retaining girls in schools, and opportunities for stimulating local market demand (on the order of a 25 percent increase for maize in Sub-Saharan Africa). Take-home rations can provide an effective economic incentive for poor families to send and keep their children, especially girls, in schools. Comprehensive community- and school-based feeding programs that offer systematic deworming, micronutrient supplementation, education on HIV/AIDS, health, nutrition, and hygiene, safe cooking facilities, drinking water, and improved sanitation can be an excellent platform for improving schools, keeping children healthy, and reaching the community.

Vitamin and mineral intake can be improved by increasing the consumption of micronutrient-rich foods, improving food fortification, and increasing micronutrient supplementation when necessary. All three of these mutually reinforcing actions should be promoted by village extension workers. Countries should give a high priority to promoting the local production of micronutrient-rich foods, such as vegetables and fruits. Both the public and private sectors can do much in developing and supplying fortified foods. Another option is the biofortification of food crops through research, an area that merits more attention.

Developing countries and the international community need to build and strengthen emergency response systems

Parallel health measures are also needed to eliminate diseases that rob people of nutrients. All children should be fully immunized and receive prompt treatment for common infections such as diarrhea, pneumonia, malaria, and intestinal parasites. The Task Force on Hunger fully supports the recommendations of the Working Group on HIV/AIDS, including measures to ensure appropriate nutritional care for people living with or affected by HIV/AIDS.

Recommendation five: reduce the vulnerability of the acutely hungry through productive safety nets

Hungry people are vulnerable to events and influences that they cannot control. These include natural disasters, armed conflicts, catastrophic illness, and political and economic instability. While investing in agriculture, education, and health remains critical to long-term food security, past gains can be threatened if people's vulnerability to short-term disasters and shocks is not tackled head on. The task force recommends the following interventions in this domain:

1. Build and strengthen national and local early warning systems, including advances in climate prediction at the hotspot level.
2. Build and strengthen the capacity to respond to emergencies.
3. Invest in productive safety nets to protect the poorest from short-term shocks and to reduce longer term food insecurity.

Mainstreaming the management of vulnerability to shocks and disasters will allow governments to protect and perhaps even enhance the returns to their investments in long-term development. That means increasing the ability to predict shocks and disasters—and to respond to them quickly when they occur. It also means managing post-crisis investments better, so that they generate assets that take people beyond where they were before the crisis.

The task force recommends that national governments, in partnership with the international community, strengthen their early warning systems, especially for hunger hotspots and pastoralist areas, many of which are often inadequately covered. Early warning systems need to be fairly sophisticated to be effective; the key to effectiveness is knowing when to intervene.

Developing countries and the international community need to build and strengthen emergency response systems. Multiyear budgeting and increased funding for organizations, such as the UN's Immediate Response Account, will help meet the escalating needs for humanitarian relief. The task force recommends that donors, where possible and appropriate, provide cash instead of food aid for relief efforts so that governments can invest more flexibly in reducing hunger among people at risk. The additional resources needed to reduce vulnerability to shocks must not be found by drawing funds away from long-term development.

Better links are needed between actions aimed at overcoming chronic malnutrition and programs addressing acute malnutrition. The successes of relief

Networks of trained rural agrodealers are recommended as a means of reaching remote areas

agencies in refugee camps need to be replicated and scaled up in the broader community during post-emergency recovery periods. One novel approach is community therapeutic care, which emphasizes treating malnourished children at home rather than in rehabilitation centers.

Safety nets should be an effective protector of last resort during shocks and an economically productive tool during noncrisis years. This involves investing in community activities that reduce vulnerability while increasing productivity. Examples include community food banks and the rehabilitation of degraded environments through food-for-work or cash-for-work schemes. If not properly implemented, large injections of cash or food aid can have a distorting effect on a local economy. Therefore, synergistic interventions based on long-term development objectives, such as programs that increase food access through interventions in the labor market, should form an important guiding principle in the design of safety nets.

Recommendation six: increase incomes and make markets work for the poor

The food-insecure either cannot produce enough food themselves or cannot afford to buy food. Properly functioning markets are critical in ensuring that people are able to earn an income, obtain the inputs they need to raise crop yields, and sell their produce at fair prices. The interventions proposed in this domain are:

1. Invest in and maintain market-related infrastructure.
2. Develop networks of small rural input traders.
3. Improve access to financial services for the poor and food-insecure.
4. Provide a sound legal and regulatory framework.
5. Strengthen the bargaining power of rural and urban poor in labor markets.
6. Ensure access to market information for the poor.
7. Promote and strengthen farmers' and community associations.
8. Promote alternative sources of employment and income.

Markets will not develop without public investment in transport and other infrastructure. A major campaign is needed to increase road-building, including paved roads and all-weather feeder roads, in large parts of Africa and also in parts of Asia and Latin America where there are high densities of poverty. Every village should have a vehicle capable of transporting products for sale and helping in health emergencies. Effective grain storage capacity at the local level will enable farmers to obtain fairer prices for their surpluses and reduce post-harvest losses to pests and fungi. Investments in small-scale processing should quickly yield benefits in increased employment opportunities at the local level.

Networks of trained rural agrodealers are recommended as a means of reaching remote areas with agricultural inputs, especially in Africa. The lack of working capital for traders, credit for farmers, and technical knowledge are the

With supermarkets becoming dominant buyers in many poor countries, governments should provide incentives for them to pursue socially responsible policies

three main drawbacks that must be overcome for this approach to work. The private sector, through these agrodealers, would implement targeted voucher programs for soil health and water resources.

Access to credit and other financial services is a particular problem for food-insecure farmers. A system of loan guarantees could provide incentives for poor people to take the risk of borrowing and for financial institutions to lend to poor people. The amounts often exceed microcredit limits, so several mechanisms will be required. Community groups established to borrow on behalf of their members can mitigate risk and make lending more attractive to financial institutions. A promising possibility is to integrate loans with saving services, allowing members to save regularly in small amounts.

Unequal bargaining power between producers and traders, exploitative behavior by companies, and uncertainties over the quality standards required of farmers complicate the transition from subsistence to commercial farming. A properly enforced system of grades and standards is especially important in overcoming such problems. Contract law should be enforced, preferably at the community level with community mediation and arbitration. In this and related areas, the government's primary responsibility is to provide a business-friendly legal and regulatory framework—together with the public goods that will create the incentives for private traders and businesses to establish and operate.

The poor are often forced to accept work at very low wages. Promoting the nonfarm sector will help raise wages by providing alternative employment opportunities. The task force recommends that organizations and programs that empower the rural landless and urban poor in labor markets be strengthened. Labor groups or cooperatives may be able to negotiate higher wages, particularly when they are needed to perform such time-critical jobs as harvesting.

A lack of market information worsens the terms of trade for poor farmers, and access to modern information technology is still rudimentary in many rural areas. But the pace of change is accelerating: governments and donors are investing in Internet technology, and combinations of technology, such as mobile phones, radios, and the Internet are being assembled to bring information to producers. Fishermen in India are now using mobile phones to seek the best price from dealers before deciding where to sell their catch.

Since most of the world's poor and hungry live in rural areas and are already engaged in agriculture, there are significant opportunities for increasing their incomes by encouraging them to gradually shift from food crops to higher value outputs, such as livestock products, and to add value through processing. Out-grower schemes, where farmers grow crops for large producers, can provide important employment opportunities for the poor. But having associations of smallholders enter high-value markets independent of large producers is more likely to increase the share of the final price that small-scale farmers obtain. With supermarkets becoming dominant buyers in many poor countries, gov-

Payments to low-income rural communities for environmental services hold significant potential

ernments should provide incentives for them to pursue socially responsible policies and stimulate local smallholder production.

Recommendation seven: restore and conserve the natural resources essential for food security

The degradation of natural resources, sometimes associated with reduced biodiversity, directly threatens the food security and incomes of poor people. Reversing degradation requires both community and national interventions, supported by inputs from the international community. The interventions recommended in this domain include:

1. Help communities and households restore or enhance natural resources.
2. Secure local ownership, access, and management rights to forests, fisheries, and rangelands.
3. Develop natural resource-based "green enterprises."
4. Pay poor farmers for the environmental services they provide.

To achieve the greatest early impact, the task force recommends targeting investments to degraded areas where hungry people are densely concentrated.

Community-based initiatives for environmental restoration may include rangeland rehabilitation, watershed restoration, establishing village ponds, restoring the vegetation of stream banks, and building vegetative filters and barriers to protect water quality. Biodiversity can be protected by establishing reserves, reforesting degraded areas, and reconstituting fisheries. Key principles for success include building ownership of initiatives among all community members and ensuring short-term gains in food security in addition to long-term sustainability.

Credible rights to land, water, forests, and fisheries are vital for facilitating investment in conservation and restoration. Many countries have legislation to enable rural communities and households to obtain such rights, but institutional constraints hamper effective implementation in many cases. Legal support services are needed to enable the poor to bring claims where their rights are denied. Media campaigns can raise awareness.

"Green enterprises" can generate valuable opportunities to generate income and strengthen livelihoods while establishing incentives to conserve. Such enterprises may trade in natural medicines, nontimber forest products, sustainably grown or certified timber, and other natural products. Success depends on fostering a combination of skills in conservation, business, and management. Access to markets is also key.

Programs providing payments to low-income rural communities for environmental services, though still at an early stage of development, hold significant potential. They include payment for biodiversity protection, watershed protection or restoration, and carbon sequestration. Since many ecosystem services are public goods, government intervention is usually required to create a functioning market.

The task force advocates a new emphasis on multisectoral and multi-stakeholder approaches

Implementing the seven recommendations

There have been many plans for ending hunger, but implementation has often been ineffective or incomplete. Because hunger is such a complex problem, the task force advocates a new emphasis on multisectoral and multistakeholder approaches that tackle the problem simultaneously, comprehensively, and in an integrated manner. The key principles to underpin implementation of hunger reduction programs include:

Identifying priority interventions. Within the seven broad recommendations presented in this report, there are 40 proposed interventions. Not every intervention will be appropriate to every country or district. An important step at the national level will be to identify the priority interventions for the conditions that prevail locally. For example, low food production caused by insufficient agricultural productivity is likely to be the primary reason for hunger in tropical Africa and remote parts of Asia and Latin America, while poverty is considered to be the primary reason for hunger in South and East Asia, Latin America, Central Asia, and the Middle East.

Developing a national strategy. Where national strategies do not exist, the key elements for their formulation include broad participation by stakeholders, including the private sector, NGOs, and donor agencies; thorough analysis of the scope and typologies of hunger at the national level, including identification of hunger hotspots; sound policy design and the integration of the Millennium Development Goals into existing national poverty reduction strategies or, where they exist, PRSPs; and a participatory and transparent monitoring process.

Strengthening capacity. Many of the task force's recommended interventions depend on building national and local capacity. Donors and national governments will need to make long-term commitments to strengthening human, technical, managerial, and institutional capacity at all levels. Capacity building, as one of the key entry points, needs to start immediately.

Adopting a multistakeholder approach. Without local action, efforts to achieve the Goals will remain top-down, supply-driven—and ineffective. All stakeholders need to be involved, particularly local community members, which will require considerable investment in the training of facilitators. Issues of gender equality should form a central component of all community action processes. The private sector can help in addressing the hunger Goal by providing affordable products and services, building links with and among local businesses, creating employment opportunities, building local capacity, supporting government efforts to attract foreign investment, and building the domestic private sector.

The hunger Goal can be achieved and hunger can eventually be eliminated from the face of the earth

Investments needed

The UN Millennium Project estimates that interventions to increase agricultural productivity and reduce chronic hunger will cost, on average, about 5–8 percent of the total costs of achieving the Millennium Development Goals in five low-income countries (UN Millennium Project 2005). This is modest in comparison with the average investments needed in education (16 percent), health (25 percent), energy (15 percent), and roads (18 percent).

Synergistic entry points

Most of the interventions detailed in this report act synergistically—in other words, when two or more are combined, the overall effect is greater than the sum of their individual effects. Interventions may also be synergistic in the sense that they address the hunger problem in more than one way—or trigger additional innovations that further strengthen antihunger efforts and those of other Millennium Development Goals. The task force identifies three local initiatives as "entry points" in the battle against hunger: community nutrition programs, homegrown school feeding programs, and investments in soil health and water. All three will need to be tailored to local conditions, combined with policy changes, regulatory reforms, and national and local incentives.

A combination of the three interventions may constitute an attractive new integrated program in rural areas facing the dual challenge of high chronic malnutrition and low agricultural productivity. Community nutrition and homegrown school feeding programs can be initiated in tandem with basic investments in soil and water. The increased local production will have a ready market in the homegrown feeding programs. The resulting synergies of better education outcomes (particularly for girls), greater agricultural production and incomes, and improved nutrition for mothers and babies will address a community's hunger from multiple angles—opening the way for other interventions.

"It can be done"

The conclusion of the task force is that the hunger Goal can be achieved and that hunger can eventually be eliminated from the face of the earth. Achieving that goal will require focused and unprecedented levels of effort from all actors. But it is well within the reach of human capabilities. The world has made progress in reducing hunger, but not quickly or broadly enough. As this report goes to press, more than 5.5 million children are dying of malnutrition-related causes each year. The actions outlined in this report, taken up by a broad coalition of stakeholders and applied in every country, can change that.

The imperatives for reducing hunger

Approximately 852 million people worldwide cannot obtain enough food to live healthy and productive lives (FAO 2004). Hunger has many impacts. It is reflected in high rates of disease and mortality, limited neurological development, and low productivity among current and future generations. It is also a major constraint to a country's ability to develop economically, socially, and politically. Women and children living in developing countries are most vulnerable to the broad and devastating effects of hunger. Hunger, poverty, and disease are interlinked, with each contributing to the presence and persistence of the other two (WHO 1997).

Recognizing the enormity of the problem, world leaders committed themselves to the Goal of reducing hunger by half by 2015. Achieving this Goal is possible. But it will require an integrated, multisectoral approach—and an unprecedented commitment of political action and resources from both developing and developed countries. The solutions to fight hunger must be holistic—incorporating the recommendations in this report in combination with those of the other task forces addressing poverty, economic development, education, gender equality, health and HIV/AIDS, environment, water and sanitation, slum dwellers, trade, and technology. This chapter defines the problem, highlights the underlying determinants, outlines its multiple costs, and restates the moral foundation for eradicating hunger.

Defining hunger

Any discussion of how to halve hunger in the world immediately runs into problems of definition. "Hunger" is a popular word that resonates strongly with all people, even those who have experienced it only briefly. In its common usage it describes the subjective feeling of discomfort that follows a period without eating. The term undernourishment defines insufficient food intake

Both food insecurity and nutritional insecurity must be overcome

to continuously meet dietary energy requirements (FAO 2003). The term food insecurity relates to the condition that exists when people do not have physical and economic access to sufficient, safe, nutritious, and culturally acceptable food to meet their dietary needs and lead an active and healthy life (FAO 1996).

Within the definition of food insecurity is a distinction between chronic and acute food insecurity. Chronic food insecurity occurs when people are unable to access sufficient, safe, and nutritious food over long periods, such that it becomes their normal condition. Acute food insecurity exists when the lack of access to adequate food is more short-term, usually caused by shocks such as drought or war.

Hunger and food insecurity are often used interchangeably, since both focus on the availability of food. But it is human nutrition that determines whether a person thrives, falls ill, or dies. Nutrition deals with the way the body absorbs and uses food. Malnutrition leads to health problems, growth retardation, poor cognitive development, and in the worst cases death. It may result from deficiencies, excesses, or imbalances in energy, protein, and other nutrients (FAO 2003). It is also caused by numerous factors ranging from the inadequate care received by a newborn baby, through the lack of essential micronutrients (vitamins and minerals) in the food consumed, to the diseases and conditions that prevent the body from properly absorbing and using nutrients (FAO 2003). In this report, we use the word hunger to encompass both food and nutritional insecurity.

The definitions are important. Both food insecurity and nutritional insecurity must be overcome—and both require equal attention in fighting hunger. But the actions to combat them may be different, if often complementary. Just as the causes of food insecurity are complex (including lack of production, market failures, the inability to afford food), so too are the causes of malnutrition (nutrient and micronutrient deficiencies, diseases, lack of hygiene). Unless decisionmakers understand the web of interconnected issues that underlies the Goal of halving hunger, there is a risk that their responses will be partial and inadequate. This report therefore seeks to disentangle the parts of hunger, as a prelude to identifying the most urgent and highest priority responses.

Determinants of hunger

Poverty, war, natural disasters, disease epidemics, political and economic shocks—all affect not only the basic determinants of hunger (physical, technological, economic, political, social, and cultural), but also the underlying determinants (household food security, care, and health environment). Several analyses show that conditions at the household level (the underlying determinants of malnutrition) are extremely important (Haddad, Webb, and Slack 1997; Webb 1998; Smith and Haddad 2000). The results also show that individuals who are malnourished have been failed by many different sectors: agri-

Parents' education, especially mothers' level of education, has significant impacts on child malnutrition

culture, health, education, social welfare, finance, and employment. To address hunger effectively requires understanding the many causes of malnutrition at the household, community, and regional levels. It also requires a multisectoral approach to develop solutions and design and implement policies specifically targeted at vulnerable populations.

Poverty

Previous research suggests that, across countries, extreme poverty accounts for close to half the variability in overall malnutrition rates. Smith and Haddad (2002), in a cross-country study of the causes of malnutrition, found that, during 1970–95, per capita income in developing countries increased significantly, from $1,011 to $2,121. This large increase was found to have facilitated an estimated 7.4 percent reduction in child malnutrition. In a study of 42 developing countries, the UN Standing Committee on Nutrition (UN ACC/SCN 1994) found a statistically significant relationship between GDP per capita growth and changes in underweight prevalence, with a 1 percent annual increase in the growth rate of GDP per capita leading to a 0.24 percent decrease in underweight prevalence. A similar study of 18 Latin American countries by the Economic Commission for Latin America and the Caribbean in 2001 found that, in 34 percent of the cases analyzed, the percentage of people living on less than $1 a day was correlated with the percentage of the population underweight. In effect, 49 percent of the cross-country variability in the malnutrition rate (low weight-for-age) and 57 percent of the cross-country variability in moderate to serious chronic malnutrition (low height-for-age) could be attributed to differences in the percentage of people living in extreme poverty (ECLAC 2004).

Education

Data suggest that the level of parents' education, especially mothers' level of education, has significant impacts on child malnutrition. If the mother attended primary school, the child is less likely to be underweight. The correlation is even stronger if the mother also received secondary education. Smith and Haddad (2000) found that women's education is associated with almost 43 percent of the reduction in child malnutrition in developing countries from 1970 to 1995 (table 1.1). This contribution is the combined result of the strong

Table 1.1
Factors contributing to reductions in child malnutrition
Percent

Factor	Contribution to reduction in child malnutrition, from 1970 to 1995
Women's education	43
Per capita food availability	26
Health environment improvements	19
Women's status relative to men's	12

Source: Smith and Haddad 2000.

Improved food availability has made a great contribution to reducing malnutrition

effect of education and a fairly large increase in its supply over the period. In a similar study, the United Nations Administrative Committee on Coordination/Sub-Committee on Nutrition (UN ACN/SCN 1993) found, especially in South Asia, that female enrollment in secondary school, and government expenditures on social services (health, education, and social security), are negatively and significantly associated with underweight prevalence.

The reduction in child malnutrition due to women's education may be due in part to the fact that education and skills training better equip women to participate in activities that can improve their overall economic and social status within the household and the community. Research also shows that educating girls can delay their marriage age, reduce their future family size, increase their earning power, and improve the nutritional status of their future children. Moreover, agricultural productivity increases dramatically when women receive the same inputs as men, including education (Smith and Haddad 2000).

Food production and access

Improved food availability has made a great contribution to reducing malnutrition. Smith and Haddad (2000) found that per capita food availability contributed about 26 percent of the reduction of child malnutrition between 1970 and 1995. The contribution was substantial in the late 1970s and early 1980s. Food production in developing countries tripled over the past 30 years. The number of rural poor fell by half. The proportion of malnourished people declined from 30 percent to 18 percent. And the real prices of the main cereal crops fell by 76 percent. But the impact of an increase in food availability on malnutrition depends on the present level of availability and access to food. Where food is scarce, an increase in availability will have a strong impact. Where food is more plentiful, the effect of an increase in availability will be smaller (Smith and Haddad 2000).

Data show an inverse relationship between food shortages and underweight children: there are more underweight children in cereal-surplus countries than in cereal-deficit ones. On reflection this is not surprising. Asian countries such as India produce enough food to feed themselves, yet both the number and rate of underweight children are extremely high. Increased supplies did not translate into comparable increases in food consumption by the poor due to the lack of purchasing power, policy failures, and the growing use of cereals and other staples for animal feed to serve wealthier consumers (Scherr 2003).

Most of Latin America and Asia produce or import enough food to feed their populations. Under these circumstances, productivity growth in agriculture is not the most effective measure for reducing malnutrition. Instead, the key is to ensure that improvements in productivity are shared across a broad spectrum of resource-poor farming households. This requires equitable access to productive assets, especially land, and to improved technologies. It is also

Inadequate sanitation, poor health facilities, and unsafe water sources contribute significantly to malnutrition

essential that markets function well enough to ensure that improvements in productivity result in lower consumer prices. The urban poor in these areas need to gain economic access to food.

In Africa, however, soil nutrient depletion and unreliable water supply are extreme. Depleted soils cannot provide sufficient mineral nutrients (nitrogen, phosphorus) for crops to grow. This translates into low food productivity and supply. Therefore, for most African countries, the initial entry point to increasing food production and access may revolve around investments in soil health and water management to improve agricultural productivity.

Sanitation, health facilities, and water

Inadequate sanitation, poor health facilities, and unsafe water sources contribute significantly to malnutrition by increasing the burden of illness for both children and adults. More than 1 billion people, one-sixth of the world's population, lack access to safe drinking water (FAO 2001a). Households dependent on well or surface water for drinking are more likely to have increased prevalence of underweight children because the water is more likely to be contaminated. And children living in households with no toilets are more likely to be underweight.

Improvements in health, sanitation, water, and other basic services contributed to 20 percent of the reduction in child malnutrition from 1970 to 1995 (Smith and Haddad 2000). Of the nearly 12 million children under age five who died in 1995, about 70 percent were affected by one or more of just five conditions: malaria, measles, acute respiratory infections, undernutrition, and diarrhea. And the death rate from disease among undernourished children is much higher than among those better nourished (FAO 2001a).

Socioeconomic and political access and inequalities

The literature on malnutrition has drawn attention to various socioeconomic factors and the functioning of markets in determining access to food. It is believed that the biggest challenge throughout the developing world is to reduce the differences in access to food across geographical areas and social strata. If the poor find it difficult to produce or purchase enough food, the lack of functioning markets makes it doubly difficult. Access to food is also limited by inefficient markets that are unable to supply sufficient quantities of seasonal food in response to demand throughout the year. These market failures exacerbate fluctuations in the price of food and affordability of food for the poor (Benson 2004).

Sociopolitical conditions affect malnutrition through inequality and exclusionary practices that disempower groups such as women, children (particularly girls), and ethnic minorities in many countries. Social exclusion results in deprivation not just in food but in a wide range of basic services, including education and health (box 1.1).

Box 1.1
Inequality and hunger in Guatemala

Source: Gallardo 2001.

Guatemala has one of the highest rates of undernourishment and underweight children in Latin America. The high level of inequality found within the country is directly related to food insecurity. Conditions affecting Guatemala include:

- Of Guatemala's population, 20 percent is rich and 80 percent is poor.
- Less than 3 percent of the population owns 65 percent of the land.
- The indigenous population accounts for about 60 percent of the total.
- The rural population represents 60 percent of the total.
- The agricultural sector accounts for 25 percent of GDP.
- International commodity price fluctuations and the shift in commodities produced have mainly affected poor peasants employed as day laborers.
- Mechanized techniques used in sugarcane harvesting have reduced the need for workers.
- Nearly all the land redistributed under land tenure reform has been returned to its former owners, the large landholders.
- Small-scale farmers tend to grow crops that deplete the natural resource base with few resources to fertilize the land.
- The diet of the rural population lacks variety and micronutrients, and consists mainly of staple grains.
- Women in the high plateau regions expend 700 calories each day, or a third of their total calorie intake, fetching water and performing other household chores.

These and other factors have led to a vicious circle of poverty, deforestation, land degradation, and malnutrition. Rural families have had to develop coping strategies, which in many cases have allowed them to overcome food insecurity. But environmental, economic, and other forces are undermining these strategies, particularly in areas susceptible to drought, floods, and, recently, armed conflict.

At the intrahousehold level, data from South Asia demonstrate that when there is discrimination in food intake between boys and girls, it is largely in favor of boys (Haddad and others 1995). The inequalities in food intake for infants in South Asia reflect cultural values and the different wages commanded by male and female adults in the labor market (figure 1.1).

This type of gender-specific exclusion from food consumption does not occur as frequently in Sub-Saharan Africa, in part because women are household heads in a larger proportion of households. But different forms of social and political exclusion in the region can have similarly negative impacts on food security and nutritional status.

HIV/AIDS

It is now well established that there are important two-way interactions between malnutrition and the spread of HIV/AIDS. Good nutrition is seen as an essential complement to the use of antiretroviral drugs to slow the progression of HIV into full-blown AIDS (Kadiyala and Gillespie 2003). Undernourished people infected with HIV/AIDS develop the full symptoms of the disease more

Figure 1.1

Men in South Asian households often get more food

Studies finding gender bias in intrahousehold food allocation

Source: Haddad and others 1995.

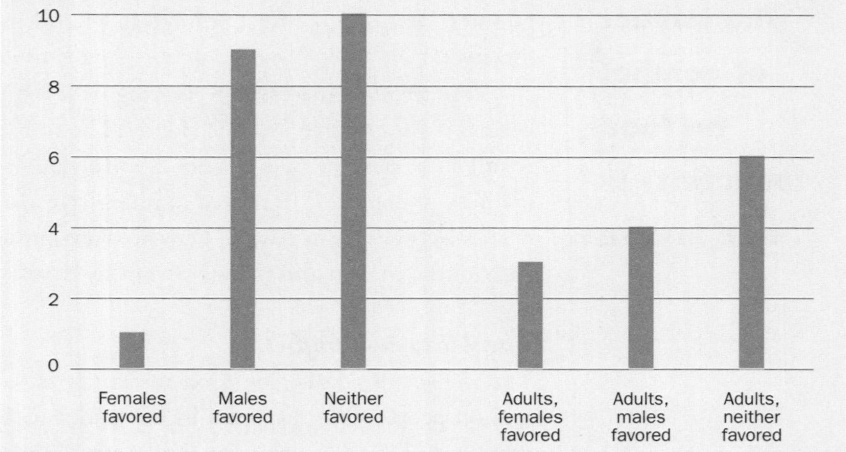

quickly than people who are well fed. People suffering from the disease need good nutrition to fight it off. Yet one of the earliest effects of AIDS is reduced consumption of food in affected households.

HIV/AIDS infection severely limits the capacity of people to work, with long-lasting damage to rural societies. When the infection is passed from mother to child, it can leave a new generation weak and without parental care. When children are orphaned, the normal flow of practical farming knowledge from one generation to another is inhibited. The labor available for agriculture and other means of earning a living is dramatically reduced, leading to a decline in production. Women, who often assume the major burden of care for the sick and perform agricultural and other tasks, are severely affected and disadvantaged. Women who have lost their husbands due to AIDS may be unable to inherit land and other assets.

HIV/AIDS has an especially devastating effect on smallholder agriculture, which remains the engine of economic development for the poor in many developing countries. The main impacts of HIV/AIDS morbidity and mortality on agriculture include reducing crop diversity and the area cropped, abandoning labor-intensive activities, and selling livestock (Drimie 2003; Haslwimmer and Chupin 1994). Other less direct factors also affect agricultural performance. For example, pastoralists in Namibia spend up to 25 percent of their time in mourning and attending funerals (Engh, Stouklal, and du Guerny 2000). The support services to agriculture also suffer. A study in Zambia found that 67 percent of extension workers interviewed had lost at least one coworker to AIDS over a three-year period (Alleyne, Kapungwe, and Kamona 2001).

HIV/AIDS interacts with famines in a catastrophic fashion. Whereas societies have usually recovered from famines, the "new-variant" AIDS-affected famines in recent years will be much more difficult to recover from (de Waal and Whiteside 2003). In the past, mortality from famines tended to be highest among the elderly, the very young, the sick, and the weak. AIDS-related

The impact of conflict on food insecurity is well known

famines increasingly affect young adults and more able-bodied members of society.

This trend is increasingly placing a heavy burden of care on those left behind—the children and the elderly. The full impact of such social disasters is still to be felt, but some societies are already showing signs of collapse and inability to cope. AIDS-related famines have already been observed in Africa, particularly Southern Africa. They are now spreading rapidly in parts of South and Southeast Asia and threatening other developing regions as well.

Instability and conflict

The impact of conflict on food insecurity is well known. In 1998 some 35 million people were displaced in low and middle-income countries, many of them due to conflict and natural disasters. Studies have sought to quantify the effects on food production in conflict zones in Africa, where farm output is the principal source of livelihood for the majority of poor and food-insecure people (Messer and others 1998; FAO 2000; Messer and others 2001).

Several analysts have shown a strong association between conflict and factors closely related to food insecurity, such as high infant mortality (Esty and others 1998) and intergroup competition over land and water (Homer-Dixon 1999). Conflict is also a very important determinant of child malnutrition. A mix of extreme poverty, inequality, and declining per capita incomes was frequently associated with civil wars in the 1990s and early 2000s, particularly when combined with heavy reliance on a narrow range of primary product exports (Collier and others 2003). Nafziger and Auvinen (2000) pointed to a similar blend of variables, along with slow growth of food production, high military spending, and a tradition of military conflict. But these studies do not specify the precise pathways for food insecurity or the other factors to combine and lead to conflict.

Other analysts contend that conflict is not an inevitable outcome of environmental scarcities and food insecurity (Messer and others 2001). They see competition between ethnic groups for political and economic power as the main explanation for violence, especially in Africa (Paarlberg 2000; Marshall and Gurr 2003). Over the past 20 years, civil conflict has created food emergencies in Angola, Burundi, Republic of Congo, the Democratic Republic of Congo, Côte d'Ivoire, Guinea, Liberia, Sierra Leone, Sudan, and Uganda (box 1.2). Although the countries affected by food emergencies may change from year to year, there has been little progress in reducing the incidence of such emergencies across the African continent (Benson 2004).

The key trigger conditions that predispose societies toward conflict may be natural, such as a prolonged drought. They may be economic, such as a change in the price of the principal food (rice in Indonesia) or cash crop (coffee in Rwanda) that deprives the rebelling population of its perceived just standard of living. Or they may be political, such as social inequalities, violations of human rights, and the denial of access to land or welfare programs, as in Central America. Frequently the food insecurity caused by conflict is heightened by economic crises, HIV/AIDS, or other disasters. The result is that even more people go hungry.

Hunger and poverty can cause conflict—and vice-versa

The second link between hunger and instability relates to "horizontal inequalities" (Stewart 2002). Large relative differences in nutrition and lack of access to economic, political, and social resources among groups differentiated along ethnic, cultural, or religious lines reduces social cohesion (Stewart 2002). Conflict becomes almost inevitable when leaders mobilize these groups for their own pursuit of power—often by constructing or enhancing group identity—and when triggers such as aid flows or political realignments accentuate group grievances. Initial studies of this hypothesis in Angola and Rwanda suggest it has some validity, at least in the countries studied (Cramer 2003). Thus, hunger and poverty can cause conflict—and vice-versa.

If we can alleviate hunger by tackling its underlying causes, we are likely to make the world and developing nations safer and more secure. Additional humanitarian resources are necessary for dealing with the consequences of both conflict and natural disasters, and the transition from conflict back to development requires huge investments in food and nutritional support.

Natural disasters and climate variability

Other major sources of vulnerability for hungry people are natural disasters and climate variability. The poor and food-insecure countries that largely depend on rainfed farming are the most vulnerable to variability in climate.

A paper commissioned by the task force (Hansen and others 2004) provides the following perspective. Climate variability affects food-insecure households in economies with a high dependence on agriculture. In southern India the coefficient of variation for net farm income over 10 years was 127

Box 1.2
Food in times of crisis in Sierra Leone

Source: Lefort 2001.

War-torn Sierra Leone has witnessed the use of food as a weapon to terrorize and suppress its people. The civil war waged by the Revolutionary United Front during the 1990s influenced people's access to food in the following ways:

- In 1998 the Revolutionary United Front commando units attacked isolated and unprotected rural areas. Among the common atrocities conducted were burning houses and mutilating villagers. The loss of one or two hands meant that the villager could no longer provide food for his or her family.
- Food supply was closely linked with the diamond industry. Food was a necessity for diamond miners, who either bought it from families at very low prices or else stole it from families or the stocks of humanitarian organizations.
- The Revolutionary United Front used food distribution as a means of encouraging people to remain in or return to the towns under control.
- The government used food distribution as a political tool—to show people it was still in control.

Agricultural productivity in Africa and Latin America could fall by as much as 30 percent in this century through climate change

percent, primarily due to climate variability. The amount of food a household is able to purchase is affected by large price fluctuations during droughts or floods. Locust outbreaks and migratory patterns also depend on climate variability, as do many other pests and diseases. A flood can cut off access to markets by damaging transport infrastructure, inundating markets, and washing away homes and crops. A drought can lead to crop losses, food price increases, reduced agricultural labor, lost revenue from secondary processing and transport of agricultural commodities, and lost energy when the water in hydroelectric dams becomes low. Technologies are available for climate prediction to assist the poor in managing their vulnerabilities to risk, based on improved knowledge of climatic risks and local predictions at seasonal time scales (Hansen and others 2004).

Additionally, the Third Assessment Report of the Intergovernmental Panel on Climate Change stated for the first time that the scientific evidence of human-induced climate change is unequivocal—and that the latest predictions are much worse than previous ones (Houghton and others 2001). The last 100 years have been the warmest on record, and the warming in the last 50 years has a clear human signature. Rainfall patterns are changing. El Niño events are increasing in frequency and intensity. Arctic ice is thinning, and tropical mountain ice is retreating.

The potential consequences of these changes are dire. Agricultural productivity in Africa and Latin America could fall by as much as 30 percent in this century. Severe droughts will occur in Southern Africa and Southeast Asia. Wetter climates and more floods are predicted for parts of East Africa and Latin America. And more smoke and haze are predicted for Southeast Asia and Central America. Higher worldwide food prices are likely to result, affecting the landless and the urban poor.

The social and economic costs of hunger

The images of hunger that fill TV screens and newspapers tend to show the devastating effects on children of acute malnutrition caused by such extreme shocks as famines and war. As critical as it is to respond to those crises, we must bear in mind that acute malnutrition affects roughly 1 in 10 of the hungry worldwide, depending on the year. Generally, most of the hungry suffer from chronic malnutrition. It is estimated that chronic malnutrition—ranging from severe, through moderate, to mild—is linked to 54 percent of child deaths worldwide, while acute malnutrition on its own accounts for roughly 10 percent (Pelletier and others 1995; UN SCN 2004). Most child deaths linked to malnutrition are thus associated with its less visually dramatic manifestations (figure 1.2).

Malnutrition and hunger are the number one risk factor for illness worldwide (WHO 2003b). For both children and adults, malnutrition reduces the body's natural defenses against most diseases. It is thus a critical factor predisposing people to infection and disease progression. Inadequate food consump-

Figure 1.2

Malnutrition is a leading cause of child deaths

Share of child deaths due to infectious diseases associated with malnutrition (%)

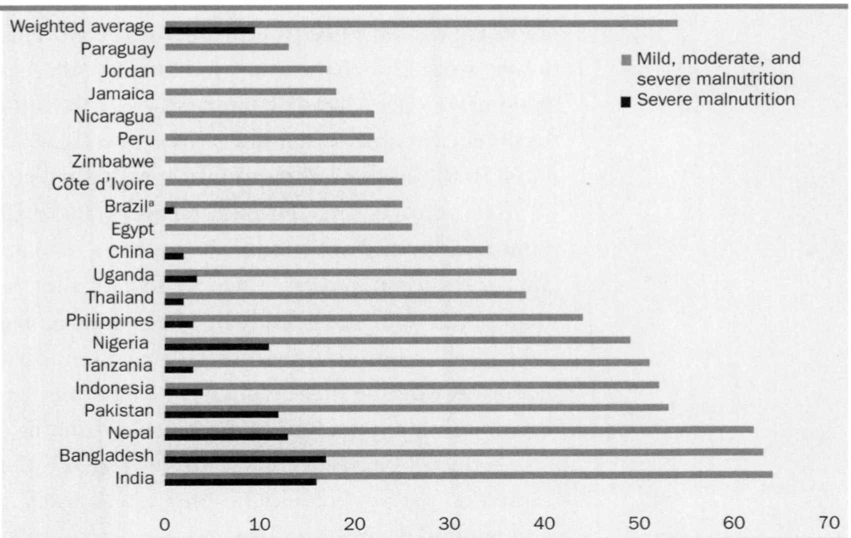

a. Data are for northeast Brazil.

Source: Adapted from Pelletier and others 1995.

Figure 1.3

Poor nutrition is one of the leading risk factors contributing to the global burden of disease

Share of world disability adjusted life years (%)

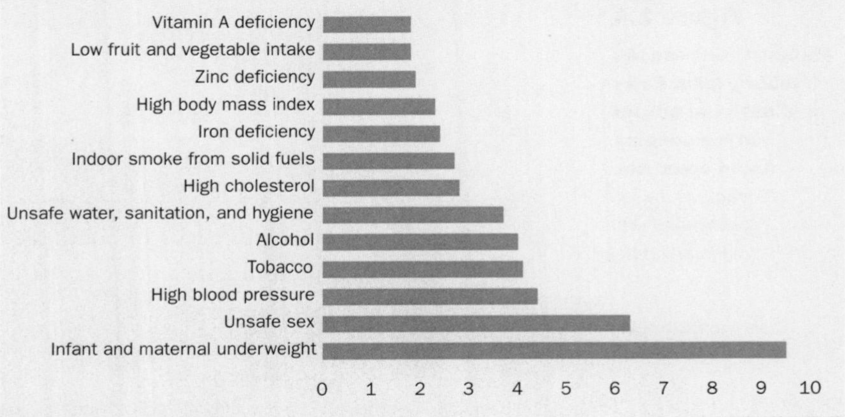

Source: Ezzati and others 2002.

tion and malnutrition account for 7 of the 13 leading risk factors associated with the global burden of disease (WHO 2003b). Nutrition thus provides a broad platform for launching efforts to reduce infection and chronic disease throughout the world (figure 1.3).

Undernourishment in childhood is also associated with poor cognitive development in children (Grantham-McGregor, Fernald, and Sethuraman 1999a,b). Indeed, poor cognitive development begins before birth with malnourished pregnant women (Hack 1998). It is also associated with reduced breastfeeding (Grantham-McGregor, Fernald, and Sethuraman 1999a). And it has been shown that reduced cognitive development, especially in the first two years of life, results in lower productivity and lifetime earnings potential (FAO 2003).

Hunger carries both direct and indirect economic costs. Its negative impact is dramatic in forgone GDP per capita. For labor productivity alone, the annual losses are at least 6–10 percent (figure 1.4). Gains in productivity of this magnitude would be headline news in any country—but they would be especially good news in developing countries seeking to compete in the global economy. Iron deficiency alone accounts for between 2 percent and 7 percent of forgone GDP in the 10 developing countries with good estimates (figure 1.5).

The impacts of hunger on an individual's labor productivity are determined early in life. Malnourished infants tend to enter primary school later and to drop out earlier. When in school, they tend to be less able to learn than better nourished children. These disadvantages in early childhood typically persist, significantly diminishing the individual's earnings throughout her or his working life. Productivity in nonmarket activities—such as care for infants, children, and other dependents—and in other household activities is also reduced. Moreover, the multiplier effect of strong and healthy human capital on the productivity of other assets—such as financial, social, natural, and physical capital—will be forgone.

Figure 1.4

Malnutrition reduces labor productivity and national output in low-income Asian countries

Productivity losses associated with malnutrition (%)

Source: Horton 1999.

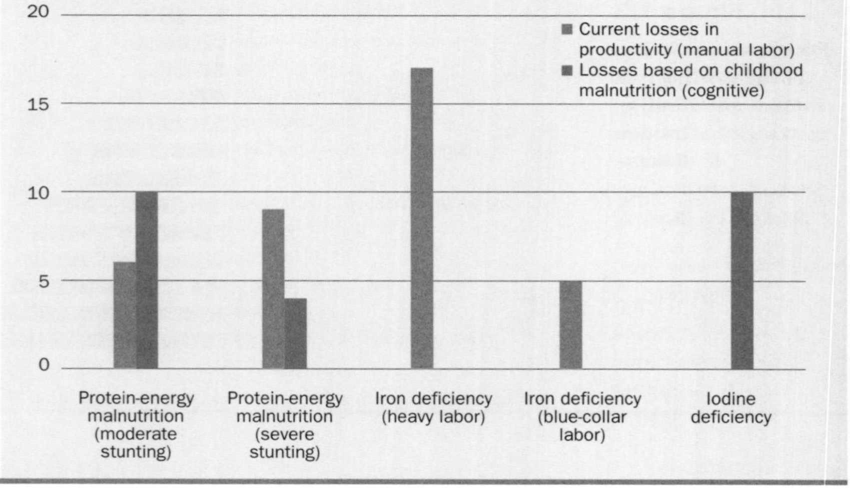

Figure 1.5

Iron deficiency anemia alone can reduce national output by 2–8 percent

Forgone GDP (%)

Source: Horton and Ross 2003.

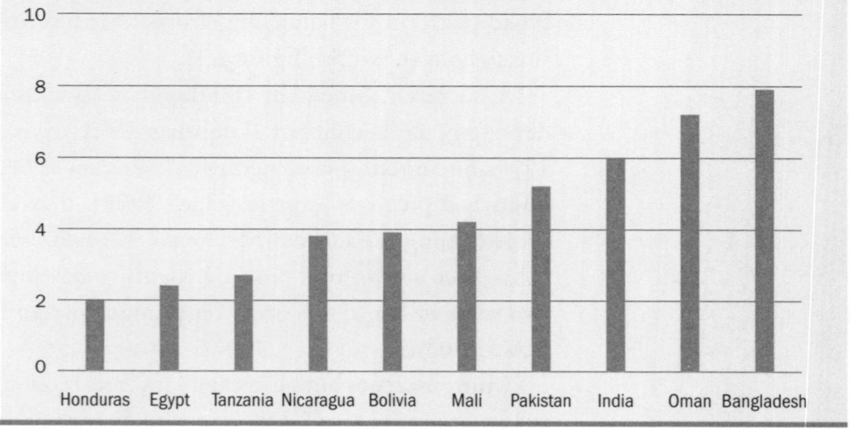

The Copenhagen Consensus, a project of the Danish Institute of Environmental Assessment, identified investment in supplying micronutrients as the second most cost-effective of all the potential development interventions included in its study, behind only a successful effort to tackle HIV/AIDS (Copenhagen Consensus 2004). Addressing child malnutrition also came in the top 10 "winners" in cost-benefit ratios. In the first "challenge paper" to emerge from the work of the Copenhagen Consensus, the preliminary results show that the economic benefits of reducing hunger consistently outweigh the costs (table 1.2).

The Copenhagen Consensus conclusions are based only on cost-benefit calculations. These costs and benefits were estimated from a number of sources, with several assumptions about baseline nutritional status or the effectiveness of interventions. However, the findings broadly support other studies on the costs and benefits of fighting hunger.

To the extent that hunger affects the lives and productivity of individuals, they are bound also to affect the economic growth performance of nations, especially those with a high incidence of chronic undernourishment. In a study for the FAO, Arcand (2001) demonstrated that, if developing countries had raised nutritional standards to adequate levels in the last half of the twentieth century, they would have improved human welfare and raised the rate of economic growth. These findings reinforce the conclusion that significant economic benefits are to be gained from measures that lead to the elimination of hunger. They suggest that it may be possible, especially in low-income coun-

Table 1.2

Benefit-cost ratios for interventions to reduce hunger

Source: Behrman, Alderman, and Hoddinott 2004.

Interventions and targeted populations	Benefit-cost ratio
Reducing low birthweight where there is a high risk (particularly in South Asia)	
Treatment for women with asymptomatic bacterial infections	0.6–4.9
Treatment for women assumed to have sexually transmitted diseases	1.3–10.7
Drugs for women with poor obstetric history	4.1–35.2
Improving infant and child nutrition in populations with a high prevalence of malnutrition	
Breastfeeding promotion in hospitals in which the norm has been the promotion of infant formula	4.8–7.4
Integrated child care programs	9.4–16.2
Intensive preschool program with considerable nutrition for poor families	1.4–2.9
Reducing micronutrient deficiencies in populations in which they are prevalent	
Iodine (women of child-bearing age)	15.0–250.0
Vitamin A (children under six)	4.3–43.0
Iron (whole population)	176.0–200.0
Iron (pregnant women)	6.1–14.0
Investment in technology to develop agriculture	
Dissemination of new cultivars with higher yield potentials	8.8–14.7
Dissemination of iron- and zinc-dense rice and wheat varieties	11.6–19.0
Dissemination of vitamin A–dense rice	8.5–14.0

tries, to induce increases in GDP growth rates by giving priority to investments reducing hunger.

Economic growth is not enough to eliminate hunger

While economic growth is usually necessary for sustained reductions in hunger, it is not enough to eliminate hunger. Some developing countries, such as India, have achieved high economic growth rates without commensurate reductions in the incidence of hunger. Others have cut hunger even when their growth has been sluggish, such as Cuba. A study by Anand and Ravallion (1993)—cited by Smith and Haddad (2000)—concluded that average income matters, but only insofar as it reduces poverty and finances key social services.

Moral and legal foundations for eradicating hunger

For all the reasons just described, extreme hunger elicits a strong response from people. The specter of famine throughout history, such as the European famines of 1815 and 1846, drove many Western humanitarian campaigns, and formed part of the rationale for increasing development assistance in the 1950s and 1960s. The famines in Ethiopia and other African countries in the 1980s led to massive public awareness campaigns, such as the charity concerts by well known musicians, to mobilize support in donor countries for hunger reduction efforts. But the historical persistence of hunger has also led to its acceptance as an inevitable part of the human condition. As a result, it has not received the absolute moral condemnation that might be expected of an issue that evokes such strong feelings.

A milestone was the recognition of the universal right to adequate food adopted by the 1996 World Food Summit. Article 11 of the 1948 Universal Declaration of Human Rights states that "Everyone has the right to a standard of living adequate for the health and well-being of himself and his family, including food. . . ." Nearly 20 years later, the International Covenant on Economic, Social, and Cultural Rights (United Nations Economic and Social Council 1966) developed these concepts more fully, stressing in article 25 "the right of everyone to . . . adequate food" and specifying "the fundamental right of everyone to be free from hunger." Delegates to the 1996 World Food Summit asserted "the right of everyone to have access to safe and nutritious food, consistent with the right to adequate food and the fundamental right of everyone to be free from hunger." They further pledged to cut in half the number of the world's hungry people. This pledge became the basis for the Millennium Development Goal for reducing hunger, formally adopted by the world's leaders at the Millennium Summit in 2000.

The 1996 World Food Summit requested that both the concept of this right—and the steps to realize it—be better clarified. Under the coordination of the UN High Commissioner for Human Rights, the request was met through the joint efforts of human rights and development experts, including food and nutrition policy analysts, international organizations, and representatives of interested governments and civil society. The process culminated

The historical persistence of hunger has also led to its acceptance as inevitable

in General Comment 12 on the right to food (CESCR 1999), which for the first time offers a comprehensive and authoritative interpretation of the human right to adequate food, as laid down in general terms in Article 25 of the United Nations Declaration on Human Rights and in Article 11 of the Covenant on Economic, Social, and Cultural Rights and in more nutritional terms in Articles 24 and 27 of the Convention on the Rights of the Child.

The Optional Protocol to the Convention on the Elimination of All Forms of Discrimination against Women entered into force in December 2000. Article 12 of the Convention provides that "State Parties shall ensure for women appropriate services in connection with pregnancy, confinement and the post-natal period, granting free services where necessary, as well as adequate nutrition during pregnancy and lactation." The ratification of the Optional Protocol gives competence to the Committee on the Elimination of Discrimination against Women to receive and consider complaints from individuals or groups within its jurisdiction. The rule of law and the enforceability of the right to food are necessary for this right to be meaningful, and the Optional Protocol is clearly an important milestone in that direction.

Having legal recourse at national and international levels is a prerequisite for making the right to food meaningful—letting people seek a remedy and accountability when this right is violated. As such, state parties to the Committee on Economic, Social, and Cultural Rights are obliged to respect, protect, and fulfill, the right to food. While not yet widespread, these provisions are beginning to gain traction in some countries (box 1.3).

The International Covenant on Economic, Social, and Cultural Rights recognizes the importance of international trade regimes, and requires countries to recognize the right to food when entering into trade agreements with other countries or international organizations. There is now sufficient international legislation on food as a human right—combined with growing awareness and emerging precedent—to support a human rights approach to hunger reduction

Box 1.3

The right to food in India

Source: People's Union for Civil Liberties 2001.

On April 16, 2001, the People's Union for Civil Liberties in India submitted a "writ petition" to the Supreme Court of India asking three questions:

- Does the right to life mean that people who are starving and too poor to buy food can get free access to government stockpiles?
- Does the right to life under Article 21 of the Constitution of India include the right to food?
- Does not the right to food, which has been upheld by the Supreme Court, imply that the state has a duty to provide food, especially in situations of drought, to people who are drought-affected and are not in a position to purchase food?

The court ruled in favor of the People's Union. While the battle continues in the courts as the states contest their obligations and their ability to meet them, the issue is guaranteed to pressure state governments to place a higher priority on combating hunger.

Box 1.4

Eleven steps in applying a human rights approach to hunger reduction

Source: Adapted from Ziegler 2002.

1. Identify groups vulnerable to food insecurity and review national legislation to determine how much these groups are protected.
2. Analyze the steps the government has taken to comply with its obligations.
3. Assess political action for access to food—and to productive resources, since they are a prerequisite to the long-term enjoyment of the right to food by the rural poor.
4. Assess the political marginalization of vulnerable groups and ensure that there is no discrimination on the grounds of ethnicity, gender, religion, or any other criterion.
5. Examine national action plans to determine whether they comply with General Comment 12 of the UN's Committee on Economic, Social, and Cultural Rights.
6. Consult the Voluntary Guidelines to Support the Progressive Realization of the Right to Adequate Food in the Context of National Food Security
7. Determine whether the right to food has been made justifiable and, if not, take steps to secure this.
8. Empower judicial institutions to enforce the right to food on the government but also on private parties, including transnational corporations.
9. Lobby to strengthen international rules and enforcement mechanisms for transnational corporations to ensure that they do not violate the right to food.
10. Lobby to review and reform international trade rules to ensure their compatibility with the right to food.
11. Put pressure on financial bodies and developmental agencies, such as the International Monetary Fund and the World Bank, to ensure that they adopt a rights-based approach to their policies and programs.

policies and strategies (box 1.4). An additional instrument has recently been developed, intended to help states in pursing a human rights–based policy: a set of voluntary guidelines to support the progressive realization of the right to adequate food in the context of national food security (FAO 2004a).

What is clear is that there are strong moral grounds for eradicating hunger, grounds sufficient for accelerating action worldwide. But eradicating hunger also can be a high-yielding economic investment. So, from both a moral and an economic perspective, there are forceful arguments for increasing the investment funds for reducing hunger. It can also be argued from a tactical perspective that reducing hunger must be a critical element of any poverty reduction strategy, recognizing that little progress in poverty reduction is likely to be possible as long as large numbers of people suffer from hunger and malnutrition. Indeed, success in reducing hunger will open the door to reducing poverty and contribute to achieving other Millennium Development Goals, especially those for health, education, gender equality, and the sustainable use of natural resources.

Who is on track or off track to meet the hunger Goal?

The hunger Goal has two indicators for monitoring progress: the percentage of the human population below the minimum level of dietary energy consumption, and the prevalence of underweight children under five years of age. Both indicators are to be measured against baseline data for 1990, the benchmark year for assessing progress in meeting all the Goals.

By looking at either of these indicators, it is clear that progress has been made in reducing the number of hungry people in the world. For example, over the last decade and across the developing world, the absolute number of preschool children who are underweight has fallen from 177 million to 134 million, while the rate of undernourishment declined by three percentage points (FAO 2003). But progress varies tremendously between subnational, national, and regional units.

The two hunger indicators measure different dimensions of hunger. The first refers to the minimum amount of food a person needs to consume to lead a normal and healthy life. It is based on data on food consumption and on inequality in the access to food, measuring the percentage of the total hungry population at a given moment. The second refers to child malnutrition, measured as low weight-for-age on the basis of child weight in an international reference population. A child is underweight if its weight is below minus two standard deviations from the median of the international reference population used for analysis by WHO and the U.S. National Center for Health Statistics and Centers for Disease Control and Prevention. Underweight is a composite measure that reflects both chronic malnutrition (low height-for-age, or stunting) and acute malnutrition (low weight-for-height, or wasting).

Hunger must be measured and analyzed at a subnational (state, province, or district) level

Hunger hotspots—measuring underweight at the subnational level

Hunger has been measured, classified, analyzed, and mapped by many agencies. The United Nations World Food Programme publishes an informative hunger map, while the FAO's *State of Food Insecurity* report analyzes trends in food security on an annual basis. Commonly available maps of hunger show which countries have high levels, but not where the concentrations are within a country or where they spread over national boundaries.

The task force strongly believes that hunger must be measured and analyzed at a subnational (state, province, or district) level. To show the variation encountered within a country, we mapped the rate of underweight prevalence at the subnational level to identify "hotspots" where hunger is intense. Hotspots are defined as the subnational units that contain more than 20 percent of children underweight. By focusing on higher percentages, hotspots reveal levels of malnutrition defined by the WHO and the expert opinion of members of this task force as "high" and "very high."

The task force acknowledges that the underweight indicator has many limitations in the way it is measured, what it measures, and what it represents. For mapping purposes, underweight was selected as the best measure for comparison across countries because recent and trend data are available for most countries. Other measures, such as height-for-age, weight-for-height, and the FAO's percentage of population chronically undernourished were also explored. In the end, these measures were not used because of the lack of adequate subnational data.[1] Data used in this analysis were for a single period of time and come from surveys that were conducted in different years during 1990–2002.

Rates of prevalence of underweight children under age five at the subnational level and the density of underweight children (underweight children per square kilometer) were mapped on the basis of available geo-referenced data.[2] Hunger hotspots were then identified on the basis of one main criterion: subnational units with more than 20 percent of children under five underweight. Other criteria, such as the number of underweight children, density of underweight children, a combination of prevalence and number of underweight children, and a combination of prevalence and density of underweight children, were also explored. However, these measures were not used because of scale variations in metrics, differences in unit sizes, and spurious bias toward more populated areas.

Using 20 percent prevalence of underweight as a cutoff point allowed us to include, based on a normal distribution for each of the regions:

- Nearly all cases in the upper three quartiles in the Sub-Saharan Africa region.
- All cases in the upper three quartiles in the South Asia region.

The 313 hunger hotspots contain 79 percent of the undernourished children under five years of age

- Nearly all the cases in the upper two quartiles in the East Asia and the Pacific region.
- Nearly all the cases in the upper quartile in the Latin America region.
- The highest cases in the upper quartile in the Middle East and North Africa region.

The results of the mapping exercise show that the highest numbers of underweight children are concentrated in relatively large areas of South Asia and Sub-Saharan Africa, with much smaller pockets in Central and South America (maps 2.1 to 2.6). Our analysis was constrained, however, by the lack of reliable data on this indicator. There is an urgent need to collect data not only on this indicator but also on wasting and stunting in all three regions. Much more investment is needed to collect subnational data, and it would be valuable to begin to standardize sampling units for population density and size. Data on indicators other than underweight children would not only enhance the comprehensiveness of this analysis but also provide us with an opportunity to analyze other aspects of hunger.

In the three regions, 313 subnational units were identified as hotspots. They are home to around 107 million preschool underweight children, encompassing some 79 percent of the estimated number of such children.

The hunger maps are useful for seeing at a glance where the hungry are located. They can also be used for targeting hunger reduction initiatives to specific regions or groups of the population particularly vulnerable to hunger. Clearly, decisions on where to target assistance must take into account information not included in the hotspots analysis. And keep in mind that hunger is a multifaceted problem and that the prevalence of underweight measures hunger only among preschool children, leaving out other age groups who may be hungry.

The Task Force on Hunger thus proposes that a new index—the hunger reduction index—be created to measure the severity of the different faces of hunger. The index should measure issues related to the availability, access, and use of food as well as resources for care, health, and sanitation that affect nutrition status.

Hunger indicator 1—percentage of the population below the minimum level of dietary energy consumption

The measure of the prevalence of hunger used by the FAO takes into account the amount of food consumption per person nationally (derived from food balance sheets) and the extent of inequality in access to food. According to this measure, 17 percent of people in the developing world were "undernourished" in 1999–2001, down from 18 percent in the mid-1990s. Over this period, because of population growth, the absolute number of food-insecure people in the developing world rose from 780 million to 798 million. This implies that the hunger Goal can be achieved only if the annual reduction can be

Figure 2.1

Most of the undernourished are in Asia

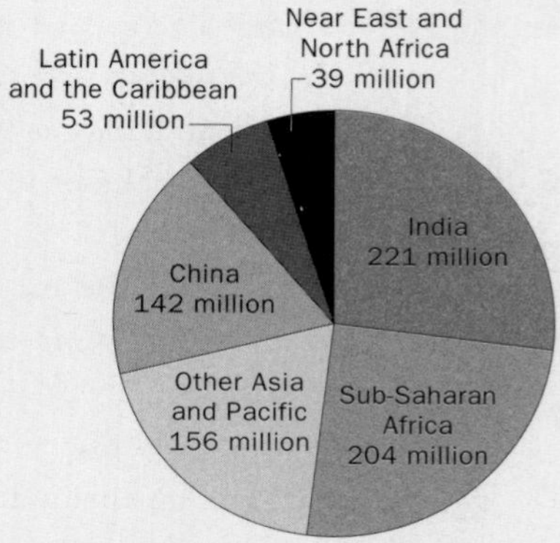

Source: FAO 2004c.

accelerated to 26 million a year—more than 12 times the pace of 2.1 million a year achieved so far (FAO 2003). The dietary intake indicator generally shows trends similar to the underweight indicator, but suggests that we should be more pessimistic about the current status of hunger.

Among the estimated 852 million food-insecure people worldwide, 815 million live in developing countries. An additional 28 million live in countries in transition, and only 9 million live in developed countries. Although the majority of undernourished people in the developing world reside in Asia (521 million) (figure 2.1), the fastest improvements in food security are also occurring there (FAO 2004c).

In most developing regions except Central Africa and the Commonwealth of Independent States, the percentage of undernourished people is declining. The latest undernourishment data at the subregional level suggest that the number of hungry people rose in South Asia, Central America, the Middle East, North Africa, and West Africa.

The rates of undernourishment in the Middle East and North Africa are as low as the rates observed in Latin America and the Caribbean. Increases in per capita domestic food supply in most countries in these regions have been responsible for the decrease seen in the past few years. In Latin America and the Caribbean, the highest rates (over 20 percent) are in Bolivia, Dominican Republic, Guatemala, Haiti, Honduras, and Nicaragua. Regional experts believe that these high rates are chiefly attributable to a fall in per capita food supply as a result of declining domestic production and import capacity—and to other circumstances associated with lack of access to food (ECLAC 2004).

Sub-Saharan Africa is witnessing the largest and fastest increase in food insecurity worldwide. Undernourishment rates are already over 40 percent—among the highest rates in the world. The total number of undernourished people has increased in East and West Africa, while in Central Africa the increase has been less dramatic (figure 2.2).

In contrast, there has been great progress in East Asia and the Pacific, especially in China, which has reduced its number of hungry people by 58 million

Figure 2.2

The number of undernourished people is rising in East, Central, and Southern Africa

Millions

Source: FAO 2004c.

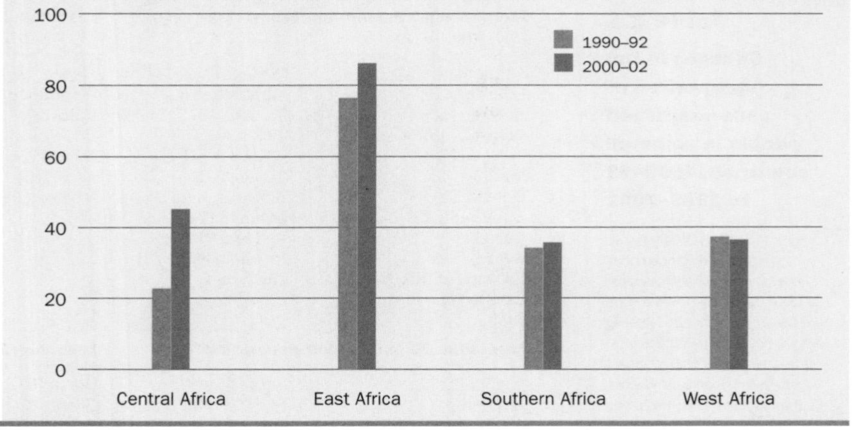

Figure 2.3

The number of undernourished people is declining most in China—and rising most in Central Africa

Source: FAO 2004c.

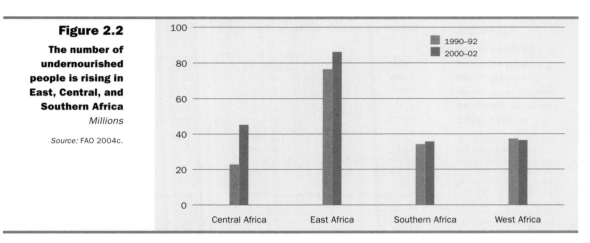

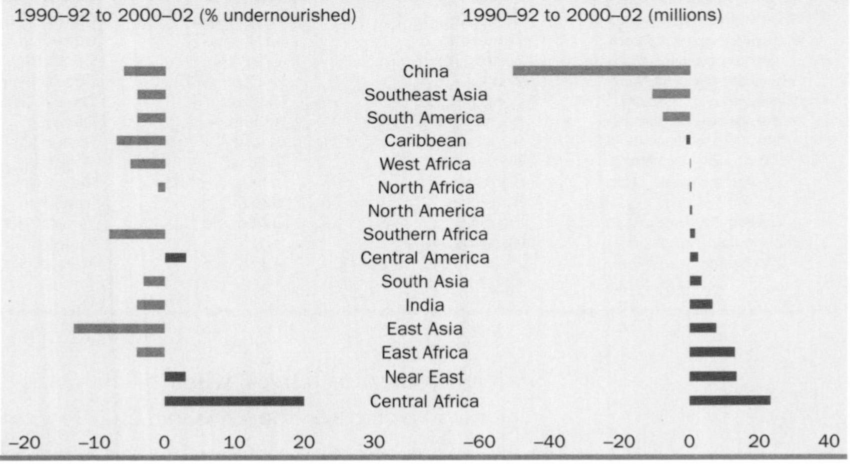

since 1990. Progress in China has slowed as the prevalence of undernourishment was reduced. India experienced an increase of 170 million undernourished between 1990–92 and 2000–02, while the prevalence of undernourishment declined from 25 percent to 21 percent in the same time period (figure 2.3).

Trend data show that undernourishment rates, already over 20 percent, are increasing in 21 countries (upper left quadrant, table 2.1). These countries require a radical change in performance and should therefore be considered a very high priority. Other countries with increasing rates should be considered high-priority areas: more needs to be done here to reverse their worsening trend.

Hunger indicator 2—the prevalence of underweight children under five years of age

Over the past decade, the prevalence of underweight among preschool children has fallen from 32 percent to 28 percent in developing countries (UNICEF 2001). Most regions have shown some improvement, though there is considerable variation among countries. Based on current trends Sub-Saharan Africa,

Table 2.1

Changes in the proportion of undernourished people in selected countries, 1990–92 to 1999–2001

More than 20 percent and increasing [1] = greater than 35%, [2] = 20–35%	Less than 20 percent and increasing [3] = 5–9%
Afghanistan [1][a] Botswana [2] Burundi [1] Congo, Dem. Rep. [1] Eritrea [1] Ethiopia [1] Gambia [2] Guatemala [2] Iraq [2][a] Korea, Dem. People's Rep. [2] Liberia [1] Madagascar [1] Mongolia [1] Panama [2] Papua New Guinea [2] Senegal [2] Sierra Leone [1] Somalia [2] Tajikistan [1] Tanzania [1] Zambia [1]	Algeria [3] Bulgaria [3] Cuba [3] El Salvador [3] Jordan [3] Latvia [3] Moldova [3] Morocco [3] Serbia and Montenegro [3] Slovakia [3] Swaziland [3] Venezuela [3]
More than 20 percent but decreasing	**Less than 20 percent and decreasing**
Angola [1] Armenia [1] Azerbaijan [2] Bangladesh [2] Bolivia [2] Cambodia [1] Cameroon [2] Central African Rep. [1] Chad [2] Congo, Rep. [2] Dominican Rep. [2] Georgia [2] Guinea [2] Haiti [1] Honduras [2] India [2] Kazakhstan [2] Kenya [1] Lao PDR [2] Lesotho [2] Malawi [2] Mali [2] Mozambique [1] Nicaragua [2] Niger [2] Philippines [2] Rwanda [1]b Sri Lanka [2] Sudan [2] Togo [2] Uzbekistan [2] Yemen [2] Zimbabwe [1]	Benin [3] Brazil [3] Bosnia and Herzegovina [3] Burkina Faso [3] China [3][b] Colombia [3] Costa Rica [3] Côte d'Ivoire [3] Croatia [3] Gabon [3] Ghana [3] Guyana [3] Indonesia [3] Iran [3] Jamaica [3] Kyrgyzstan [3] Macedonia, TFYR [3] Mauritania [3] Mauritius [3] Mexico [3] Myanmar [3] Namibia [3] Nepal [2] Pakistan [3] Paraguay [3] Peru [3] Suriname [3] Thailand [3] Trinidad and Tobago [3] Turkmenistan [3] Uganda [3] Viet Nam [3]

Note: Numbers in brackets give ranges for the proportion of undernourished. Table does not include countries for which there were insufficient data. The following developing countries and countries in transition have lower than 5 percent prevalence: Argentina, Albania, Belarus, Chile, Czech Republic, Ecuador, Egypt, Estonia, Hong Kong (China), Libya, Korea, Kuwait, Lebanon, Lithuania, Malaysia, Uruguay, Romania, Russia, Saudi Arabia, Slovenia, Syria, Tunisia, Turkey, Ukraine, United Arab Emirates
a. Estimates of the proportion of undernourished for 1999–2001 are not available; estimates for 1998–2000, published in FAO 2001a, were used instead.
b. Includes Taiwan, China.

Source: Total population from UN Population Division, 2000; undernourishment from FAO 2003.

with few countries on track, will not achieve the hunger Goal (figure 2.4). The region will be farther from the Goal in 2015 than it is today. By contrast, Asia and Latin America on a regional basis are projected to meet or come close to meeting the hunger Goal. It is important to emphasize the significant variation within regions—particularly in Asia, where China's rapid progress to reach the Goal offsets the slow progress in India and elsewhere.

According to a study by Chhabra and Rokx (2004), six of the world's developing countries have already halved the percentage of their underweight children: Kazakhstan, Romania, Dominican Republic, Jamaica, Mexico, and Venezuela. Ten others have prevalence rates that are considered low—at less than 3 percent. Another 25 countries are likely to halve their prevalence rates if they continue to progress at the same rate they achieved after 1990. But despite their positive trends, they must renew and continue their efforts to improve the nutritional status of preschool children and other groups to meet the hunger Goal.

Thirty-eight countries showing unsatisfactory progress are not on track to meet the hunger Goal, as reflected in this indicator. And a further 71 countries have insufficient data or no data on which to base a judgment on progress (figure 2.5). That 71 countries do not have sufficient data is alarming: if gov-

Figure 2.4

The prevalence of underweight children is greatest in South Asia and rising only in Sub-Saharan Africa

Prevalence of underweight children under age 5, 1990–2005 (%)

Source: UNSCN 2004.

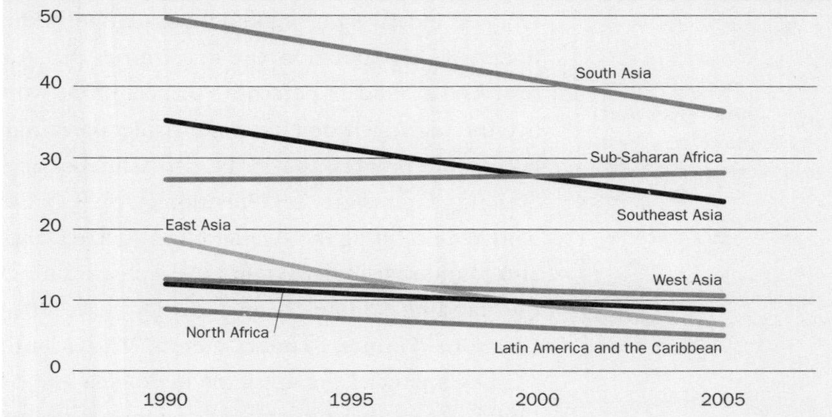

Figure 2.5

Still a long way to the target for Asia and Africa

Prevalence of underweight children under age 5, actual and projected (%)

Source: WHO 2003b.

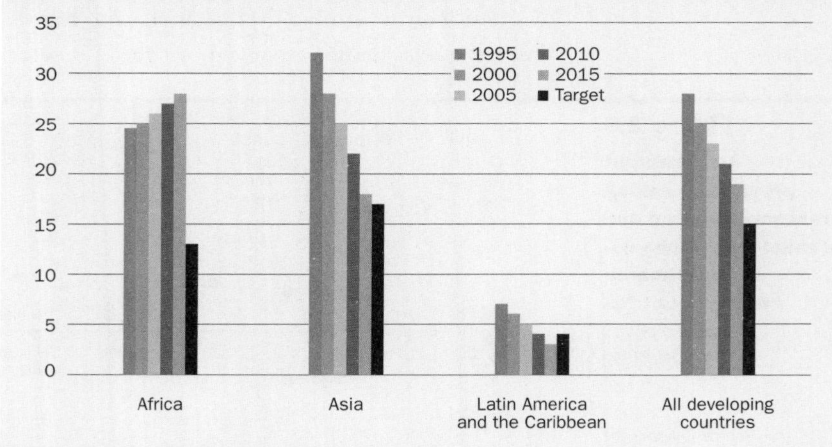

ernments are committed to halving hunger, collecting and monitoring the data to measure their progress toward this goal should be a priority.

Underweight children in Africa

Sub-Saharan Africa has the highest number of countries with increasing rates of malnutrition for children under five—with the highest rates tending to be for landlocked countries and those with a large part of their population in the interior.

In view of the trends expected for the next decade, a special focus is needed on Eastern Africa, which seems likely to suffer from growing hunger, with the prevalence of underweight children under five expected to rise by 36 percent between 1990 and 2005. This dismal forecast reflects civil war, macroeconomic mismanagement, commodity price shocks, and natural disasters such as droughts and floods (UN SCN 2004).

Although Eastern Africa gives cause for special concern, the situation is worrying in most Sub-Saharan African countries. Almost 57 percent of the region's underweight preschool population (around 14 percent of the world's underweight population) live in countries that are making unsatisfactory progress. And around 21 percent (5 percent of the world's underweight population) live in countries where rates are rising alarmingly (figure 2.6). But there has been some progress. According to Chhabra and Rokx (2004) and the UN Standing Committee on Nutrition (UN SCN 2004), underweight prevalence has been declining in Nigeria, Niger, Ghana, and Malawi. Chhabra and Rokx also found that underweight rates were declining in countries not included in the Standing Committee on Nutrition survey: Benin, Botswana, Côte d'Ivoire, Equatorial Guinea, Gambia, Kenya, Mali, Mauritania, Rwanda, and Togo.

Discrepancies are apparent in Angola and Madagascar, where UN SCN (2004) found that underweight rates were decreasing but Chhabra and Rokx (2004) found that they were increasing. Only six countries—Benin, Botswana, Côte d'Ivoire, Gambia, Mauritania, and Togo—have made enough progress over the past decade or so (above the 2.7 percent average decline)[3] to meet

Figure 2.6

Underweight prevalence among preschool children and annual rate of change in Sub-Saharan African countries

Annual change, 1987–2003 (%)

Source: Chhabra and Rokx 2004.

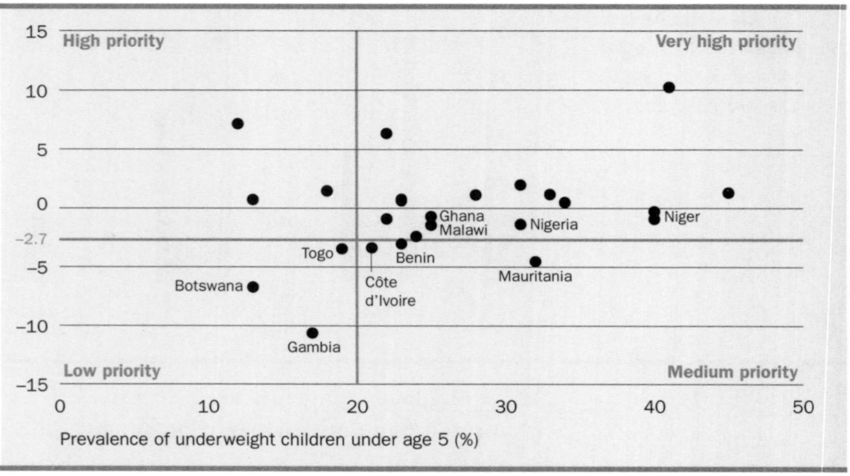

Figure 2.7

Underweight prevalence among preschool children in Sub-Saharan African countries

Share of world's total underweight children under age 5 (%)

Source: ORC-Macro 2004; national Human Development Reports, 1990–2002; African Nutrition Database Initiative; UNICEF 2002, 2003b, 2004; CIESIN 2004; UN Population Division 2002.

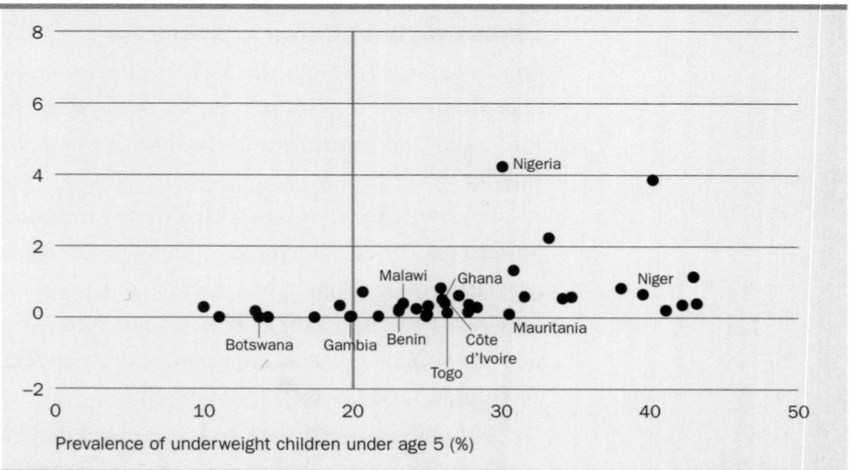

The negative trends in Sub-Saharan Africa reflect the deteriorating conditions facing the poor and hungry

the hunger Goal on the basis of current trends (Chhabra and Rokx 2004). But these countries represent only 5 percent of the population of Sub-Saharan Africa.

The remaining 21 countries (of the 47 in this region) do not have enough data to estimate progress (Chhabra and Rokx 2004). Among them, two deserve high priority: Ethiopia (with around 5.2 million underweight children under the age of five) and the Democratic Republic of Congo (with around 5.7 million underweight children). Both are home to 25 percent of the region's underweight preschool population (6 percent of the world's underweight population).

In absolute numbers, around 32 million preschool children—about 1 in 4 children under five—are underweight in Sub-Saharan countries. The highest numbers of underweight children (around 14 million out of the 32 million in the region) are found in three countries: Nigeria, Ethiopia, and the Democratic Republic of Congo (figure 2.7).

These negative trends in Sub-Saharan Africa reflect the deteriorating conditions facing the poor and hungry in a growing number of the region's countries. Poverty has increased. HIV/AIDS has had a devastating impact. Wars persist. And gains in agricultural productivity remain elusive (UNDP 2003; UN SCN 2004).

Underweight status and trends in the Middle East and North Africa

Countries in the Middle East and North Africa fall into two contrasting groups. Seven countries—Algeria, Djibouti, Jordan, Morocco, Oman, Syria, and Lebanon—have made considerable progress and seem likely, on current trends, to achieve the hunger Goal. Four countries—Egypt, Bahrain, and particularly Iraq and Yemen—urgently need intensive efforts to reduce underweight rates (figure 2.8). Some 56 percent of the region's underweight preschool population (1 percent of the world's underweight population) lives in these four countries. There are not enough data to determine trends for the remaining six countries, representing about 44 percent of the region's underweight population (Chhabra and Rokx 2004). There are roughly 3.3 million underweight children in the entire region, or around 2.5 percent of the world total (figure 2.9).

Subnational distribution of underweight children in Africa

Data for 366 subnational units (states, provinces, or districts) in Africa were gathered (units with data at the national level were excluded). Subnational data were not available for southern Sudan, northeast Kenya, Liberia, or southeast Republic of Congo—areas that have recently experienced conflict and are therefore likely to be facing serious food insecurity and possibly acute malnutrition. Most African countries have high rates of underweight children (20 percent or greater), as do most of their subnational regions. In many countries, including Burundi, Eritrea, Ethiopia, Madagascar, and Sudan, rates of

Figure 2.8
Underweight prevalence among preschool children and annual rate of change in Middle Eastern and North African countries
Annual change, 1987–2003 (%)
Source: Chhabra and Rokx 2004.

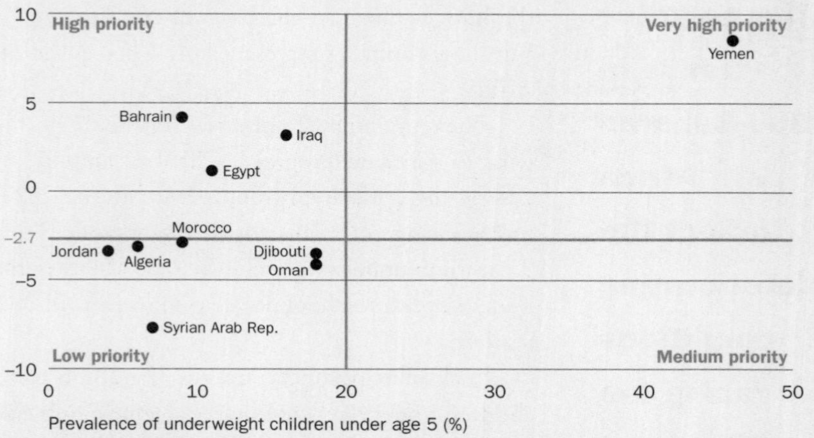

Figure 2.9
Underweight prevalence among preschool children in Middle Eastern and North African countries
Share of world's total underweight children under age 5 (%)
Source: ORC-Macro 2004; national Human Development Reports, 1990-2002; African Nutrition Database Initiative; UNICEF 2002, 2003b, 2004; CIESIN 2004; UN Population Division 2002.

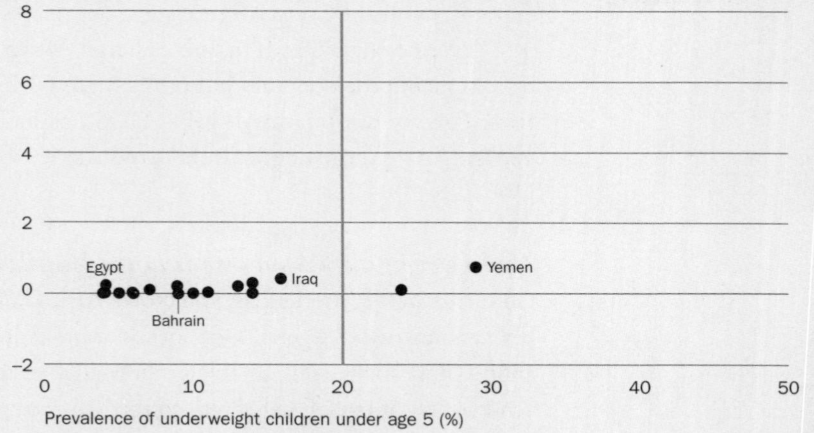

40 percent or more were found in at least half of their subnational regions (map 2.1).

The highest rates and numbers of children underweight are concentrated in subnational units in Angola, Chad, the Democratic Republic of Congo, Ethiopia, Madagascar, Malawi, Mozambique, Niger, Nigeria, Somalia, Sudan, Tanzania, and Uganda. Drawing attention to these areas does not suggest that hunger is not an issue in the rest of Africa—only that hunger is concentrated in the aforementioned places. Of the 366 subnational units analyzed, 229 have underweight rates equal to or higher than 20 percent (areas that are somewhat distinguished by both their population sizes and densities of underweight children), which are home to about 28 million preschool children who are underweight, around 88 percent of the region's underweight children and 21 percent of the world's. The subnational unit with the highest prevalence rate is the middle region of Burundi, which has a rate of around 55 percent. Oromiya, in Ethiopia, is the region with the highest number of underweight preschool

Map 2.1

Prevalence of underweight children in Africa

Percent

Source: CIESIN 2005; ORC-Macro 2004; African Nutrition Database Initiative; UNICEF 2002, 2003b, 2004.

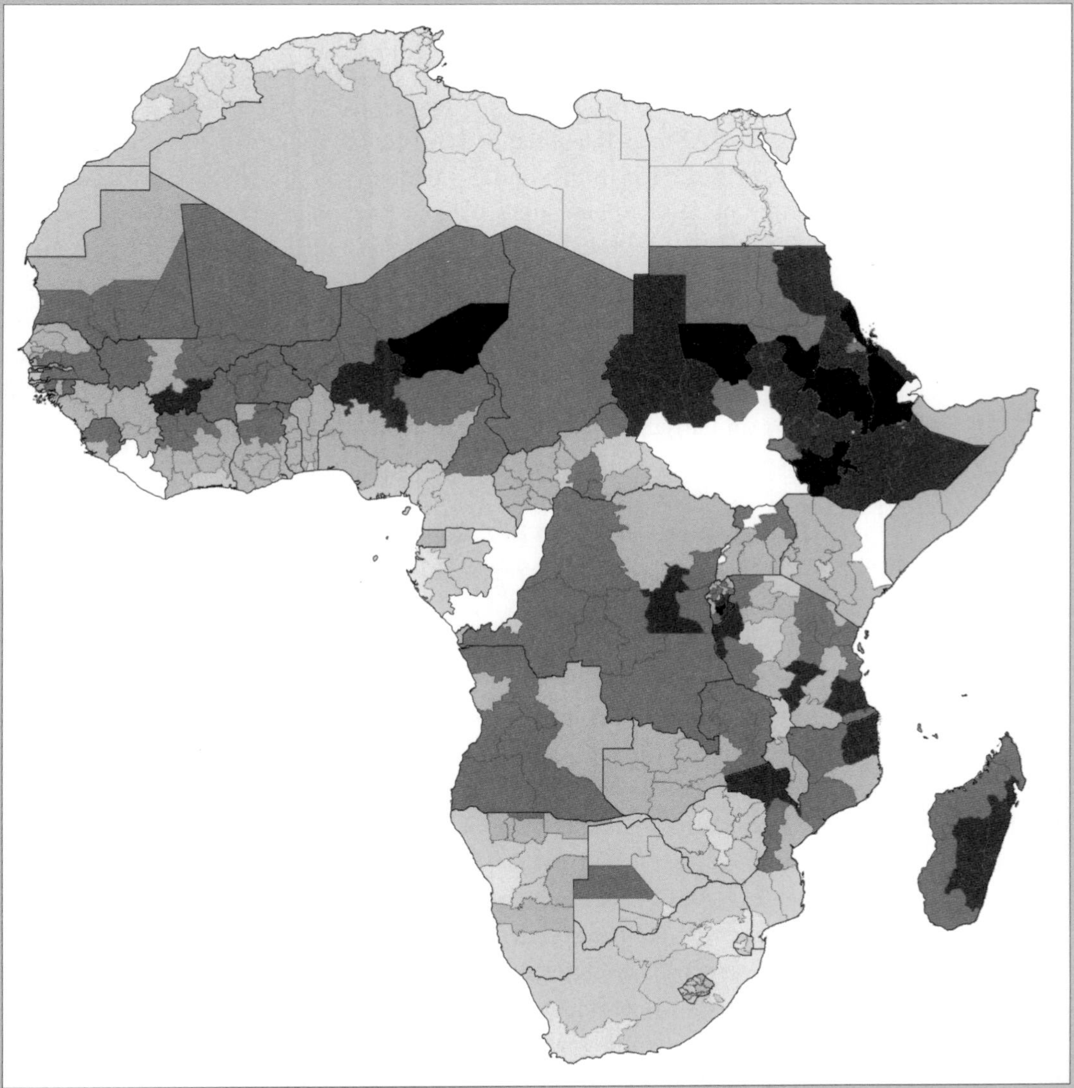

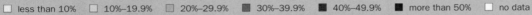

less than 10% | 10%–19.9% | 20%–29.9% | 30%–39.9% | 40%–49.9% | more than 50% | no data

China has shown the most spectacular progress

children (around 1.7 million). Six subnational units have numbers higher than 1 million—three in Ethiopia (Oromiya, Southern, and Amhara) and three in Nigeria (Northeast, Southeast, and Northwest).

The population density of underweight children varies considerably within and across countries. In Ethiopia population densities range from 0.4 to 107.4, but the regions with the highest proportions of underweight children do not differ in their densities from regions with lower proportions of underweight children. Sparsely populated countries like Mauritania, despite having rates of underweight children in the range of 20–40 percent in all regions, also have small populations of underweight children relative to densely populated countries.

The subnational data often distinguish urban centers—such as Bangui (Central African Republic), Addis Ababa (Ethiopia), Antananarivo (Madagascar), and Kigali (Rwanda)—perhaps combined with parts of the surrounding areas. These areas tend to have somewhat smaller percentages of underweight children (though in many instances still above 20 percent) but at much higher population densities than elsewhere in their respective countries. Urban areas may have somewhat smaller shares of underweight children, but these children live in much higher concentrations than children elsewhere. If it were possible to disaggregate all regions by their urban areas, it is likely that similarly high densities of underweight children would become evident (map 2.2).

Underweight children in Asia

The East Asia and Pacific region is making the best progress of all developing regions in reducing preschool malnutrition. Three of the 22 countries in this region, with 77 percent of its total population, are making impressive progress to halve hunger by 2015 (Chhabra and Rokx 2004) (figure 2.10). Of the three countries—China, Indonesia, and Samoa—China has shown the most spectacular progress. Indeed, its most recent national human development report claims to have already met the hunger Goal (UN 2004). Viet Nam, Cambodia, Lao People's Democratic Republic, and the Philippines are also making progress, but not fast enough to achieve the goal. Almost 34 percent of the region's underweight preschool population live in these four countries, representing around 4.4 percent of the world's underweight population. No data were available for Fiji, Kiribati, Papua New Guinea, or the Democratic Republic of Korea (Chhabra and Rokx 2004).

In absolute numbers, around 17 million underweight preschool children, or around 13 percent of the world's total underweight children, live in the East Asia and Pacific region. The highest numbers (around 10.5 million of the 17 million underweight in the region) are in Indonesia, Philippines, and Viet Nam (figure 2.11). The situation in the Philippines is the most critical one. It has a high underweight population (around 2.5 million) and its average annual

Map 2.2

Population density of underweight children in Africa

Children per square kilometer

Source: ORC-Macro 2004; African Nutrition Database Initiative; UNICEF 2002, 2003b, 2004; CIESIN 2004; UN Population Division 2002.

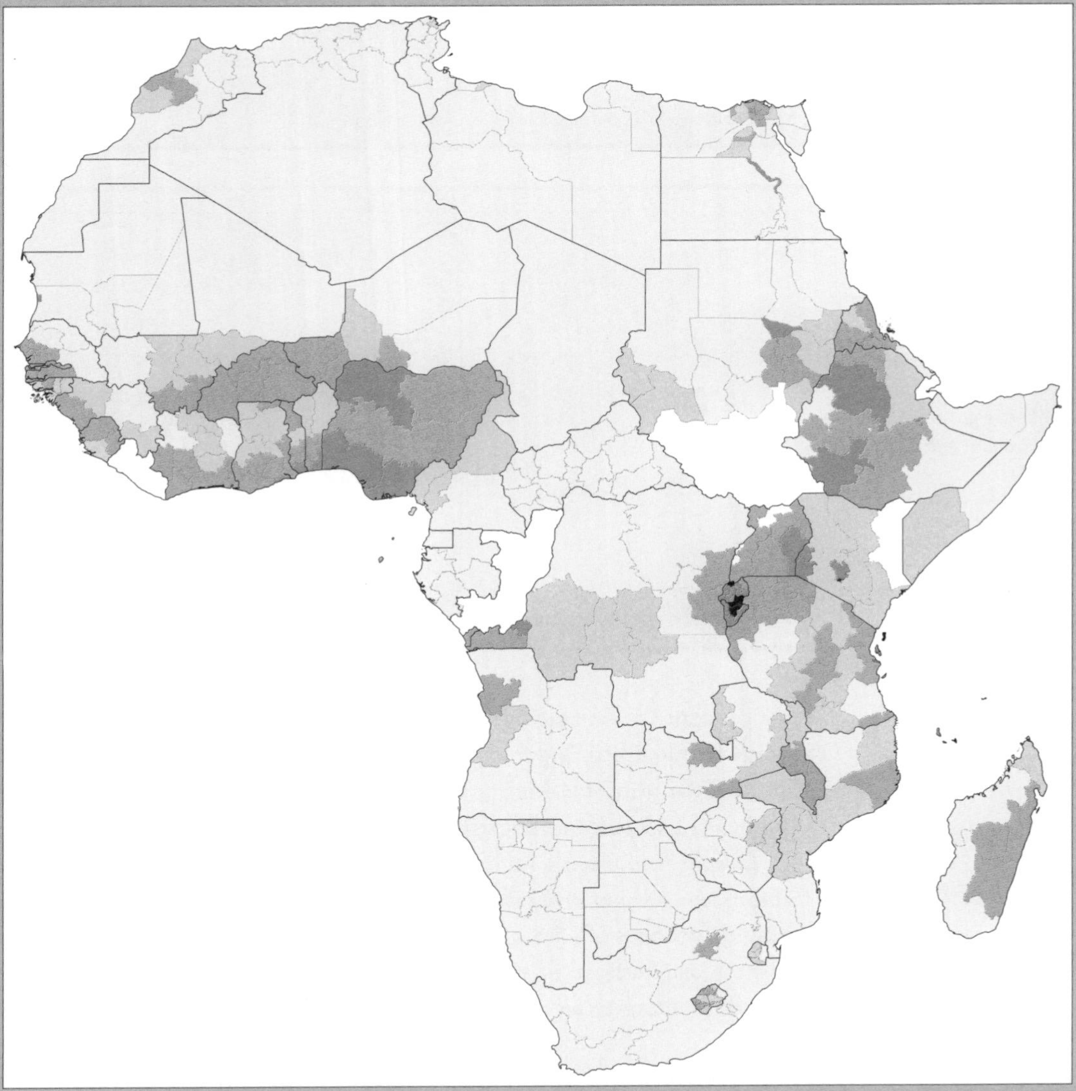

less than 1 | 1–2 | 2–8 | 8–25 | 25–50 | more than 50 | no data

Figure 2.10

Underweight prevalence among preschool children and annual rate of change in East Asian and Pacific countries

Annual change, 1987–2003 (%)

Source: Chhabra and Rokx 2004.

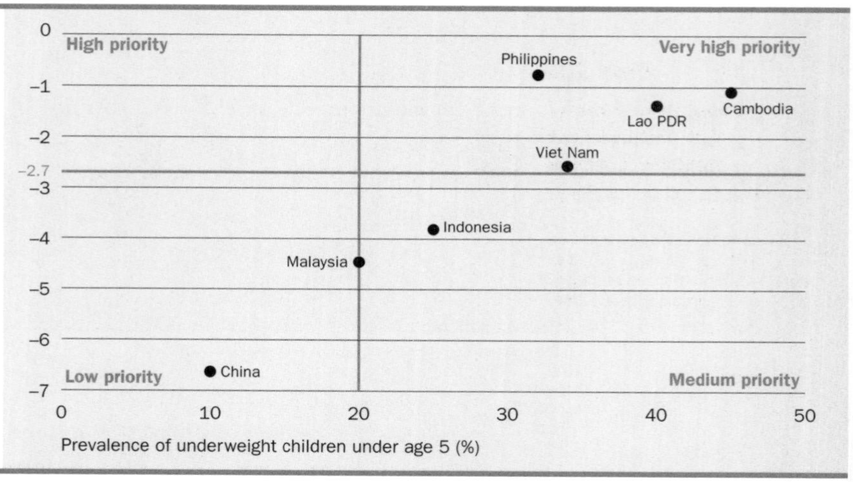

Figure 2.11

Underweight prevalence among preschool children in East Asian and Pacific countries

Share of world's total underweight children under age 5 (%)

Source: ORC-Macro 2004; national Human Development Reports, 1990–2002; African Nutrition Database Initiative; UNICEF 2002, 2003b, 2004; CIESIN 2004; UN Population Division 2002.

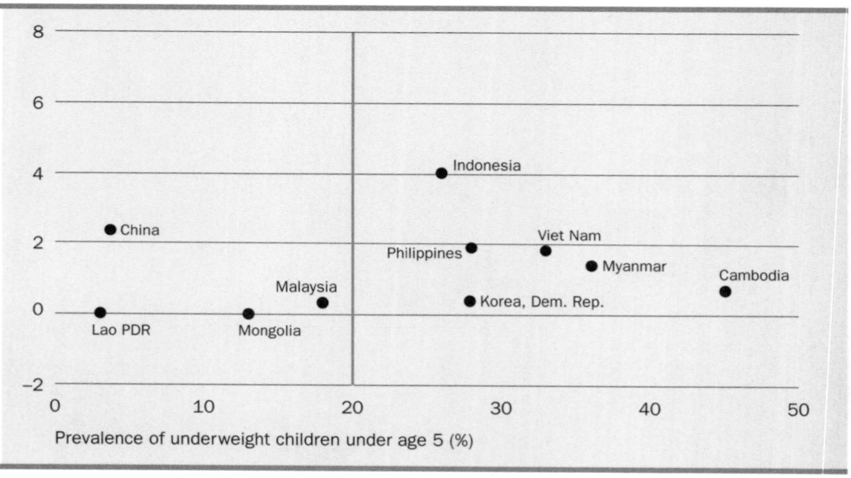

rate of progress is very slow if compared with the annual average rate to achieve the hunger Goal (–0.76 percent versus –2.7 percent). The absolute numbers in Viet Nam are almost as high as the ones in the Philippines. Its rate of progress is higher (–2.55 percent) but still not high enough to meet the hunger Goal.

Despite Indonesia's high number of underweight children (around 5.4 million), the pace of progress toward achieving the hunger Goal is impressive, averaging declines of –3.8 percent. Ongoing efforts and commitments to fight hunger must increase in this region, especially in the Philippines and Viet Nam, if the hunger target is to be attained.

Underweight status and trends in South Asian countries

In South Asia the underweight rates observed are as high as those observed in many Sub-Saharan African countries. But the total number of hungry people is considerably larger. Bangladesh, India, Sri Lanka, Pakistan, and Nepal are home to the vast majority of the underweight preschool population in South

Asia—making this region the worst affected in terms of absolute numbers of underweight children. The eight countries in this region are home to 76 million underweight preschool children, around 57 percent of the world's total (figure 2.13).

Special attention must go to this region, particularly to India, Bangladesh, and Pakistan. India alone is home to around 55 million underweight preschool children (about 40 percent of the world's total). Bangladesh and Pakistan each have more than 8 million underweight preschool children and underweight rates higher than 45 percent. The annual average rate of progress toward achieving the hunger Millennium Development Goal is better in Bangladesh (–2.17 percent) than in Pakistan (–1.28 percent) and in India (–1.6 percent). But it is still lower than the rate of progress needed. At current rates of progress, these countries are unlikely to achieve the hunger Goal. Even if they can halve

Figure 2.12
Underweight prevalence among preschool children and annual rate of change in South Asian countries
Annual change, 1987–2003 (%)

Source: Chhabra and Rokx 2004.

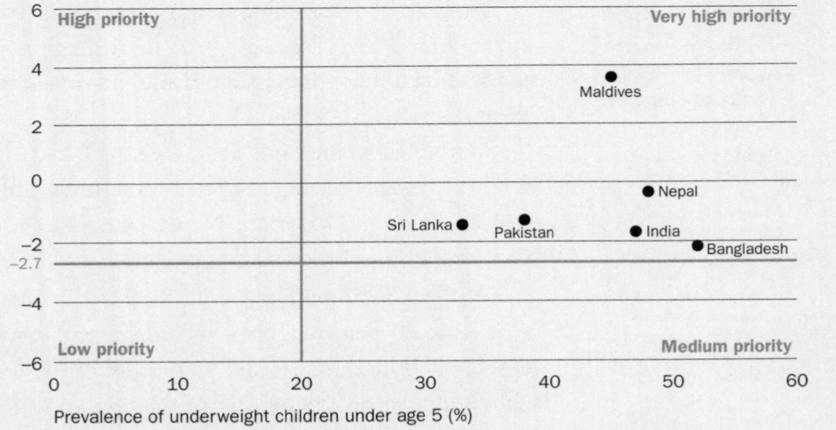

Figure 2.13
Underweight prevalence among preschool children underweight in South Asian countries
Share of world's total underweight children under age 5 (%)

Source: ORC-Macro 2004; national Human Development Reports, 1990–2002; African Nutrition Database Initiative; UNICEF 2002, 2003b, 2004; CIESIN 2004; UN Population Division 2002.

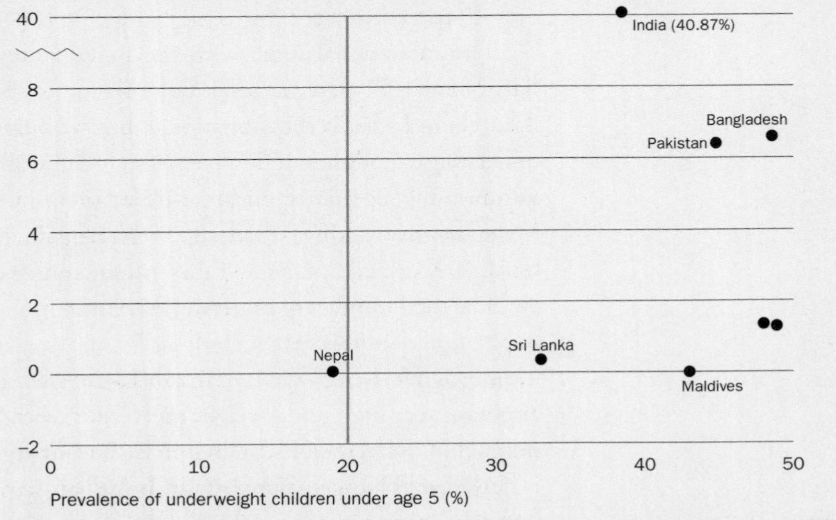

South Asia stands out as having very high rates and numbers of underweight children

these rates by 2015, they will still have unacceptably high prevalence rates (figure 2.12). More must to be done to reverse this worsening trend.

Afghanistan and Nepal have similar rates but lower absolute numbers (between 1 and 5 million). Pakistan has lower prevalence rates (between 30 percent and 40 percent) but higher absolute numbers (more than 5 million). In Maldives the absolute number is low (around 1,000 underweight children) but the prevalence rate has been increasing in the past decade or so. Insufficient data were available for Afghanistan and Bhutan.

Subnational distributions of underweight children in Asia

The task force's subnational analysis of underweight distribution evaluated data for 172 subnational units in Asia. This excludes units with data where subnational data were not available, including Iraq, Yemen, Oman, and Saudi Arabia.

The size of these subnational units varies tremendously across countries and regions. This is especially true in this region where, in India and Pakistan, subnational units represent states and provinces, while in Bangladesh they represent districts.

South Asia stands out as having very high rates and numbers of underweight children. The highest rates and numbers of underweight preschool children are in India, Pakistan, Nepal, Bangladesh, Uzbekistan, Myanmar, Viet Nam, the Philippines, Indonesia, and Afghanistan.

Of the 172 subnational units analyzed in Asia, 76 had underweight rates of at least 20 percent. They include approximately 78 million underweight preschool children or around 95 percent of the region's total underweight preschool population (58 percent of the total global underweight population). In Bangladesh, India, Nepal, and Pakistan, all subnational units have prevalence rates above 20 percent—and all the units in Bangladesh and Nepal have levels over 40 percent (map 2.3).

The subnational units with the highest prevalence rates were Sylhet in Bangladesh (57 percent) and Balochistan in Pakistan (56 percent). Uttar Pradesh, in India, is the subnational unit with the highest absolute number of underweight children under five (close to 9.3 million). Twenty-two units have numbers higher than 1 million—12 of them in India: Uttar Pradesh, Bihar, Maharashtra, Madhya Pradesh, West Bengal, Rajasthan, Andhra Pradesh, Gujarat, Karnataka, Orissa, Tamil Nadu, and Assam.

The total number of underweight children, and their correspondingly high population densities, particularly in South Asia, stand out as an order of magnitude higher than those in Africa or Latin America. Cambodia and Myanmar also have very high underweight prevalence, with Myanmar also having a high number of underweight children in each of its regions (map 2.4).

Although hunger is important in Afghanistan, Indonesia, the Philippines, People's Democratic Republic of Korea, Sri Lanka, Viet Nam, and even Oman,

Map 2.3
Prevalence of underweight children in Asia
Percent

Source: ORC-Macro 2004; national Human Development
Reports, 1990–2002; UNICEF 2002, 2003b, 2004.

☐ less than 10% ☐ 10%–19.9% ☐ 20%–29.9% ☐ 30%–39.9% ■ 40%–49.9% ■ more than 50% ☐ no data

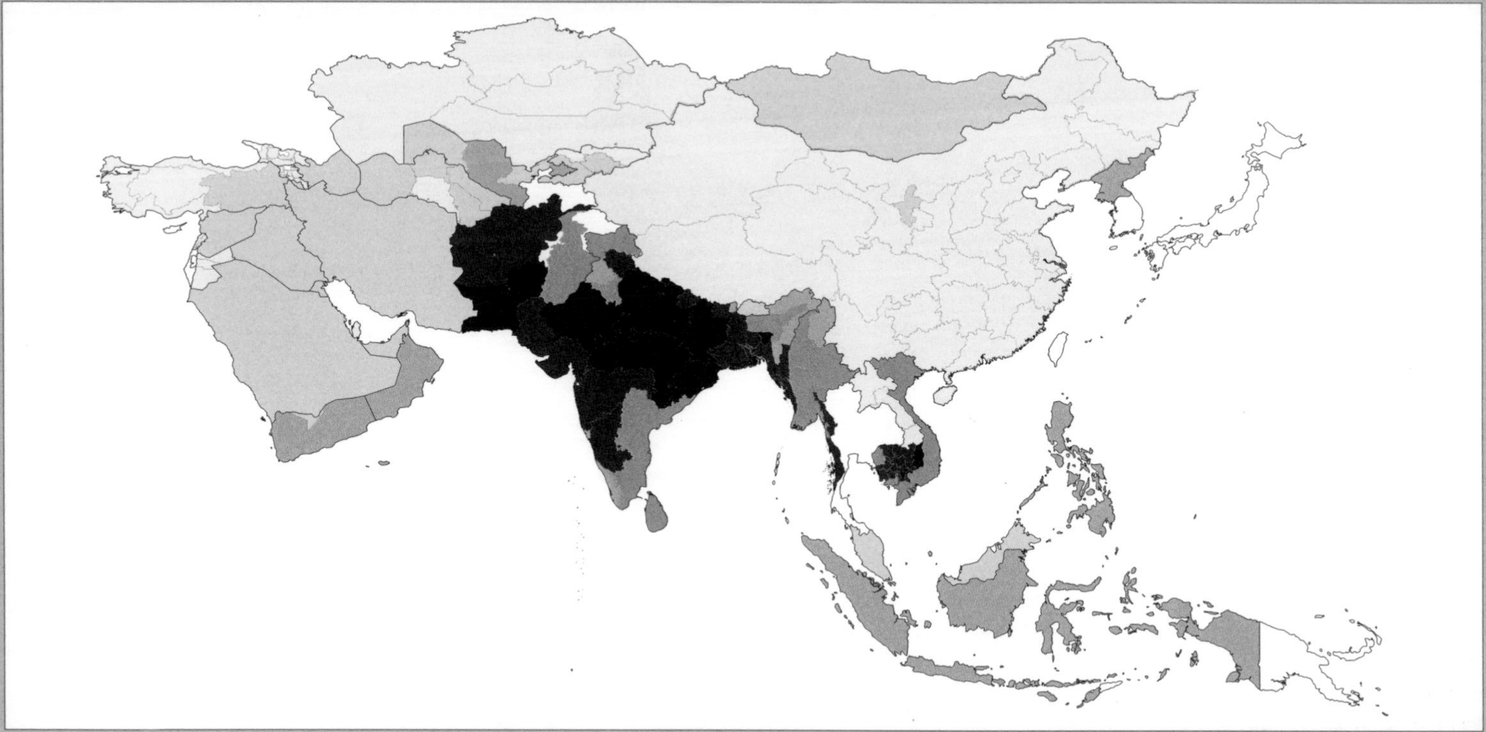

Map 2.4
Population density of underweight children in Asia
Children per square kilometer

Source: ORC-Macro 2004; national Human Development Reports, 1990–2002; UNICEF 2002, 2003b, 2004; CIESIN 2004; UN Population Division 2002.

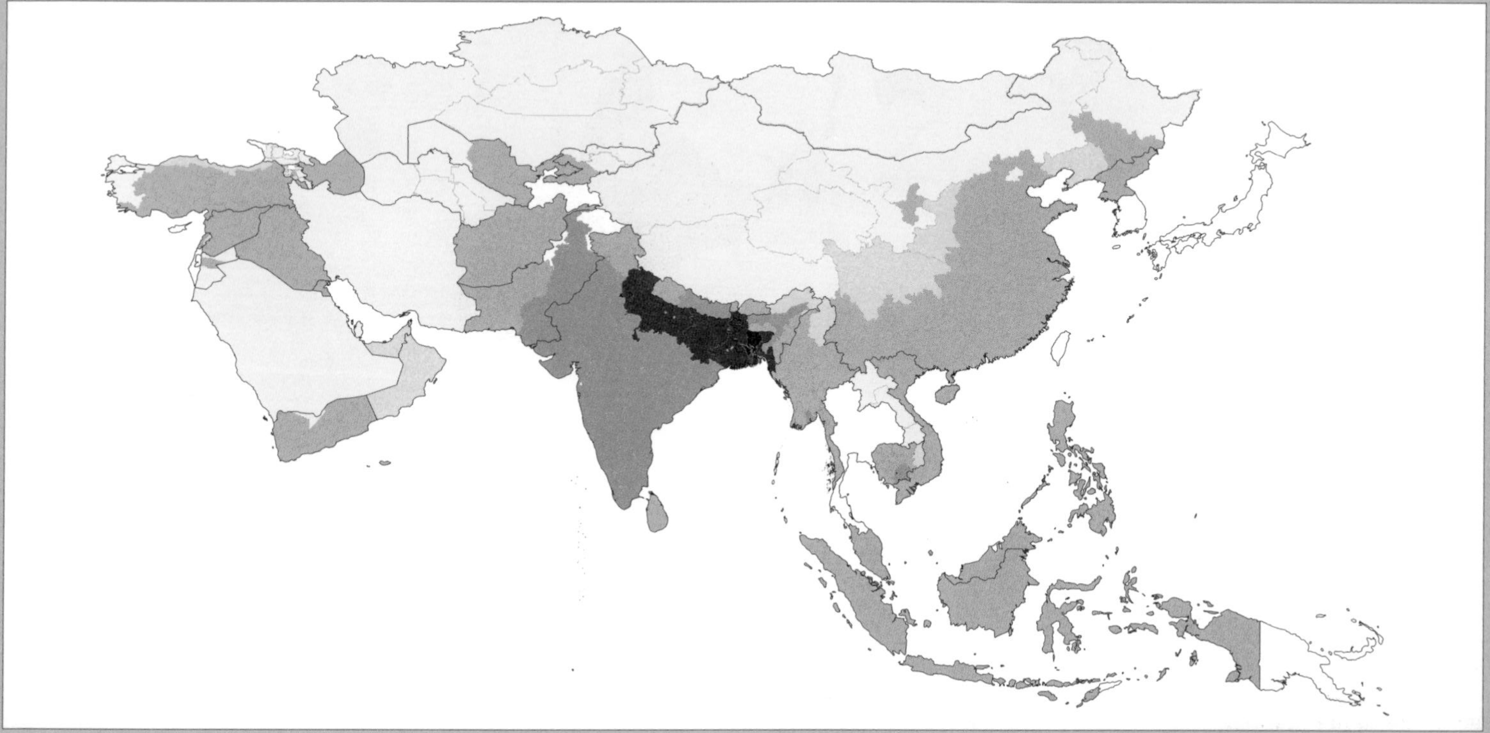

Spatial disaggregation would assist in the specification of hunger hotspots

conclusions based on national data are too aggregated to justify commentary. Subnational views of these countries would indicate a much more refined picture of hunger for analysis and policymaking. Similarly, the sheer size of South Asia calls for higher resolution data, since spatial disaggregation would assist in the specification of hunger hotspots. (The population and land area of several Indian states exceed those of Cambodia, which has data for 17 subnational units.)

Underweight children in Central Asia and Europe

Based on current data, Kazakhstan and Romania have already halved underweight nutrition in preschool children against their 1990 baseline figures. The highest concentration of underweight preschool children is in Turkey and Uzbekistan. Turkey is on track to meet the target well before 2015, but there are no trend data to assess progress in Uzbekistan. Eight countries—Yugoslavia, the Russian Federation, Croatia, Georgia, Czech Republic, Moldova, Ukraine, and Armenia—have shown satisfactory performance. And all now have low rates (less than 3 percent) of preschool underweight. Azerbaijan needs urgent attention since it is the only country where the prevalence of underweight is increasing (figure 2.14).

Special attention needs to go to data collection and monitoring in this region, where data for 16 of 27 countries were either completely lacking or insufficient for trend analysis.

In absolute numbers, the region is home to around 1.5 million underweight preschool children, or around 1 percent of the world's underweight population (figure 2.15).

Underweight children in Latin America and the Caribbean

There are roughly 4 million underweight preschool children in Latin America, or around 3 percent of the world's underweight population. Underweight rates in this region are substantially lower than in Sub-Saharan Africa and Asia. Over the past decade, the percentage of underweight preschool children has fallen from about 13–14 percent to 8–9 percent. Seven countries in the region—Bolivia, Colombia, El Salvador, Guyana, Haiti, Peru, and Uruguay—are making good progress toward achieving the hunger Goal. Four countries—Dominican Republic, Jamaica, Mexico, and Venezuela—have already halved hunger. Chile and Costa Rica have rates lower than 3 percent, similar to the rates observed in developed countries (figure 2.16).

Only two countries in the region have rates of underweight prevalence higher than 20 percent: Guatemala and Honduras. Guatemala is making marginal progress, while Brazil, Honduras, and Nicaragua are not making enough progress to achieve the Goal. Panama is the only country in the region where underweight prevalence is increasing, especially among the indigenous population (Chhabra and Rokx 2004). The highest numbers of underweight pre-

Figure 2.14

Underweight prevalence among preschool children and annual rate of change in European and Central Asian countries

Annual change, 1987–2003 (%)

Source: Chhabra and Rokx 2004.

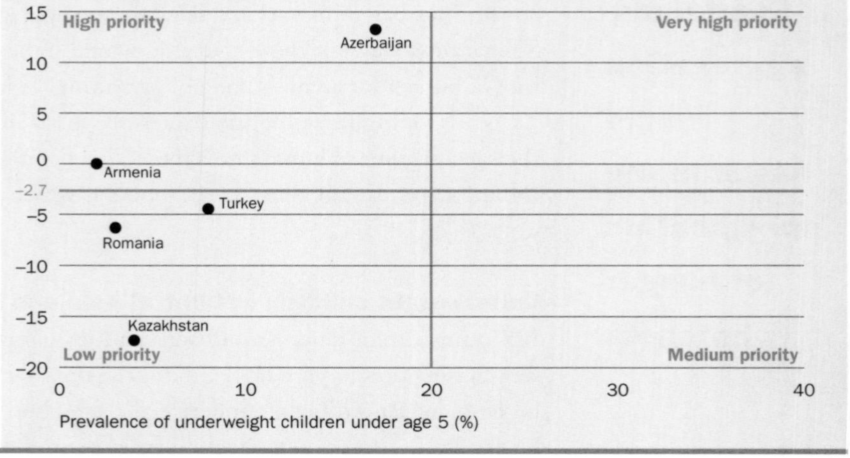

Figure 2.15

Underweight prevalence among preschool children in European and Central Asian countries

Share of world's total underweight children under age 5 (%)

Source: ORC-Macro 2004; national Human Development Reports, 1990–2002; African Nutrition Database Initiative; UNICEF 2002, 2003b, 2004; CIESIN 2004; UN Population Division 2002.

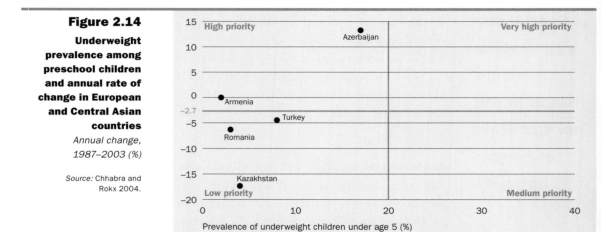

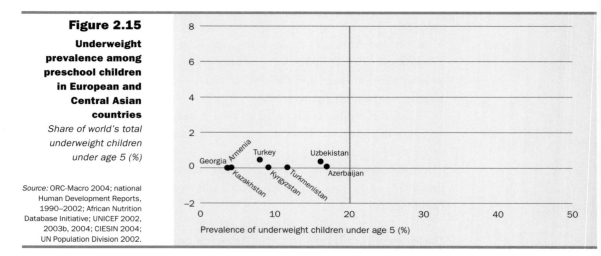

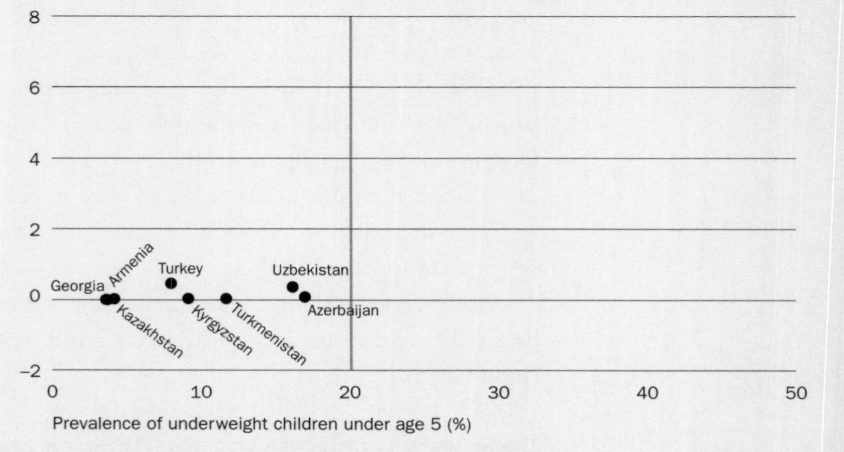

school children (around 850,000) are found in Brazil and Mexico (figure 2.17). No data were available for Ecuador, French Guyana, Paraguay, or Surinam.

Subnational distribution of underweight children in Latin America

The task force's subnational analysis showed that child underweight figures are substantially lower for Latin America than for either Africa or Asia. Data were available for 106 subnational units, but none of these units were in Mexico, Ecuador, Chile, Argentina, Venezuela, or Cuba. Of the 106 subnational units, only 8 have underweight rates equal to or higher than 20 percent. They are home to approximately 400,000 underweight preschool children or around 17 percent of the region's underweight population (0.3 percent of the world's total). The subnational data for Haiti are comparable to those found in some places in Africa. The Latin American surveys have many subnational units (similar to many of the African nations) which allows fuller analysis of the

Figure 2.16
Underweight prevalence among preschool children and annual rate of change in Latin American countries
Annual change, 1987–2003 (%)

Source: Chhabra and Rokx 2004.

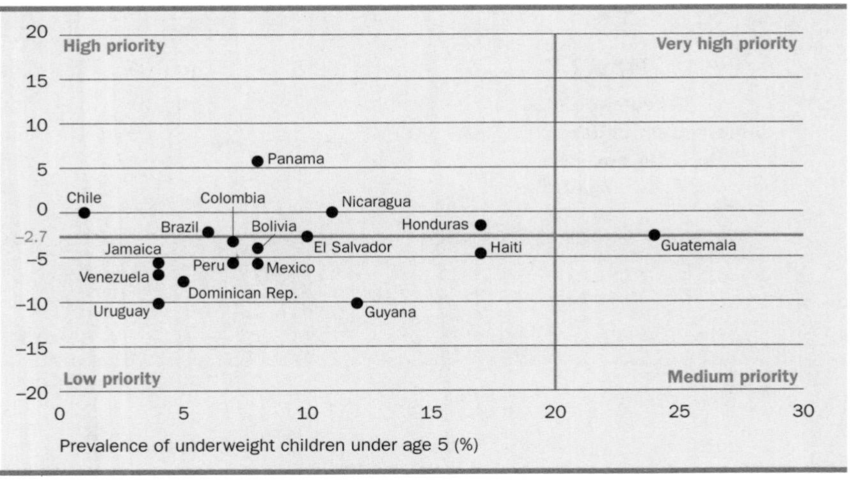

Figure 2.17
Underweight prevalence among preschool children in Latin American countries
Share of world's total underweight children under age 5 (%)

Source: ORC-Macro 2004; national Human Development Reports, 1990–2002; African Nutrition Database Initiative; UNICEF 2002, 2003b, 2004; CIESIN 2004; UN Population Division 2002.

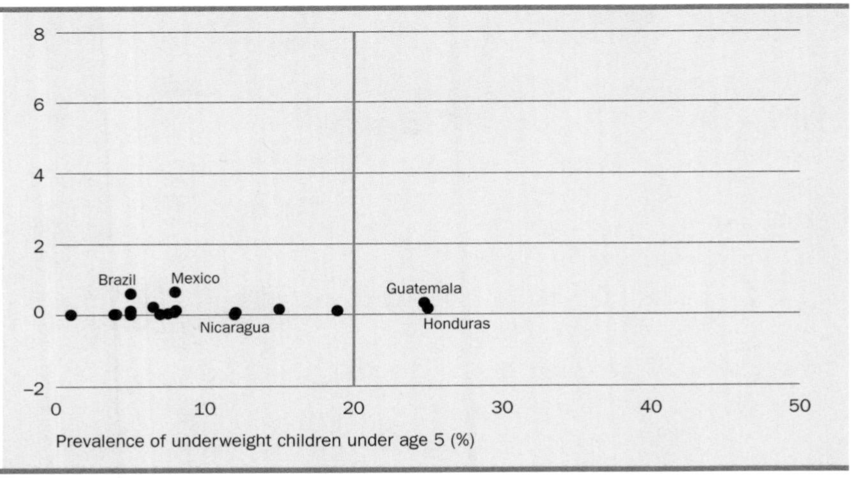

distribution of the problem, and thereby an increased ability to target it in the region (map 2.5).

The highest prevalence rates and numbers occur in Guatemala, Haiti, and Nicaragua. Three subnational units in Guatemala have the highest rates: Northwest (33.4 percent), Southwest (29.4 percent), and Northeast (29.1 percent). The lowest underweight rate was observed in Monquegua, in Peru (0.4 percent).

Only one subnational region, Guatemala's Southwest, has a prevalence and population size above the critical thresholds commonly found in Africa or Asia. Like countries in Asia, however, several populous countries have only national data, including Argentina, Chile, Ecuador, Honduras, Mexico, and Venezuela. Subnational data would highlight which, if any, subnational regions have underweight rates, and dense populations of underweight children, that stand far above their national averages. Given the low levels of underweight prevalence in Latin America, it may be even more important to identify regions—

Map 2.5

Prevalence of underweight children in Latin America

Percent

Source: ORC-Macro 2004; national Human Development Reports, 1990–2002; UNICEF 2002, 2003b, 2004.

☐ less than 10% ☐ 10%–19.9% ☐ 20%–29.9% ☐ more than 30 ☐ no data

Map 2.6

Population density of underweight children in Latin America

Children per square kilometer

Source: ORC-Macro 2004; national Human Development Reports, 1990–2002; UNICEF 2002, 2003b, 2004; CIESIN 2004; UN Population Division 2002.

☐ less than 0.1 ☐ 0.1–0.3 ☐ 0.3–2.0 ▨ 2–7 ■ more than 7 ☐ no data

Map 2.7
Index combining normalized rates of underweight prevalence and population density of underweight children

Source: ORC-Macro 2004; national Human Development Reports, 1990–2002; African Nutrition Database Initiative; UNICEF 2002, 2003b, 2004; CIESIN 2004; UN Population Division 2002.

Note: This index combines the proportion of children underweight and the population density of underweight children for each surveyed region. To create the index. each measure is normalized such that its new average, over all regions, is 0, and its standard deviation is 1. The two normalized values are added for each region to create the new index. The mapped classes are quintiles of the full distribution of the index.

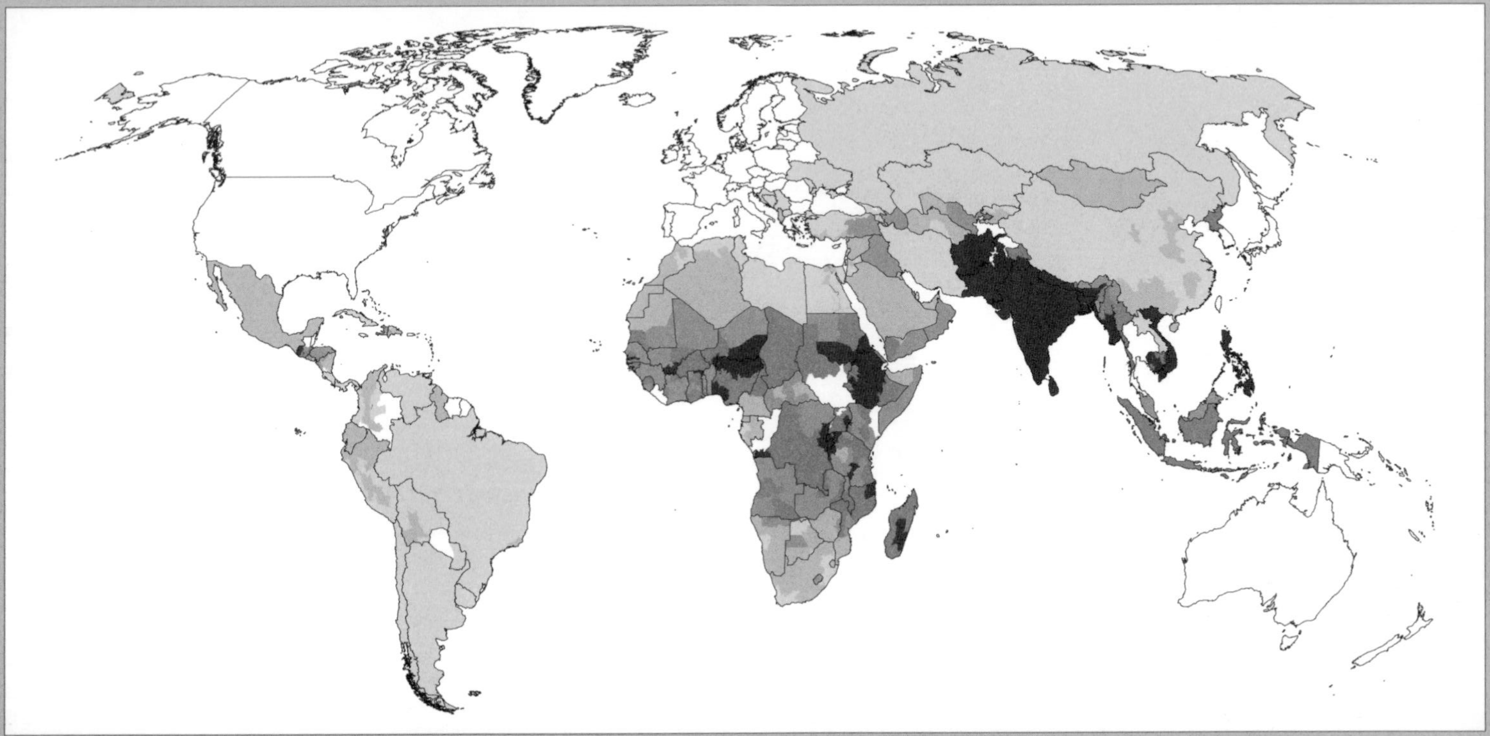

☐ lowest ☐ low ☐ middle ☐ high ■ highest ☐ data not available

Prevalence and density can be instrumental for targeting and shaping the design of hunger alleviation programs

including the large urban areas, and their associated slum populations—that have higher levels of hunger (map 2.6).

Future efforts to characterize global hunger should include additional efforts to determine subnational rates in some of the world's most populous countries and subnational regions.

A global view of the prevalence and density of underweight children

The data in this section show the distribution of underweight children from two perspectives: prevalence and density. Both perspectives can be instrumental for targeting and shaping the design of hunger alleviation programs. The task force took the additional step of combining these two perspectives in a global map, to show simultaneously prevalence and density.

To do so, we created an index combining normalized rates of underweight prevalence and population density of underweight children for each region. To create the index, each of the two measures was normalized so that its new average over all regions was zero, with a standard deviation of one. The two normalized values were added for each region to create the new index. The full distribution was divided into quintiles (map 2.7). The darkest regions have the highest prevalence and the highest density of underweight children. The lightest regions have lower prevalence and density. The medium shades represent intermediate combinations of these factors (CIESIN 2004).

A strategic approach for halving hunger

This chapter outlines the Task Force on Hunger's approach for halving hunger by 2015. We begin by describing the principles that should guide strategy formulation and implementation at the country level. We then describe the vulnerability analysis of food insecurity that guided our strategy, outlining the tools used to formulate our recommendations and providing an overview of these recommendations, which the following chapters elaborate in greater detail. A critical element of our approach is that national poverty reduction strategies or PRSPs, where they exist, must focus on the policy and investment needs to reach the Goals. Such national strategies can be powerful tools for overcoming hunger and achieving all the Goals. But they must be deployed and implemented for that purpose. National poverty reduction strategies should be based on needs assessments and plans that include all the Millennium Development Goals and are developed through an open, consultative process that involves all the key stakeholders from national to local levels.

The core recommendation of the UN Millennium Project is to put the Millennium Development Goals at the center of national and international poverty reduction strategies through a series of specific and practical efforts by each developing country and its development partners. The principles that guided the formulation of such national strategies should also guide implementation. The fundamental principle behind focusing on hunger is that unless hunger is dealt with successfully, the achievement of the other Goals will be compromised. Some of the guiding principles of the Task Force on Hunger include forging a global partnership, promoting good governance, mainstreaming gender equality, adopting a people-centered approach, and investing in science and technology.

These principles and the resulting recommendations are determined partly by the lessons learned from past successes and failures in reducing hunger—

The international community needs to strengthen global partnerships to fight hunger and attain all the Goals

and partly from recent international initiatives and agreements that pave the way for the renewed drive to eliminate hunger. Some principles will need to be observed by national governments in developing countries, others by the international community that supports their efforts.

Forging a global partnership

It is clear that the international community—developed and developing countries alike—needs to strengthen and build upon existing global partnerships to fight hunger and attain all the Goals. The essence of these partnerships should be as follows:

- Developing country governments agree to review, evaluate, and reform policies for their impact on hunger and to remove the constraints that impede progress toward hunger reduction.
- Developing countries agree to make allocations for hunger reduction in national budgets that reflect the importance of addressing the social and economic costs of hunger and specify the resources needed to attain the hunger Goal.
- Developing countries focus on the empowerment of the poor and ensure gender equality so that the food-insecure can take the necessary actions to improve their livelihoods.
- Developed countries honor their commitments to allocate adequate amounts of new money to the fight against hunger and put in place suitable policy reforms at the global level (such as those for trade and untying aid).
- The donor community agrees to harmonize its efforts and offer long-term commitments to support well-formulated national poverty reduction strategies to fight hunger, to improve the targeting of aid to the poor, and to measure results.
- Multilateral agencies work with developing countries to put in place holistic strategies to halve hunger.
- Governments take steps toward the progressive realization of the right to adequate food.
- The international community, such as the Intergovernmental Committee on World Food Security, agrees to review the institutional arrangements in place to combat hunger; make necessary reforms; document and disseminate promising practices to relevant global, regional, national, and local entities; and monitor the impact of macro-level policies on vulnerable livelihood systems.

These principles are in line with the intention of the UN Millennium Declaration, which commits the world's political leaders to work together toward a set of development objectives, subsequently specified as the Millennium Development Goals. This new partnership will require long-term investments with a horizon of well over a decade to reach the threshold of self-sustaining growth.

Participatory governance should be expanded and deepened

One of the reasons why development projects have failed in the past is that they have ended prematurely. Longer term commitments for agricultural productivity, physical and institutional infrastructure development, and capacity building are necessary for efforts to achieve scale and impact.

Through the UN Millennium Declaration the world has made a deal: poor countries commit to good governance and development policies based on sound science and the scaling up of best practices—while rich countries commit to providing greater financial and technical assistance, market access, and knowledge transfers. This deal brings hope that the inefficiencies of past development efforts will be replaced by real progress, based on shared rights and responsibilities.

Promoting good governance

The UN Millennium Declaration is based on an understanding that achieving the Goals depends in part on greater transparency of government and greater and more equitable application of the rule of law, in accord with human rights. Participatory governance should be expanded and deepened, and fair and transparent ways of conducting transactions should be followed. The rule of law should apply to all, independent of gender, social position, or ethnic origin. Many developing country governments have since made strong commitments to improve governance, and many have begun the needed reforms, including legislative measure to protect people's right to food.

The UN Millennium Project (2005) distinguishes between two different types of "poor governance." The first type is where a low-income government wishes to carry out reforms but lacks the resources to do so. The public management systems are consequently very weak. The problem is the inadequacy of public resources to train, retain, and properly compensate public officials. In these circumstances, weak governance can be addressed as an "investment problem," requiring several years of investment in improved public management and administration.

A second, very different type of poor governance is volitional. In these cases, national leaders don't wish to reform. Corruption is rampant, and the political elite represent a narrow group in society. This situation is much harder to address. Conditionality from the outside rarely makes a difference, and increased development aid might easily be diverted rather than properly invested.

Countries that have committed to or embarked on the path to good governance merit support from donor countries and agencies. There will be a continuing need to tackle the local aspects of good governance that affect the freedom of people to fight poverty and hunger. Good governance must also be based on human rights. States should implement their obligations on the right to adequate food and in so doing make use of the Voluntary Guidelines to Support the Progressive Realization of the Right to Adequate Food in the

Ensuring control of assets will be required if women are to have the means of producing or purchasing food

Context of National Food Security, adopted by the Committee on World Food Security in September 2004.

The fight to reduce hunger will depend to a great extent on improvements in local governance. Poor people are particularly affected at the local level by the inequitable access to resources, the retention of power by local elites, the existence of multiple official and informal obstacles to doing day-to-day business, and the continual requirement to pay bribes for simple services. Poor people are thus often excluded from decisionmaking and planning at the community and local levels. These aspects of poor governance can be deeply rooted in societies. They can also prove intractable, even when the country has embarked on reform toward good governance at the national level.

The real challenge lies in addressing the weakness of institutions at all levels of government. Reforming local government will be vital to weaken the hold of local elites and provide incentives for poor families to produce and trade. The maze of national to local legislation that often requires people to go through numerous transactions to carry out their day-to-day business (such as obtaining a permit to export produce) should be simplified as it stifles initiatives to invest and produce. Serious action is needed to overcome corruption at all levels. Donors should support multilevel approaches to establish or rehabilitate institutions and ensure effective coordination among them.

Mainstreaming gender equality

Addressing issues of gender equality is a fundamental precondition to overcoming the persistent causes of hunger. Ensuring access to and control of assets (social, financial, natural) will be required if women are to have the means of producing or purchasing food. Adequate attention at the national level and promoting its application to the local levels are critical to ensuring proper implementation and results.

Women produce more than half the food in Latin America and South Asia (Hayzer 2003) and 80 percent in Africa (FAO 1997). They not only supply much of the labor for agricultural production but also are responsible for most of the household economy. They fetch water, gather firewood, cook for the family, market surplus produce, and provide most childcare. They are the key to the health and nutrition of infants and children. If women are unable to plan their pregnancies—and properly space births—they and their children suffer poor nutritional outcomes. These same women often have less opportunity to breastfeed their children—further worsening the poor nutritional status of newborns. Because they also educate children and pass on knowledge, ensuring their access to educational opportunities (Millennium Development Goal 3) is vital not only in its own right but also to improve the health and nutritional status of themselves and their children.

Despite the central importance of women in reducing poverty, producing food, and improving livelihoods, they are still systematically bypassed by most

Well designed programs should decentralize decision-making and financial authority

formal—and some informal—extension and development services, projects, and programs. So an important first step toward women's empowerment and full participation in rural development and food security strategies is to collect and analyze gender-disaggregated data to understand role differences in food and cash crop production—as well as men's and women's different managerial and financial control over production, storage, and marketing of agricultural goods (FAO 1997).

The developing world must move beyond rhetoric to put gender equality into practice if the hunger Goal, and all the other Goals, are to be met. The aim should not be to simply remove barriers. It must be to ensure women's rights and to empower them to develop and apply their skills and knowledge in all aspects of rural development. If this does not happen, our efforts to eliminate hunger will fail.

Adopting a people-centered approach

The expectation of increased funding is central to reaching the Goals, but experience over the past 30 years has shown weaknesses and limitations in supply-led, top-down approaches. Well designed programs should decentralize decisionmaking and financial authority to the local level, where appropriate, while putting in place means for the poor to participate in and monitor local government. The design of national hunger reduction strategies, with local communities at the center of the design and implementation, will provide the best means of enabling local people to identify and deal with local governance challenges. Harnessing the knowledge, creativity, and innovation of poor people can lead to much greater development effectiveness (Chambers, Pacey, and Thrupp 1989).

There is an overwhelming need to respond to the specific needs of poor, food-insecure people, rather than simply provide standard and predetermined services. Genuinely participatory approaches have been shown to yield benefits in efficiency and equity. A people-centered approach gives all stakeholders, including food-insecure people, a sense of ownership, allocating resources according to their preferences and tapping their skills and knowledge (Osami 2001). The task force recognizes the importance of significantly increased funding for agriculture, nutrition, rural development, and hunger reduction programs. But politics and policy should be driven by country needs and once funds have been secured, the money must generate results by supporting local initiatives. Any strategy to reduce hunger must therefore have as a central tenet the empowerment of the poor through full participation in decisionmaking and implementation.

Investing in science and technology

Science and technology have the potential to transform food and nutritional security in poor countries. Much has already been achieved in increasing crop

Developing countries should ensure that science and technology are integrated into national processes for setting priorities

yields, improving nutrition, understanding links between environment and poverty, and providing access to information and knowledge. But the lack of adequate policies to mobilize the powers of science and technology remains a serious obstacle to further progress. In addition, scientific institutions have given too little attention to the review, validation, and documentation of local practices and their incorporation into relevant development policies.

The contribution of science and technology to improving the yields of the world's major food staples has been tremendous. The most impressive yield gains in food crops occurred in the Green Revolution, with the development of short-stemmed rice and wheat varieties during the 1960s (Runge and others 2003). Similarly dramatic cases could be made for measures to improve crop management and agronomic practices for the sustainable use of marginal lands, to enhance genomic information and its use in plant breeding, and to increase the use of information and communication technologies in providing technical and market information. Other examples include measures to overcome micronutrient deficiencies through breeding varieties rich in micronutrients or providing supplemental fortified food to counter micronutrient deficiencies.

Science and technology, despite their contributions to development, often do not have a high enough profile in the policy formulation processes of developing countries. This may be partly due to poor communication strategies from scientists. The style and content of scientific publications are seldom user-friendly, and research typically concentrates on expanding new areas, devoting limited attention to capitalizing on previous research. An immediate requirement is to improve the flow of information about research—its achievements and potential—to policymakers. Two recent exercises show how this can be done. The InterAcademy Council (2004) has reexamined science and technological strategies for improving agricultural productivity in Africa. And the International Assessment of Agricultural Science and Technology (IAAST 2003) recently launched an assessment of the value of agricultural science and technology for development over the next 50 years.

Science and technology should be among the priorities of developing countries. Developing countries should ensure that science and technology are integrated into national processes for setting priorities, such as the PRSP, and assigning budgets to them. The following are among the urgent priorities for investing in science and linking it with policy.

- Increase funding for technical and policy assistance to developing countries on issues related to agriculture, nutrition, and rural development.
- Increase funding to the international research system of the Consultative Group on International Agricultural Research and to national agricultural and natural resource management research in developing countries.
- Increase investment in the capacity to monitor hunger and malnutrition in developing countries.

The drive to halve hunger will need to tackle a wide range of political, socio-economic, and technical issues

- Provide information to policymakers on the potential of science and technology for development.
- Establish poverty reduction strategy committees on science and technology, and establish national priorities for investment.
- Align science and technology activities with gender and other socially relevant issues to ensure their relevance.

Vulnerability analysis—a tool for setting priorities

As outlined in chapter 1, hunger has multiple causes. To be fully effective, the drive to halve hunger will need to tackle a wide range of political, socio-economic, and technical issues. Our strategy therefore takes the form of seven recommendations spanning the different fields that require attention. Each recommendation is to be achieved through a set of interrelated interventions that define what needs to be done.

The recommendations are based on an analysis of vulnerability to food insecurity. By understanding the risks poor people are exposed to and the means they have for minimizing those risks, it is possible to determine the priority interventions that can be expected to have a major impact on reducing hunger.

The definition of food security states that a food-secure person has access to adequate nutritious food at all times. People are food-insecure because they are exposed to various risks that can lead to food and nutritional shortages. People and households differ in their capacity to cope with these risks—and as a result, some go hungry while others do not.

The food-insecure are vulnerable in the sense that even a minor shock can deprive their access to food and nutrition. For example, in a year of drought, all smallholder farmers in the drought-affected area will be exposed to the same hazard (a risk that has materialized). Those who depend entirely on rainfed agriculture will suffer, while households that have a second source of income, perhaps from off-farm employment or remittances from working relatives, will be able to buy food. Vulnerability, therefore, is the expression not only of exposure to risk but also of the ability to cope with these risks.

The following vulnerability and food security framework indicates the range of risks to which vulnerable households may be exposed, the kinds of coping capacity that households might employ, and the key outcomes that result from the interaction of hazards and coping strategies (figure 3.1). The five coping capacities in this framework—resource management, production strategies, income and price levels, consumption patterns, and nutrition outcomes—are outlined below and provide a structure to understand how resilient households are to the risks they face.

First, poor people depend disproportionately on natural resources for food, agricultural inputs, and their livelihoods. In many cases these natural resources, especially soils, have been degraded a great extent. Restoring and conserving the natural resource base has great potential for increasing food security in the longer term.

Figure 3.1

Vulnerability and food insecurity framework

Source: Adapted from WFP 2002; Webb and Rogers 2003.

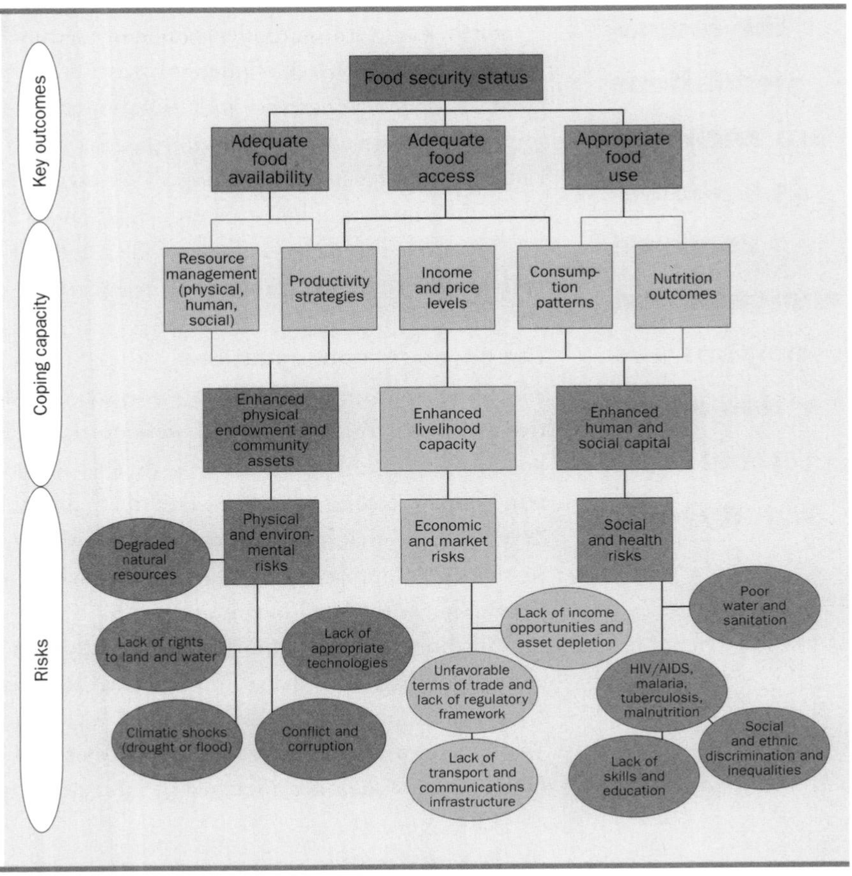

Second, about half the world's hungry are thought to be involved in agricultural activities as members of smallholder farming households. Increasing the productivity of smallholder farmers—women as well as men—results directly in hunger reduction through increases in food availability and farm income, leads to an overall increase in food supply, and promotes nonfarm income generation.

Third, many hungry people simply cannot afford to buy food. This results from a lack of income-earning opportunities, often related to the lack of functioning markets in remote places. Activities that open new markets or employment opportunities for the poor and allow them to increase their incomes are vital in the fight against hunger.

Fourth, people who are poor and hungry are forced to follow consumption patterns based on lower quantity and low cost foods (starchy staples, for instance), which are also poor in nutrients, vitamins, and proteins. In many cases, the need to alter consumption patterns is the result of catastrophic shocks, such as severe droughts or war. Establishing safety nets and other mechanisms that protect vulnerable people when shocks occur is an important strategy for reducing hunger.

The recommendations are anchored in a people-centered approach that emphasizes action at the local community level

Fifth, malnutrition results from many causes, including lack of food, inadequate food quality, lack of micronutrients, inadequate nurturing of babies and children, poor water quality and sanitation facilities, and common diseases. To improve the nutrition of vulnerable people, it will be necessary to tackle these causes comprehensively, including all the various groups affected. If this can be done, the impact will be enormous.

These five coping capacities provide a point of departure for the Task Force on Hunger's recommendations.

The seven recommendations

The Task Force on Hunger's recommendations fall into seven areas. The first two respond to the need for both developed and developing countries to build political action and put in place the policies to end hunger. The remaining five build on the coping capacities, described above, that vulnerable people have developed and that have the potential to lead them out of poverty and hunger. As such, the approach is anchored in a people-centered approach that emphasizes action at the local community level.

All the recommendations are synergistic at several levels. They are mutually reinforcing, such that if implemented together their impact would be far greater than the sum of the impacts that each can achieve by itself (figure 3.2). The synergies among the recommendations and with the other Millennium Development Goals are discussed in more detail in chapter 11.

At the global level

1. Move from political commitment to action. This recommendation is directed toward the international community as well as governments in developing countries. The main areas for action are advocacy, public awareness, and funding. It will be especially important to put pressure on donor governments to fulfill their commitments to increase aid, cancel debt, and eliminate trade subsidies. At the same time, developing country governments will need to take steps to fulfill their commitments to move toward greater accountability and better governance and to promote and protect human rights. The Task Force on Hunger believes that the greatest advances will be achieved in hungry countries that are sufficiently well governed or committed to good governance, coupled with long-term support by donors.

At the global and national levels

2. Reform policy and create an enabling environment. The international and national policies that affect the fight against hunger are often in need of review and reform. The priority activities are to ensure that hunger reduction is reflected in national planning processes (especially poverty reduction strate-

Figure 3.2
Task force recommendations at the global, national, and community scale

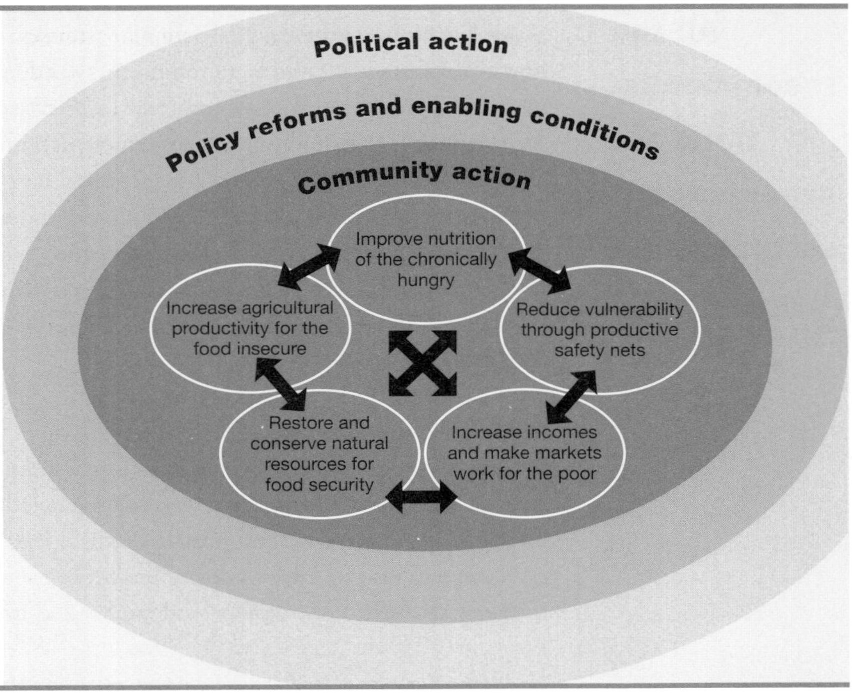

gies) and to increase allocations to agriculture and rural development in both national budgets and aid budgets. Other needs include strengthening agricultural research (national and international), linking agriculture and nutrition, building the capacity to fight hunger, empowering women as the major combatants, and addressing other important policy issues, such as land tenure.

At the national and local levels

3. Increase the agricultural productivity of food-insecure farmers. Smallholder agriculture remains the engine of economic development in nearly all developing countries. It is central in reducing both hunger and poverty. Priorities for action on food crops include improving soil health, improving and expanding small-scale water management, and increasing the availability of improved seeds and other planting materials. It will be vital to diversify farm enterprises by strengthening the livestock, tree, and fisheries/aquaculture components of mixed farming and aquatic ecosystems. A third challenge is to strengthen the support services to agriculture, notably research, extension and post-harvest management to minimize losses. Women farmers, researchers, and extensionists need to be empowered to play a central role alongside men.

4. Improve nutrition for the chronically hungry and vulnerable. Chronic undernourishment affects vast numbers of people across the developing world. We recommend a life-cycle approach that ensures adequate nutrition for the hunger-

All the recommendations are synergistic at several levels

prone at various sensitive ages. Particular attention needs to go to improving the nutrition of pregnant and lactating mothers and infants under two, since interventions directed to these groups help to break the cycle of intergenerational deprivation. It is also important to reduce malnutrition in children under five and in school-age children and adolescents. There are possibilities for multiple benefits and synergies accrued through food and nutritional interventions and education in schools to reach these age groups. Nutritional supplementation is vital to eliminate micronutrient deficiencies throughout the life-cycle, and parallel health measures are needed to eliminate the diseases that rob people of nutrients.

5. Reduce the vulnerability of the acutely hungry to disasters and shocks. This recommendation reflects the vulnerability of hungry and poor people to events they cannot control. Priority interventions include the strengthening of early warning and emergency response systems at both national and international levels. It will also be vital to devise productive social safety nets such as food-for-work schemes, community food banks, and micro-credit groups.

6. Increase incomes and make markets work for the poor. A major reason why agricultural production remains low in many developing countries is the lack of functioning markets for agricultural inputs and outputs to serve the poor. To remedy this situation we recommend reducing the costs of purchased agricultural inputs through voucher schemes, opening output markets, developing networks of rural input traders, improving access to credit and market information, strengthening farmer associations, reducing transaction costs by building rural infrastructures such as storage facilities, and improving transport infrastructure (particularly rural roads).

7. Restore and conserve the natural resources essential for food security. Many ecosystems on which the poor depend are so badly degraded that the productivity of the land has been all but lost. We recommend action to enable the poor and hungry to restore their natural assets through such measures as producing community action plans, establishing secure rights to assets, and developing schemes that offer payments for environmental services, particularly the storage of carbon. There are growing opportunities for communities to develop "green enterprises" that trade in sustainably managed forest and other products.

Recommendation one

Move from political commitment to action

The world's political leaders have repeatedly committed to ending hunger, but so far have fallen short of achieving this goal. As a quantitative, time-bound goal—first adopted by the World Food Summit (1996), reiterated at the Millennium Summit (2000), and reaffirmed at the World Food Summit five years later (2002) and the World Summit on Sustainable Development (2002)—the hunger Goal enjoys unprecedented global political endorsement. The World Food Summit of 1996 outlined a comprehensive Plan of Action to halve hunger by 2015 and established a system for monitoring progress by the FAO Committee on World Food Security. In addition, the Monterrey Consensus of 2002 promised increased financing for development by both donor countries and developing country governments.

In 2003 the FAO's Anti-Hunger Programme identified priority actions to reach the hunger Goal through investments in agriculture and rural development to enhance direct and immediate access to food for the most seriously undernourished (FAO 2002a). Focusing on small farmers, the Anti-Hunger Programme aims to create more opportunities for rural people, representing 70 percent of the poor, to improve their livelihoods on a sustainable basis. This was followed by the 2003 Maputo Declaration on Agriculture and Food Security in Africa, which recommitted participants to increase their investments in agriculture and rural development and called for expanded official development assistance and debt relief (African Union Assembly 2003). The challenge now is to translate widespread political support into concrete action in the policy, institutional, and budgetary arenas.

To bridge the gap between commitment and results, the global community must translate its promises into greater resource mobilization, heightened public awareness, more participation in planning by the poor and hungry, and greater policy coherence in areas that affect food security and development.

Countries at all stages of economic development must address the structural issues that hamper progress toward eliminating hunger

The Task Force on Hunger puts forward the following five interventions to move from political commitment to action:

1. Advocate political action to meet intergovernmental agreements to end hunger.
2. Strengthen the contribution of donor countries and national governments to activities that combat hunger.
3. Improve global public awareness of hunger issues and strengthen advocacy organizations.
4. Strengthen developing-country advocacy organizations that deal with poverty reduction and hunger alleviation.
5. Strengthen data gathering and monitoring and evaluation.

Background

Moving from political commitment to long-term global action is critical to achieving the hunger Goal. As chapter 2 shows, the world has made some progress in reducing hunger. But achieving the hunger Goal will require a significant acceleration and expansion of hunger reduction efforts, coupled with vigorous processes of policy and institutional reform. Neither can occur without increased action by public leaders.

To back up their commitments, countries at all stages of economic development must address the structural issues (political, economic, and social) that hamper progress toward eliminating hunger. Governments in developing countries need to greatly increase the scale and efficacy of their national hunger reduction programs. Some developing countries—notably India, China, Brazil, Ethiopia, and Sierra Leone—have already begun to back up their commitments by refocusing their efforts to overcome hunger (boxes 4.1 and 4.2). Developed country governments need to increase and improve development

Box 4.1
From commitment to action in China

China's strong economic performance over the past two decades—especially in the 1990s, when economic growth averaged more than 9 percent annually—has led to a massive structural transformation in the Chinese economy and a considerable reduction in poverty. Between 1978 and 2000 the number of poor living on less than $1 a day fell from 250 million to 30 million (UNDP 2003). And between 1990 and 2000 the number of chronically hungry fell by more than 80 million (FAO 2004c).

Contributing to China's success: policy and institutional reforms that permitted the rural poor to gain access to social services and production assets, together with significant public investments in rural education, agricultural research, extension, irrigation, and other forms of infrastructure. The application of modern agricultural technologies has led to a spectacular takeoff in crop yields, leading to the production of an additional 100 million tons of cereals annually by 1990 (Fan, Zhang, and Zhang 2002). These changes made agriculture and the rural sector the country's engine of economic growth.

assistance (especially for agriculture and nutrition) and to reform agricultural and trade policies.

Stronger political action to end hunger will require bold leadership, energetic and well organized political advocacy, and clearly articulated public demand. A combination of these elements is essential to mobilize systematic planning, assure the long-term commitment of adequate financial resources, improve institutions and policies, and develop innovative programming.

While numerous global events threaten to distract or derail hunger reduction efforts, there are positive trends as well. The spread of democracy, the growing recognition of food as a human right, and the increasing support for antihunger advocacy groups and political leaders are helping to build the

Box 4.2

India's strategy for eliminating endemic hunger

Source: M.S. Swaminathan 2004.

Despite impressive gains in food production in recent decades, India is the home of a large number of chronically undernourished children, women, and men. A recent analysis of the reasons for food insecurity in rural and urban India identified inadequate purchasing power as the primary cause of under and malnutrition. This can be attributed to inadequate employment and livelihood opportunities arising from high population pressures on land and the slow growth rates of nonfarm employment opportunities.

Based on substantial grain reserves, the Government of India operates a wide range of nutrition safety-net programs. These include the world's largest integrated child development service and a national school meal program. The government recently established an Employment Guarantee Scheme, which provides 25 percent of wages in cash and the rest in wheat or rice (5 kilograms per day). Despite these social support programs, the incidence of both endemic and hidden hunger remains high. To meet the national goal of significantly reducing hunger by August 15, 2007, a National Food Security Summit, held in New Delhi in February 2004, proposed the following seven-point action plan:

- Develop integrated life-cycle nutrition programs and increase programs targeting adolescent girls, pregnant women, and children from ages 0–2.
- Expand the use of community grain banks based on local grains (millets, pulses, and so on) to improve food security at the local level.
- Establish a food guarantee program combining the principles of employment guarantee and food-for-work programs. Engender the food-for-work program to expand women's employment opportunities.
- Sustain, strengthen, and spread self-help groups by ensuring backward linkages with technology and credit and forward linkages with markets.
- Enhance the productivity of cropping and farming systems through packages of technology, services, and public policies.
- Promote a food-based approach to nutrition security through widespread cultivation and consumption of vegetables, fruits, millets, legumes, and tubers and by strengthening integrated production systems of crops, livestock, and fish.
- Ensure access to clean drinking water, environmental hygiene, primary health care, and elementary education.

These steps will help eradicate the image of India as a country with mountains of grain and millions of hungry people.

Special attention must be paid to good governance

momentum to achieve the hunger Goal. For example, hunger-affected communities and local groups are doing more in hunger reduction campaigns and calling for political action to raise the profile of hunger and malnutrition on the political agenda.

At the local level, grassroots groups in Africa have used the poverty reduction strategy process to challenge corruption, strengthen democracy, and improve health and education services directed to the poor and hungry. At the international level, an FAO-supported Intergovernmental Working Group, established at the World Food Summit, developed voluntary guidelines for nations on achieving the right to adequate food, adopted by the FAO Committee on World Food Security in September 2004 and the FAO Council in November 2004. The International Alliance Against Hunger, established at the 2002 World Food Summit, linked governments, international organizations, and civil society in a promising example of antihunger coalitions across borders and sectors (box 4.3). Globally, there is growing recognition of how North American, Japanese, and European farm subsidies impede development—and there is greater willingness to argue forcefully for change (Beckmann and Byers 2004).

At the country level, special attention must be paid to good governance, as a key ingredient to fight hunger and promote economic development. Corruption, excessive bureaucracy, inadequate planning and control, and insufficient institutional capacity hold back the successful implementation of even the best conceived policies. In addition, conflict remains one of the key factors blocking development and hunger alleviation. The primary responsibility for avoiding and resolving conflict lies with national political leaders. But the international community can also contribute to the prevention and resolution of conflicts.

Box 4.3
The International Alliance Against Hunger

Source: FAO 2001b.

The International Alliance Against Hunger is the title of the final declaration of the *World Food Summit: Five Years Later.* The Alliance provides a forum for advocacy, promotes joint actions by its members, and facilitates information exchange through Web sites, newsletters, and progress reports, bringing together the strengths of different groups into a joint effort. The Alliance includes food producers and consumers, international organizations, academics, donors, policymakers, religious groups, and nongovernmental organizations—all raising awareness about hunger.

National alliances against hunger are the heart of the overall effort, because the main responsibility for reaching development goals lies with a nation and its people. Each country sets its national targets through its legislative bodies and lays out the steps to move forward, including implementing programs that target the hungry. It works in close collaboration with the Rome-based agencies (the Food and Agriculture Organization, the International Fund for Agricultural Development, the International Plant Genetic Resources Institute, and the World Food Programme), nongovernmental organizations, civil society organizations, and the UN System Network on Rural Development and Food Security.

National governments need to be held accountable to fund and implement scaled-up programs to address hunger

The international community should support efforts by developing country governments to establish effective governance and increase accountability at political and official levels. The African Peer Review Mechanism of the New Partnership for African Development is a valuable tool for supporting such efforts and should be more widely used. Yet the challenge remains whether and how to support development efforts in countries with poor governance. The task force suggests maintaining some level of engagement, both for humanitarian reasons and as an investment in the promotion of political, economic, and social change over a longer time frame. Donor investments can also help strengthen legal, financial, and auditing systems to improve governance.

The key message for political leaders is that halving world hunger is well within our means. What has been lacking is sufficient action to implement and scale up known solutions. In July 2004 UN Secretary-General Kofi Annan sent out such a message to the political leaders of Africa. At a meeting in Addis Ababa, he called for a "uniquely African Green Revolution in the twenty-first century" (box 4.4). His vision was of a new kind of revolution with a wider focus on social and environmental sustainability, aimed at simultaneously addressing the biophysical, socioeconomic, and political causes of hunger. "Hunger is a complex crisis," he said. "To solve it we must address the interconnected challenges of agriculture, health, nutrition, adverse and unfair market conditions, weak infrastructure, and environmental degradation. Knowledge is not lacking." What is lacking, as ever, is the will to turn this knowledge into practice.

"Success will require African governments to commit themselves wholeheartedly to the Millennium Development Goals, by developing national strategies consistent with the timeline and targets for 2015. We will also need more convincing action from the developed countries to support those strategies: by phasing out harmful trade practices, by providing technical assistance, and by increasing both the volume of aid to levels consistent with the Goals."

Advocate political action to meet intergovernmental agreements

Political leaders have repeatedly committed themselves to ending hunger, only to fail to act on their commitments. National governments need to be held accountable to fund and implement national scaled-up programs to address hunger. Establishing measurable indicators of progress, and reporting them publicly, can help strengthen accountability.

Several upcoming events will provide opportunities to reaffirm and act on existing commitments. For example, March 2005 will see publication of the report of the U.K.'s Commission on Africa, July 2005 the G8 Summit,[1] hosted by the United Kingdom and focusing specifically on development, and September 2005 the high-level UN event to assess progress on the Millennium Declaration. Hunger will be given high profile at these events. The Task Force on Hunger encourages individual governments to champion the issue

Box 4.4

Toward a Twenty-first Century African Green Revolution

Source: Sanchez 2004.

The original Green Revolution is one of the crowning development achievements for the latter third of the twentieth century. In the developing countries where the revolution occurred, food production tripled between 1965 and 2000, the number of rural poor fell by half, the proportion of malnourished people dropped from 30 to 18 percent, and the real prices of the main cereal crops declined by 76 percent. Determined scientists and policymakers identified the key entry points: the need for high-yielding varieties of rice and wheat—and the crop management practices that would allow these varieties to express their full potential. Other factors were also put in place, such as enabling government policies, new or expanded irrigation schemes, mechanization, seed production, better infrastructure, and stronger national research systems.

While the Green Revolution generated remarkable success in parts of Latin America and Asia, it had little success in Africa. The contribution of improved crop varieties to yield increases were 70–90 percent in Asia, Latin America, and the Middle East, but only 28 percent in Sub-Saharan Africa. There are two major biophysical constraints in Africa: low and declining soil fertility, and scarce or uncertain water supply. The lack of infrastructure, such as rural roads, is also a major constraint to increased productivity. Greater investments to overcome these constraints are essential if Africa is to experience its own Green Revolution.

Many valuable lessons have been learned from the first Green Revolution. It focused too much on monocultures and grain crops, reducing agro-biodiversity. It neglected some environmental concerns, such as water pollution in areas of intensive, high-input-based production. This has led to the recognition that a new, more equitable and sustainable Green Revolution is needed. It should integrate landless, small-scale farm households and community participation in research for the effective design and delivery of new technology suited to local conditions. The focus must be on the poorest of rural households, which generally involve women farmers, who were largely bypassed in the original Green Revolution. Closing the gap between scientists' priorities and those of food-insecure farmers, especially women, is essential for a more equitable and sustainable Green Revolution.

To accomplish this, a new science is emerging, based on better natural resource management and on genetic improvement. We know more about the crucial need to diversify farm enterprises, to work with communities to determine their specific needs, and to preserve the agro-ecosystems and the ecosystems that agriculture interacts with. New technologies must match the realities experienced by the majority of poor producers in nonirrigated, environmentally fragile areas. There is now much greater emphasis on creating a policy environment conducive to innovation on small farms, and a greater focus on gender issues, as well as the need to make markets work for poor producers. With agriculture once again seen as an engine of economic growth, the political will can be rekindled to succeed where past efforts have failed.

during preparations for these meetings. In addition, regional meetings organized around specific Goals could provide a valuable forum for policymakers to exchange information and collaborate in turning commitment into action.

The eighth Goal calls for a "Global Partnership for Development"—reciprocal undertakings that both developed and developing countries must act on if they are to meet the Goals. In accord with the Millennium Declaration,

Reforms in public policy, national priorities, and budgeting are key political actions

the Task Force on Hunger recommends that developed country governments increase and improve their official development assistance, especially for agriculture and nutrition, and reform their agricultural and trade polices.

The initial focus should be on accountability for implementing the 1996 and 2002 World Food Summit commitments, and satisfactory completion of the Doha Development Round—both of which are crucial for to achieving the hunger Goal. A key part of the negotiations under the Doha Round relate to agricultural trade and support policies, which should be reformed on terms favorable to developing country agriculture. The OECD policies that require major reform include reductions in domestic production supports, trade-distorting price guarantees, export subsidies, and tariffs and quotas on imports (particularly higher value products from the developing world). Trade negotiations have spurred the formation of new alliances among developing countries, as well as advocacy by international NGO networks. These alliances and networks should continue and intensify their work.

The impacts of trade liberalization will vary among countries and subgroups. In the long term, the extent of trade liberalization benefits captured by developing countries will depend on the competitiveness and comparative advantage of their agricultural sectors. In the short term, many of the poorest farmers will not be sufficiently integrated into the global economy to enable them to gain much from trade policy reform. For them, the development of domestic and regional markets offers the greatest potential for near-term benefit.

Developing country governments must, in turn, improve the quality and increase the scale of their national hunger reduction programs, targeting hotspots where the majority of the hungry live. There are many examples of governments in the developing world that have already acted effectively to reduce hunger and malnutrition. Key ingredients of success have included establishing and maintaining domestic peace, applying the rule of law, and making public investments in rural infrastructure and agricultural research to increase farm productivity and reduce rural poverty (Paarlberg 2002).

Reforms in public policy, national priorities, and budgeting are key political actions to be taken by developing country governments. The next chapter discusses these reforms in more detail. Undertaking effective policy reform will involve addressing the needs of vulnerable groups, including women, tribal people, and those living in marginal areas. Because these groups are largely disempowered in national political processes, prioritizing their needs will require the political courage to reverse the status quo.

Success in hunger-related programs can be greatest when governments work in partnership with NGOs and local communities to build support and bring about change. President Luiz Inacio Lula da Silva's commitment to ending hunger in Brazil is an example of effective political action and popular support for hunger eradication (box 4.5).

Box 4.5

Brazil's Zero Hunger Program

Source: Brazil 2002.

The government of Brazil has developed and accorded high priority to an integrated and comprehensive strategy for reducing hunger, the "Zero Hunger Program." The program's strategy is to link five key actions:

- Providing opportunities to excluded people through employment and agrarian reform.
- Using the government's increased commitment to hungry people to broaden awareness and political commitment within Brazilian society. The program has mobilized civil society and private sector participants, supported by the central government.
- Increasing the basic food supply through support to family agriculture.
- Lowering the cost of food through popular restaurants, agreements with supermarket chains, alternative trade channels, equipment modernization, and reduced taxes.
- Providing emergency interventions, such as food coupons, a basic food basket, free school food, food banks, food security stocks, and mother-child nutrition programs.

Strengthen the contributions of donor countries and national governments to activities that combat hunger

To achieve the hunger Goal, donor countries and national governments must increase their commitment of resources to hunger reduction initiatives. One method of assessing political commitment is to compare national spending on agriculture and rural development with that on other national priorities, such as defense (tables 4.1 and 4.2). Highly food-insecure countries spend two to three times as much on defense as on agriculture.

The already low levels of public investment in agriculture have declined still further over the past decade (table 4.2). On average, developing countries now invest just 0.6 percent of their agricultural GDP in public agricultural research, compared with 2.6 percent for developed countries. The average annual growth of public agricultural research expenditures in developing countries in the first half of the 1990s was significantly below that of the late 1970s, and in Sub-Saharan Africa it was lower than in 1970.

In countries where 20–35 percent of the population is undernourished, agricultural spending averaged 7.6 percent of total budgets in 1992 and only 5.2 percent in 1998. In countries with more than 35 percent of the population food-insecure, agricultural spending in 1992 was 6.8 percent of total budgets, falling to a mere 4.9 percent in 1996. These levels of spending are far lower than the share of agriculture in these countries' GDP. By contrast, in countries with less than 2.5 percent of the population undernourished, the share of government spending on agriculture comes closest to matching agriculture's importance in the economy (FAO 2002b).

Compounding this problem, development assistance for agriculture has declined in real terms from the early 1980s to the early 1990s (FAO 2003). From 1993 to 2000, external assistance to agriculture fluctuated around levels

Table 4.1
Share of defense spending in government budgets
Percent

Region	1992	2001
Latin America and Caribbean	6.2	6.9
Middle East and North Africa	..	..
Sub-Saharan Africa	8.4	..
East Asia and Pacific	23.7	16.4
South Asia	16.8	14.7
Europe and Central Asia	15.2	9.6

Source: World Bank 2003.

Table 4.2
Share of agriculture in total government spending
Percent

Region	1992	1998
Latin America and Caribbean	3.9	1.9
Middle East and North Africa	3.7	1.1
Sub-Saharan Africa	6.6	3.9
East and Southeast Asia	5.9	5.2
South Asia	10.4	5.4

Source: FAO 2001a.

close to half those recorded over 1982–86. The World Bank, for example, reduced its lending for agriculture from nearly $6 billion in 1986 to $2.7 billion in 1996.

There are many reasons for the decline. These include the inherent complexity, risk, and high transaction costs of agricultural projects; the growing number of environmental and social safeguards that must be built into projects; the perceived ineffectiveness of past projects; the lack of professional capacity in organizations responsible for implementation; and the reduced demand from the developing countries themselves (FAO 2001b). Moreover, low agricultural commodity prices have created a less attractive climate for investment and led to lower rates of return. National governments often have a very low capacity to manage donor-funded projects, particularly when their investment in rural infrastructure and support services to small farms has been neglected (Goodland and Cleaver 2002).

Given the close connection between agriculture and the livelihoods of poor rural people, the combination of declining investments in agriculture and rising military expenditures is extremely worrying—and an indicator of the real priorities of governments and donor agencies, despite their stated commitments. To reach the hunger Goal, official development assistance and commitments from developing country governments for hunger-related sectors must be significantly increased.

The task force recommends that governments implement the existing agreements, such as the Monterrey Consensus, which reaffirmed the minimum target of 0.7 percent of GDP for development assistance, as well as the Marrakesh Agreement under the Doha Development Round. Agreements such as the Maputo Declaration, which committed greater support specifically toward

Campaigns should emphasize that eliminating hunger is feasible

hunger and food security, should also be implemented. The task force also recommends that donors increase assistance to sectors related directly to hunger reduction, such as agriculture, nutrition, water, sanitation, and agriculture-related markets.

To secure increased aid and ensure that it is effective, developing countries will need to present sound and actionable hunger reduction programs and policies. Both aid and recipient programs must be well targeted and transparently managed. Both donors and governments should hold themselves accountable for the efficacy of their programs, as measured by outcomes in hunger reduction.

Improve public awareness of hunger issues and strengthen advocacy organizations

Building public awareness of hunger and the issues that surround it can provide political leaders with the mandate and support they need to take action. Antihunger coalitions can articulate arguments for action that are both morally and practically compelling. Civil society organizations can work together to create global awareness campaigns both at the national and international level. In this way they can greatly strengthen the public demand for action. Mass public awareness campaigns are needed to build public understanding of the dimensions, causes, and consequences of hunger. Campaigns should also emphasize that eliminating hunger is feasible. Presenting credible data, actionable solutions, and compelling success stories will strengthen the case.

To build broad public support it is necessary to create a groundswell of popular opinion at the local level. In developing countries this can and should involve mechanisms that enable the poor and hungry to participate in the dialogue. Effectively organized campaigns should involve the participation of all stakeholders, including citizens, NGOs, research organizations, and the mass media. Opinion leaders such as businessmen and women, religious leaders, and public personalities can serve as effective spokespeople for communicating key messages.

For example, the U.S. Alliance to End Hunger brings together diverse institutions working to strengthen the political will to end hunger in the United States and worldwide. It includes advocacy organizations, charities, religious bodies, foundations, think tanks, universities, the private sector, unions, civil rights organizations, farm organizations, and individuals. In Europe, Euronaid, an advocacy coalition of 38 major NGOs involved in food aid and security, has been instrumental in generating political commitment in the EU for hunger reduction. It has initiated improvements in European food aid and lobbied vigorously for measures to improve food security in the worst affected countries (boxes 4.6 and 4.7).

A key mechanism for ensuring that broad political commitments lead to long-term action is to develop partnerships both vertically (from community to national and international levels) and horizontally (across sectors). For

Box 4.6
Building a global campaign—lessons from Jubilee 2000

Source: FAO 2002b.

Jubilee 2000 Campaign, an international coalition of NGOs and civil society organizations created in the early 1980s, successfully lobbied OECD countries to relieve the debt of highly indebted poor countries (see www.jubilee2000uk.org). Although much more needs to be done, the lessons from the campaign's experience are that campaigns should:

- Outline clear, simple, time-bound goals and restate them relentlessly.
- Have tight, symbolic deadlines.
- Appeal to a shared sense of justice.
- Build coalitions of highly networked civil society groups.
- Maximize the use of both modern and traditional communications technology to mobilize public support.
- Ensure high-quality research and monitoring.
- Target key leaders and secure assurance of their support.
- Focus energy on decisionmaking events and the accountability of individual leaders.

Box 4.7
Campaigning can be cost-effective

Source: Beckmann 2004.

In the United States the impetus for policies to help reduce hunger domestically and internationally has often come from concerned citizens and grassroots communities. Bread for the World, a nationwide grassroots movement, mobilizes about 250,000 letters to the U.S. Congress each year on issues important to hungry people. In almost every year of its 30-year history, it has helped bring about significant changes in U.S. policy, such as support for debt relief for the world's poorest countries and, in 2004, a 33 percent increase in poverty-focused official development assistance. According to Bread for the World, every dollar it spends on advocacy brings in $100 of public funding for antihunger programs.

example, the United Nations World Food Programme works with more than 1,100 NGOs to complement its food aid with technical and nonfood inputs. These partnerships draw on grassroots networks, local knowledge, and a wealth of field-based experiences. Partnerships at the local level are also essential for stimulating the urgent action in the countries where needs are greatest. Local NGOs, such as REST in northern Ethiopia, have developed strong relationships with community groups and state organizations that have a common interest in overcoming food insecurity and malnutrition.

Strengthen developing country advocacy organizations that deal with poverty reduction and hunger in poor countries

Strengthening public advocacy is also critical in developing countries, where local NGOs have few resources but can lobby for political action to reduce hunger. Democracy and transparency are needed to create the political space for NGO lobbying and to ensure successful working partnerships with governments. Local NGOs can act as facilitators to assist food-insecure groups to articulate and voice their concerns to government. Greater financial support is needed for such antihunger efforts as the International Alliance Against Hunger. Charitable foundations and private corporations can donate both

Benchmarks can serve as a powerful tool for building public awareness and political accountability

financial support and other inputs, such as technologies, to public sector and civil society antihunger efforts as part of their corporate philanthropy and social responsibility strategies. The strengthening and networking of local community and advocacy groups over the past decade is one of the most promising developments in the struggle against hunger. It shows how effective action can emerge from a system of governance that connects the needs of the malnourished to a local government that is empowered with the necessary technical and institutional capacity (Garrett 2000).

However, those most concerned with hunger reduction—the hungry—are usually disenfranchised and marginalized, not only by their age, gender, and ethnicity but also by their all-consuming struggle for survival. Poverty, illiteracy, ill health, limited infrastructure, and social factors limit hungry people's access to information—and thus their ability to participate in political processes. Effectively addressing this problem requires a thorough understanding of the factors that limit the political power of vulnerable groups and of the strategies that can build support for these groups in the broader community.

Governments wishing to strengthen collective action by and for the hungry should first identify and deal with any factors that prevent the food-insecure from working together. Guaranteeing control over resources or programs for food-insecure communities or individuals can provide a tremendous stimulus to collection action. But care should be taken not to exclude vulnerable groups, such as women or ethnic minorities (Meinzen-Dick and di Gregorio 2004).

Although it is often difficult for disadvantaged groups to gain political influence, current policy instruments, such as poverty reduction strategies, can provide a mechanism for organized groups to acquire a stronger voice (Meinzen-Dick and di Gregorio 2004). But tapping into this potential requires specialized knowledge of how such systems operate (Krishna 2002). The Task Force on Hunger recommends that, in addition to increased financial support for community-based advocacy groups, capacity building and training should be expanded to ensure their participation in national policymaking.

Strengthen accurate data collection, monitoring, and evaluation

Key ingredients in working toward the Goals are accurate data collection and benchmarks for monitoring and evaluating. Such benchmarks, when clear and credible, can serve as a powerful tool for building public awareness and political accountability. At the international level, one mechanism for ensuring accountability and monitoring progress is the United Nations Development Programme's *Human Development Report,* which tracks annual shifts in the human development index by country. A number of UN system organizations—such as the FAO, WHO, United Nations Educational, Scientific and Cultural Organization, the United Nations Children's Fund, the Joint United Nations Programme on HIV/AIDS, and the World Bank—are already monitoring country progress in achieving the Goals. The UN Department of Economic and Social

Developing relevant and robust monitoring and evaluation processes is challenging

Affairs compiles a composite report, inserting the data into the annual report of the UN Secretary-General on the Millennium Declaration's implementation. Even so, improvements in measuring, analyzing, and reporting on country progress are important to attaining the goals and must continue.

It is also important that global and national monitoring and evaluation systems are reflected in local efforts to monitor progress toward the Millennium Development Goals. The task force recommends that key indicators for each Goal and a composite index should be used to measure a country's overall progress toward achieving the Millennium Development Goals. National governments, multilateral organizations, and civil society should work together to strengthen such monitoring and accountability systems.

Developing relevant and robust monitoring and evaluation processes focused on specific Goals is challenging. Particularly difficult is building agreement on sound, uniform methodology, monitoring data collection and analysis, and conveying findings to the public and to policymakers. But efforts show how it can be done. For example, Alliance 2015, a consortium of six major European NGOs, has published an assessment of the EU's contribution to the Goals, with special emphasis on Goal 6 for combating HIV/AIDS, malaria, and other diseases. Monitoring and reporting systems also need to be developed at the national and local levels. All these activities should be built into national strategies for achieving the hunger Goal.

Actions needed to implement recommendation one

Advocate political action to meet intergovernmental agreements

Advocate action through international and regional agreements such as the African Union, the New Partnership for African Development, the Association of Southeast Asian Nations, the Caribbean Community and Common Market, and others. Organize regional meetings around specific Goals to strengthen and focus efforts. Establish measurable indicators of progress, and report them publicly. Ensure that the Goals and progress reports are brought to the attention of key government officials. Milestones for success would be the references to hunger reduction and commitments of budget support stated in international declarations, and progress reports on those commitments.

Strengthen the contribution of donor countries and national governments to activities that combat hunger

Implement development finance declarations, including the Monterrey Consensus, specifically the target of committing 0.7 percent of GDP for development assistance, and the Marrakesh Agreement under the Doha Development Round. Implement agreements on hunger and food security, such as the Maputo Declaration and others. Increase official development assistance for sectors related directly to hunger reduction, such as agriculture, nutrition, water, sanitation, and agriculture-related markets.

	Key ingredients for success include donors creating credible and actionable antihunger programs and policies, developing countries assigning priority to hunger reduction in national policies, and both groups practicing cooperation, transparency, and accountability in these actions. Milestones for success include attaining goals outlined in national and multilateral declarations and commitments.
Improve global public awareness of hunger issues and strengthen advocacy organizations	Create mass public awareness campaigns to build public understanding of the dimensions, causes, and consequences of hunger. Campaigns should emphasize that eliminating hunger is within our reach and should present sound data, credible and actionable solutions, and compelling success stories. Strengthen campaigns by building the capacity of advocacy groups, increasing funding, and providing access to information. Encourage collaboration and partnerships, building transparency and trust between advocacy groups and partners. Involve mass media, particularly television and the Internet. Campaigns should involve all stakeholders including government, the private sector, NGOs, civil society organizations, and international agencies.
Strengthen developing country advocacy organizations that deal with hunger reduction and poverty alleviation	Strengthen collective action by and for the hungry, and expand the participation of developing country civil society institutions in national policymaking to ensure that hunger is addressed. Governments must create the political space for vulnerable groups to voice their demands and for NGOs and civil society organizations to push for policies that reduce hunger. Governments and international partners can support civil society groups by increasing funding, building capacity through training, and expanding partnerships and linkages with other groups. Key groups include civil and religious organizations, national organizations, NGOs, farmer associations, and national governments.
Strengthen accurate data collection and monitoring and evaluation	Devise benchmarks to monitor and evaluate progress toward reaching the hunger Goal. Strengthen monitoring efforts by UN agencies and the Committee on World Food Security. Fund and empower multistakeholder independent bodies to undertake data collection and monitoring at local and regional levels, as part of national strategies to achieve the hunger Goal. Convey findings clearly to the public and policymakers.

Recommendation two

Reform policies and create an enabling environment

In the fight against hunger and poverty, general and sectoral policies can be powerful and constructive instruments that affect all dimensions of food security. For example, monetary, fiscal, and trade policies have a direct influence not only on the price of food, but also the stability of the economic system and the overall investment and employment climate. In addition, favorable social and gender-specific policies can influence the extent to which the poor and the vulnerable, especially mothers and children, have access to food. But policies poorly formulated or implemented at any level of government can directly impede progress and create conditions that keep the poor trapped in hunger. A favorable policy framework is thus needed to maximize the impact of increased political action and implementing the local interventions described in the next chapters.

To create an enabling environment to end hunger, governments need to implement laws and policies at all levels, national to local, that are conducive to hunger and poverty alleviation. That environment is essential to attracting private investment in agriculture and rural development and to promoting growth, employment, and poverty reduction. It should also ensure an inclusive and participatory policy process—from design to implementation—that truly empowers all stakeholders. National policies, which may be necessary to ensure macroeconomic stability, may have negative effects on hunger and poverty and should be addressed through countermeasures to assist the poor. The process of policymaking should ensure, as much as possible, inclusiveness and participation by all stakeholders.

Governments should monitor the implementation of policies and programs and be held accountable for their impact. The quality and transparency of public administration, a participatory approach to policy designs and implementation, and a commitment to gender equality are essential elements of a

National policymakers need to recognize the multiple drivers of food and nutritional insecurity

pro-poor and environmentally friendly policy framework. The Task Force on Hunger proposes the following 10 interventions under this recommendation:

1. Promote an integrated policy approach to hunger reduction.
2. Restore the budgetary priority of the agricultural and rural sectors.
3. Build developing country capacity to achieve the hunger Goal.
4. Link nutritional and agricultural interventions.
5. Increase poor people's access to productive resources.
6. Empower women and girls.
7. Strengthen agricultural and nutrition research.
8. Remove internal and regional barriers to agricultural trade.
9. Increase the effectiveness of donor agencies' hunger-related programming.
10. Create vibrant partnerships to ensure effective policy implementation.

Background

In most developing countries the government is the supplier of essential public goods and services including legislation and regulation governing the generation and distribution of national wealth and income. The persistence of hunger can often be attributed to shortcomings in national policies and governance. Good governance—which includes the rule of law, transparency, lack of corruption, conflict prevention and resolution, sound public administration, and respect and protection for human rights—is therefore of critical importance in ensuring sustainable food security (Pinstrup-Andersen 2001).

Although governments bear the primary responsibility for addressing food insecurity and malnutrition, policy formulation should be in partnership with all stakeholders, including civil society and the private sector. Indeed, the broad participation of all stakeholders is essential to the success and sustainability of any hunger reduction program—as well as those designed to attain the other Goals. For example, in formulating national nutrition policies, the contribution of local governments, civil society, healthcare practitioners, educators, and women's groups will all be important.

When policies are poorly formulated or implemented, they can obstruct or harm food security. In many hungry countries, poor legislation and enforcement, cumbersome bureaucracy, and rampant corruption compromise the efficiency and effectiveness of antihunger programs by increasing transaction costs, thus limiting investment, productivity, and employment opportunities. A willingness to re-examine policies, combined with a commitment to change them where necessary, together with the establishment of accountability are keys to combating hunger.

Sustainable hunger reduction policies must be equitable and environmentally sustainable. They must also empower all groups in the society to participate. Pro-poor policies and institutions are needed to improve human capital and expand human potential, broaden access to productive resources and mar-

National poverty reduction strategies offer the best opportunities for multisectoral planning

kets, and promote the generation and adaptation of knowledge and technology to the benefit of the hungry. Appropriate social safety nets for especially vulnerable segments of the population should be devised and integrated into the policy framework.

To create this conducive policy environment, policymakers need a thorough understanding of the impact of existing policies on hunger through an impact analysis and evaluation. Next, they must identify the key enabling policies to reduce hunger, and assess their probable impact and modes of implementation. Needs assessments should be participatory and inclusive. Then they must formulate policies in an inclusive and participatory manner so that the needs of the poor are fully reflected and the poor are empowered through the process. Once this is accomplished, policymakers must identify and close the financial gap between available country resources and the total budgetary requirement for meeting the hunger Goal by reallocating domestic resources and mobilizing development assistance. These steps are prerequisites for the success of the interventions described below.

Promote an integrated policy approach to hunger reduction

To reduce hunger, national policymakers need to recognize the multiple drivers of food and nutritional insecurity—broadly characterized as a lack of food supply, lack of economic access to food, and poor biological utilization of food. Intervention in only one domain, such as increasing food production by food-insecure producers, is unlikely to be fully effective and will not benefit all vulnerable groups. National food and nutrition policies are needed, featuring coordinated and integrated multisectoral strategies. Strategies to reduce hunger should at a minimum involve agriculture, health, education, social security, transportation, natural resource management, and finance. Gender equality and empowerment should form integral parts of all policies, programs, and interventions.

National poverty reduction strategies and PRSPs, where they exist, offer the best opportunities for multisectoral planning. The task force recommends integrating the Goals into every low-income country's poverty reduction strategy or equivalent national planning process, with a specific focus on what is needed to achieve the hunger Goal. This is especially recommended for low-income countries that are falling behind in their efforts to achieve one or more of the Goals. In middle-income countries with significant pockets of extreme hunger, poverty reduction strategy–type processes will need to focus on ways of targeting populations in greatest need.

Policies to reduce hunger should stimulate increased food production, improve nutrition for vulnerable groups, develop input and output markets, spur the creation of agricultural and off-farm jobs, improve access to clean water and adequate sanitation, strengthen health and education services, and empower women. These policies need to be monitored and evaluated at the

National governments must commit to increase public funding to the sectors essential to overcoming hunger

national and local levels throughout implementation. The focus of all these policies should be on the food-insecure poor. For example, policies to increase food productivity should focus specifically on food-insecure farmers as a first priority, rather than benefiting food-secure farmers already integrated into the market economy. Although the employment opportunities generated by food-secure commercial farmers are a valuable contribution to economic growth, the benefits will not necessarily trickle down to poor and hungry farmers. Hunger must be tackled directly.

Policymakers involved in poverty reduction strategy processes need to recognize that there are wide differences in the nature and causes of food and nutritional insecurity across and within different parts of Africa, Asia, and Latin America—within the subnational levels and between rural and urban areas. As a result, "one-size-fits-all" policy blueprints, even within a country, are rarely appropriate. Policy prescriptions need to be tailored to local needs and resources. For example, India produces abundant food but has large numbers of hungry people—so the top priority of policy reforms should be to increase economic access to food. In many African countries, both food production and purchasing power are low—so policies that increase food production and diversify income-earning opportunities are both important. It is also vital to recognize the common causes of hunger that transcend national borders, such as gender discrimination and the isolation of poor people from markets. On these issues, governments can learn much from success stories in other countries.

Cities and periurban areas have problems that differ markedly from those of rural areas in terms of availability and access to food, market development, natural resources management, and access to basic services. Specific policies are needed to address these problems. For example, despite the existence of urban agriculture in many cities, urban dwellers rely much more on purchased food—so a steady and affordable food supply is essential to their food security. Efficient food marketing systems are the first pillar of urban food security, because they affect the price of food and its quality and safety. As rapid urbanization creates increasing demand for commercial food supplies, policies must be in place to strengthen the infrastructure for distributing food and the systems for ensuring that it reaches the poor and hungry.

Restore the budgetary priority of the agricultural and rural sectors

Creating effective policies and institutions will not be enough. National governments must also make a commitment to increase public funding to the sectors essential to overcoming hunger. This can be done by increasing support for agriculture to at least 10 percent of the national budget—and linking it to additional investments in infrastructure, such as rural trunk roads and feeder roads, railways, ports, health posts, schools, and communications facili-

Nonfarm rural activities form an essential part of the risk management and coping strategies of the rural poor

ties. Kenya and Uganda now invest less than 5 percent of their government budgets in agriculture despite the fact that 70 percent or more of their people are rural and depend primarily on agriculture for their livelihoods. In contrast, Ethiopia, which has a similar proportion of rural people, has recently begun investing 15 percent of its national budget in agriculture. In July 2003, the African Union adopted the Maputo Declaration on Agriculture and Food Security in Africa, endorsing NEPAD's Comprehensive Africa Agricultural Development Programme's recommendation that countries should invest at least 10 percent of their budgets in agriculture and rural development. The Task Force on Hunger recommends that African governments invest at least 10 percent of their budget specifically on agriculture and the public goods needed for agriculture to develop—in addition to the needed investments in rural energy, infrastructure, health, education and other rural sectors.

The increasing recognition of the potential of agriculture and rural development in reducing hunger and poverty is a sign that development assistance providers are ready to respond to such demands. The international community—donor agencies, the UN and other specialized agencies, and international NGOs and private companies—will need to provide significant additional support to hungry countries, in a sustained and predictable manner. Over the long term rich countries should provide budget support and technical advice, remove trade barriers, and accelerate debt cancellation—in addition to restoring investments in agriculture and providing similar increases for other measures to reduce hunger in ways that integrate both gender equality and environmental concerns.

Agriculture alone cannot sustain the livelihoods of poor rural families. Hence nonfarm rural activities form an essential part of the risk management and coping strategies of the rural poor. The aim of rural hunger alleviation policies should be to facilitate the participation of the poor in nonfarm activities and the creation of employment opportunities in the rural areas. Effective policies and institutions are needed to develop rural infrastructure, build entrepreneurial capacity, and ensure competitive and fair markets for small rural enterprises. Increasing the asset base of poor households (liquid assets, education, access to credit) will allow them to participate in more remunerative off-farm employment activities.

Build developing country capacity to achieve the hunger Goal

The perceived lack of absorptive capacity in poor countries is often used to argue against large increases in development assistance. But this impediment can itself become the focus of public investment, with emphasis on enhancing the technical and managerial capacity for policy and program implementation in the sectors relevant to overcoming hunger. Building local capacity should be the central goal of both national government and donor-funded activities. Yet there is a need to develop a better understanding of the underlying causes of

A corps of para-professional extension workers could be created

the lack of capacity, its symptoms, and its solutions. For example, it is important to determine whether poor performance is due to a lack of technical skills, weak incentives for performance, or political constraints.

It is also important to determine at what level this capacity issue should be addressed and what can be done at which levels. The process of developing a capacity strategy should be fundamentally owned and created by developing countries, with support from donors. Developing countries should be responsible for setting the agenda and leading the process of identifying their needs, through broad consensus and a clear sense of resources and capacity gaps. Capacity development is a long-term process and donors need to support developing countries' agendas with longer term commitments to see sustainable results.

One type of capacity development would be massive on-the-job training of staff in government, NGOs, the private sector, and community-based institutions—in specific interventions to help meet the hunger Goal. In this case, policies should also be implemented to promote local university education in nutrition, agriculture, and business. Such broad training efforts will create the absorptive and implementation capacity for larger investments. A corps of paraprofessional extension workers could be created for agriculture, nutrition, and health, residing in villages identified as hunger hotspots.

Other capacity development efforts might deal more with structural incentives that lead to poor performance. What do countries do when pressures, sanctions, and lack of incentives induce nonproductive behaviors and limit transparency and competition? For example, many poor countries cannot afford an effective public sector. They lack adequate resources for decent salaries—and checks on political abuse. In such a situation, conventional approaches to capacity development, such as restructuring and systemic improvements, will not work. The problem may be related to efficient management systems and the lack of proper monitoring and evaluation systems. The answer may lie in helping countries improve their overall approach to governance, accountability, and democratization.

At the local level, investment in people is crucial to any antihunger campaign. Provided the people concerned remain healthy and actively engaged in relevant work, policies aimed at human capacity development will have highly positive long-term effects. Investments in capacity building at the local level should cover the education, childhood nutrition, and healthcare sectors in addition to agriculture and natural resource management. Across sectors, special attention should be placed on the needs of children and women, with a sharp focus on gender equality. Policies to build capacity should encourage the participation of communities in the planning, implementation, and monitoring of antihunger programs. Decentralization without attention to governance issues will fail if it merely establishes new local elites and does not liberate the skills and talents of ordinary people.

Governments should create institutional structures to integrate agriculture and nutrition policy at all levels

As discussed in chapter 3, national policies that promote basic skills, education, literacy, and numeracy, especially for women and girls, are a key component in capacity building. This requires policy reforms to improve enrollments and educational quality in primary, secondary, and university programs. National policies to ensure universal, high-quality primary education for girls and boys should be established in all developing countries. The Task Force on Education and Gender Equality examines these issues in greater depth.

Link nutritional and agricultural interventions

Nutritional and agricultural interventions are essential to hunger reduction—and could be more effective if designed and implemented in complementary ways. Yet all too often they are undertaken by separate institutions with little coordination between them. The task force recommends that hunger reduction programs increase their efforts to integrate nutritional and agricultural aspects in their work, taking opportunities to try out new ideas whenever possible.

Greater budgetary support is needed for both nutrition and agriculture, especially in remote rural areas and city slums. The structure and priorities of national governments often give inadequate attention to nutritional programs—in ministerial mandates and priorities, and in national poverty reduction strategies. As a result, national food security programs often ignore nutrition, focusing solely on agricultural development. To ensure that hunger and malnutrition are effectively addressed, policymakers must ensure that the two are linked across all hunger-related policies and programs.

Governments should create institutional structures to integrate agriculture and nutrition policy at all levels (from ministries to communities). Cross-sectoral coordination can be encouraged at legislative and executive levels, such as ministries of agriculture, education, and health—and within national food security coalitions. Policymakers can formulate agricultural policies and investments to bring nutritional benefits, and assure that nutritional interventions are fully funded parts of the country's agricultural development strategy. They can also formulate nutritional policies and programs to stimulate agricultural production, through home gardens, school feeding with locally produced foods, and so on. These links can be encouraged in communities by teaching "home science" in primary and secondary school (including nutrition, health, and sustainable livelihoods).

Increase poor people's access to land and other productive resources

Appropriate policies and institutions are needed to facilitate secure access to productive resources, such as land and capital, and to stimulate employment opportunities essential for pro-poor economic growth. Secure access to land is essential for resource-poor farmers to invest in maintaining and enhancing long-term productivity through soil conservation, tree planting, and other

Governments should create and enforce land and inheritance laws that do not discriminate against women

means. The unprecedented increase in agricultural productivity in China, for example, is widely attributed to greater access to land and other natural resources through land reforms and other rural development initiatives—such as improving irrigation and roads, building rural credit cooperatives, establishing technological extension services, investing in health and education, and providing a community-based social security system (Vepa, Anneboina, and Manghnani 2004).

When individual land tenure is not the most appropriate solution, community-based approaches can be effective. Research has shown that many traditional land tenure systems can provide adequate security without introducing costly, contentious, and complex land registration and titling systems. But official registration and titling of land should be considered where traditional land tenure systems do not ensure equitable and efficient use of land resources.

Special efforts are needed to ensure women's access to and control of land. Often, customary laws grant control of land tenure to men, depriving women farmers, many of them heads of households, not just of decisionmaking power but of assets vital to their survival. If a husband dies, his relatives often gain land rights, further dispossessing the widow. When women do own land, their holdings tend to be smaller, less fertile, and more remote than those of men.

Governments should create and enforce land and inheritance laws that do not discriminate against women. Care must be taken to ensure that land reform programs, together with the break-up of communal land holdings, do not lead to the transfer of exclusive land rights to only males as heads of households, as is often the case. This ignores both the existence of female-headed households and the rights of married women to a joint share (FAO 1997). National and local governments should also carry out public education campaigns to promote understanding of the negative impacts of discriminatory land tenure and inheritance practices on women and society.

Over the past 15 years, countries as diverse as Brazil, India, Nepal, The Gambia, and Cameroon have set aside public lands for use or co-management by indigenous and local communities. Legal reforms have strengthened community forest tenure in Bolivia and the Philippines, while China and Viet Nam have allocated public forest land to individual households. The recognition of indigenous rights and community ownership—and the successful cases of management handover now documented—present a good opportunity for more countries to adopt these policies, which seem likely to improve the livelihoods of millions of forest inhabitants. Critical investments will be required to facilitate this transition by supporting the assessment of claims, the mapping of land to be handed over, the delineation of individual properties where appropriate, the reform of legal frameworks, and the establishment of new regulations and enforcement mechanisms (White and Martin 2002).

Land tenure is as important in cities as the countryside. Hungry people who live in slums and have no property rights are permanently excluded from

In Africa the activities most relevant to hunger are the domain of women

the mainstream economy and face far greater economic risk and uncertainty. The Task Force on Improving the Lives of Slum Dwellers covers this topic in greater detail.

Empower women and girls

In Africa the activities most relevant to hunger—farming, preparing food, caring for children, and managing households—are the domain of women. They produce 80 percent of the food and provide 90 percent of the water and fuel consumed by their households. Yet they own only 1 percent of the land, receive only 7 percent of agricultural extension time and resources, and obtain only 10 percent of the credit available to small-scale farmers (FAO 1997). The situation is similar in Latin America and South Asia, where women produce more than half the food (Hayzer 2003).

High rates of malnourishment, illiteracy, early marriage, and inadequate access to reproductive health services create a vicious circle of deprivation that is passed on from mother to child. The low social, economic, and legal status of women is therefore a major barrier to increased food production and improved nutrition at the intrahousehold and community levels. That is why political leaders at all levels should work with community groups to empower women and girls through legal, policy, and institutional reforms. These should be coupled with the targeted provision of healthcare and education, universal access to reproductive health services, and improved access to land, water, credit, and agricultural extension services for women. Policies also need to be put in place to recruit and train more women extension agents, whose advisory services should be linked with women workers in literacy, numeracy, and community health and nutrition programs.

The priorities for mainstreaming gender equality in the pursuit of hunger elimination include:

- Adjust agricultural policies so that they support the needs of women farmers—by improving access to productive resources, increasing the number of women extension agents recruited, and linking women more directly through agricultural advisory services with literacy, numeracy, reproductive health, and nutrition programs.
- Assure women's property rights to land, water, trees, and fisheries by enforcing constitutional rights and increasing access to credit, extension services, and information.
- Inform communities, through public awareness campaigns and school curricula, about behavior and attitudes that harm the nutrition of girls and women—and thus the nutrition of all.
- Ensure that more women play leadership roles in elected bodies and in government programs related to hunger. Key ministries and institutions involved in addressing hunger should increase the number of women professional staff who interact with the public. Governments should

The emphasis should be on rainfed areas—and on helping food-insecure producers

encourage women's participation in social, political, and economic processes and where necessary establish laws requiring equal opportunities and benefits for women and men.

- Encourage the formation of women's self-help groups to initiate community-level actions.
- Adopt the goal of universal access to reproductive health. Both men and women should be educated about the importance of family planning and spacing children as well as the critical need to use condoms to stop the spread of HIV/AIDS and other sexually transmitted infections.
- Review and reform legislation that negatively affects women and their role in combating hunger. In particular, women need to be given access to and control of resources and credit services.
- Adapt education curricula to meet the needs of girls as future farmers, businesswomen, caregivers, and educators.
- Develop and introduce, through agricultural and natural resources research and development, technology that will ease the workload of rural women.

Strengthen agricultural and nutrition research

The unprecedented growth in agricultural productivity in the past century was primarily a result of investments in agricultural research, which can generate new knowledge and technologies to benefit the poor and increase food security (Borlaug 2001). But the belief that most agricultural problems in Africa can be solved by deploying existing technologies has led to a decline in research funding by governments, donors, and international financial institutions since the 1980s.

Public agricultural research systems in most developing countries consist of research institutes and universities that operate independent of extension agencies and farming communities—and are poorly connected to them. The result is inefficient use of national resources, duplication in research agendas, a lack of synergies, research objectives separate from farmer needs, and the limited transfer of research results to poor communities. National science and technology policies should be designed and adequately funded to create effective working partnerships between farmers, universities, research centers, and extension services. This more collaborative and participatory system would replace the outdated linear and top-down approach that has failed in most developing countries.

The Task Force on Hunger endorses the analysis and conclusions of the InterAcademy Council report, "Realizing the Promise and Potential of African Agriculture" (IAC 2004) and the Consultative Group on International Agricultural Research's vision and strategy, "A Food Secure World for All" (CGIAR 2000). The emphasis should be on rainfed areas—and on helping food-insecure producers sustainably increase and stabilize production. For example, there is

Strategies should link with and support the innovation initiatives of communities

evidence from India and China that research and development investments in rainfed areas can result in productivity growth and poverty reduction substantially greater than similar investments in irrigated agriculture (IFPRI 2002b).

The task force recommends increasing national research investments to at least 2 percent of agricultural GDP by 2015. Of this, 1.5 percent should go to agricultural research, as recommended by the InterAcademy Council—embracing sustainable crop, livestock, fish, and tree production systems and associated natural resource and ecosystem management—and 0.5 percent to nutrition research. This would more than double the current funding for such research. These strategies should seek to link with and support the innovation initiatives of communities. The majority of the agricultural and nutrition research funding should address the needs of poor farmers in marginal lands (box 5.1).

The international agricultural research centers coordinated by the CGIAR are grossly underfunded in relation to the huge challenges posed by the expanded agenda they now pursue. Additional funding for these centers should be devoted to the priority interventions identified in this report. Moreover, many of the innovations are not being systematically fed into national rural development plans and processes. This shortcoming needs to be addressed by an explicit, appropriately funded effort to accelerate research and link the work of the centers to national and regional development planning. This initiative will enhance the credibility, relevance, and impact of the CGIAR system.

The task force has also identified the need to strengthen research on human nutrition. Despite recent initiatives on biofortification and a long history of

Box 5.1

Poor farmers on marginal lands

Source: Nelson and others 1997.

Nelson and his colleagues analyzed the distribution of the poor among favored and marginal lands in developing countries. Favored lands are rainfed and irrigated cropland in areas that are fertile and well drained, with even topography and adequate rainfall. These lands are in comparatively intensive use, with low risk of degradation. Marginal agricultural lands are those used for agriculture, grazing, or agroforestry, but often characterized by variable topography, poor fertility, inaccessibility, fragility, and heterogeneity, and at risk of degradation. Forests, woodlands, and arid lands were also included in marginal lands.

The authors approximated rural poverty by applying average national percentages of poverty to the respective areas. The resulting estimates were 325 million poor on favored lands and 630 million poor on marginal agricultural, forested, and arid lands.

An important implication of these findings is that strategies to reduce poverty and hunger will require major investments in marginal lands, even assuming high rates of out-migration from marginal lands to favored lands and urban areas. Given that agricultural production (crops, livestock, fisheries, forests) remains the predominant source of livelihoods and food security in the marginal lands, investments in these sectors—and in maintaining the resource base and ecosystem stability—must play a critical role in poverty and hunger reduction.

Many developing countries and regions would benefit greatly from policy reforms and legislation enabling increased cross-border trade

nutrition policy research, there is a clear need to bring nutritional researchers into the CGIAR research community through interdisciplinary partnerships and strategic alliances. The task force has noted that the links between the agricultural and nutrition research communities are weak and ad hoc. It thus recommends that donors increase funding to the CGIAR from current $400 million to $1 billion by 2010—and that the CGIAR centers prepare a plan for scaling up research and capacity building that will support the recommendations in this report.

Remove internal and regional barriers to agricultural trade

For developing countries, trade is an important source of wealth generation and economic growth. It can generate the foreign exchange that countries need to import essential technologies (such as farming equipment or spare parts for manufacturing). These technologies in turn boost the productivity and competitiveness of domestic producers, who may then gain access to larger, wealthier markets abroad (McCulloch, Winters, and Cirera 2001). Greater efficiency of local private sectors also benefits domestic consumers through lower prices and greater choice of goods and services.

Many developing countries and regions would benefit greatly from policy reforms and legislation enabling increased cross-border trade. The share of developing countries' trade with other developing countries is large and growing rapidly. Yet formal and informal trade barriers severely limit the volume and profitability of such trade, blocking potential economic gains. Governments should reform national and regional trade policies to open markets. They should also address the corruption that inhibits cross-border trade flows.

When transporting agricultural inputs and outputs in Africa, traders encounter multiple barriers that drastically increase their transaction costs. These barriers range from legal and casual fees to massive delays at border crossings and checkpoints. Policy and legal reforms are needed, together with adequate training and enforcement to crack down on corruption, and infrastructure investment to improve roads, storage facilities, and border crossings. To make this happen, economic blocs—such as the East African Community, the Common Market of Eastern and Southern Africa, and the Economic Community of West African States—should forge new regional agreements. Regional trading blocks among developing countries are preferable to separately negotiated bilateral arrangements but should not be a hindrance to the progress in multilateral talks on trade liberalization.

International trade regimes are unfairly weighted against developing countries. Farmers in developing countries face high levels of protectionist policies from both developed and developing countries, as well as complex phytosanitary and veterinary regulations. Massive producer subsidies paid by OECD governments to their farmers depress the world prices of commodities,

Investments in agriculture, nutrition, and humanitarian food aid are seldom well linked

making imports into developing countries abnormally cheap and creating a strong disincentive for local production.

The domestic agricultural sectors and trade policies of OECD countries are problematic and should be liberalized to open opportunities for developing country production and trade in commodities in their comparative advantage. OECD policies that require major reform include domestic production supports, trade-distorting price guarantees, export subsidies, tariffs and quotas on imports, and protectionist safety and quality regulations.

Unilateral and multilateral trade reforms in agriculture have the potential for considerable poverty alleviation. However, policies must be in place to offset any negative affects that particular groups of poor people may suffer from liberalization (McCulloch, Winters, and Cirera 2001). To increase the trade reform's pro-poor effects, governments must establish complementary policies to ensure that increased agricultural incomes reach the poor, such as through extension services, market and communications infrastructure, training and addressing gender imbalances. The Task Force on Open, Rule-Based Trading Systems addresses this area in greater depth.

Increase the effectiveness of donor agencies' hunger-related programming

Although international donors contribute generously to hunger reduction efforts, their investments in agriculture, nutrition, and humanitarian food aid are seldom well linked. Massive relief efforts to combat humanitarian disasters often dwarf contributions to long-term development. For example, during the 2003 famine in Ethiopia, the United States Agency for International Development (USAID) invested $500 million in emergency food aid—compared with $50 million for development programming in agriculture, health, nutrition, water, and sanitation put together (USAID 2003, 2004). The key to preventing or reducing the impact of these humanitarian crises is to better combine the two forms of investment so that they are mutually supportive.

Such imbalances are exacerbated by the basic mechanism of donor intervention. The project cycle is usually short in term (three to five years) and seldom funded to address problems on a national scale. Projects are typically saddled with cumbersome procurement procedures and reporting requirements, taxing the capacity of local governments and other recipients to respond (Goodland and Cleaver 2002). The dispersion of donor projects in a country can be substantial. For example between 2000 and 2002, some 18 aid agencies in rich countries funded no fewer than 1,371 different projects in Tanzania, which also received funding from the World Bank, the IMF, the African Development Bank, and similar regional or international bodies (CGD and Foreign Policy 2004). The impact could be greater with even a modicum of cooperation: using shared coordinating mechanisms, adopting

Box 5.2
Global partnerships for rural development

Source: ECOSOC 2004.

To meet the internationally agreed development goals such as those established in the Millennium Declaration, recent sessions of the Economic and Social Council of the United Nations focused on the importance of an integrated UN system approach to rural development. Based on the outcomes of the 2003 high-level meeting on "Promoting an integrated approach to rural development in developing countries for poverty eradication and sustainable development," the UN Secretary-General issued a report on a coordinated and integrated UN system approach to promote rural development in developing countries. The heads of major UN agencies and ministers of rural development and development cooperation participated in three simultaneous roundtable discussions on:

- Sustainable rural development and natural resources management for poverty eradication.
- Integrated approach on implementation of the Goals in the area of rural development.
- Global partnerships for rural development.

Subsequently, during the council's 2004 substantive session of June 28–July 23, 2004, a resolution was submitted on a "Coordinated and integrated United Nations system approach to promoting rural development in developing countries, with due consideration to least developed countries, for poverty eradication." This report referred to the UN System Network on Rural Development and Food Security as a national and international forum that "can assist to exchange and disseminate information, experiences and best practices, reinforce ties between organizations of the United Nations system and other stakeholders and mobilize support for government efforts to implement rural development and food security."

common monitoring procedures, and developing robust systems for sharing results and knowledge.

Better coordination could result in joint donor support for national food security and rural development by consolidating financial reporting, coordinating procurement, and eliminating tied aid. A good impetus toward a common approach has recently been provided by the OECD peer review system—to assess the performance of member state aid programs.

So far, changes in donor behavior have been slow to materialize. To make a real impact before 2015, new mechanisms will have to be found to bring donors together around agriculture, nutrition, and rural development. Poverty Reduction Strategy Papers, an instrument for donor coordination at the country level, are promoting a welcome shift from project aid to program assistance, largely through direct budgetary support. But this alone may not be a sufficient or suitable vehicle for coordination.

Create vibrant partnerships to ensure effective policy implementation

The international community needs to create and support vibrant partnerships among developing country governments, civil society, the UN system, and international donors—partnerships that link performance with public accountability and funding for all the Goals.

Such partnerships could form the basis of an independent civil society review mechanism, including participatory monitoring in rural areas. Partners would monitor the activities of bilateral and multilateral donors so that international assistance could be tied to the formulation and implementation of agreed policies. They would also promote awareness in developed countries of the inconsistency between an active international cooperation policy, a closed agricultural trade policy, and debt payment burdens that often exceed aid flows (box 5.2).

Actions needed to implement recommendation two

Promote an integrated policy approach to hunger reduction

Prepare an MDG-based poverty reduction strategy with an integrated, multisectoral approach to meeting the hunger Goal. Poverty reduction strategies should be developed with broad stakeholder participation and include a needs assessment and costing for meeting the hunger Goal, plans to address necessary funding requirements and policy reforms, and systems to monitor and evaluate progress. Align annual budget allocations and MTEFs (medium-term expenditure frameworks for donors) with the MDG-based poverty reduction strategy. Strategies to reduce hunger should involve the health, education, social security, agriculture, transportation, natural resource management, and finance sectors.

Key ingredients for effective policy integration include a focus on the food-insecure and the rural poor, information sharing, and capacity building. Key actors include relevant ministries of the national government, donors, and traditionally underrepresented groups, such as rural government, grassroots leaders, and women. By 2007 all countries should have a poverty reduction strategy or other policy and implementation strategy to achieve the hunger Goal.

Restore budgetary priority to agriculture and the rural sectors

Allocate at least 10 percent of the national budget to agriculture, through national budget processes (involving stakeholder consultation) and donor investments. Substantiate the role of agriculture as the engine of economic growth and development. Link this to increased complementary investments in rural roads, energy, education, healthcare, finance, and communication infrastructure.

Increased budgetary priority for agriculture should be complemented by greater investments in food security and nutrition. A major focus should be expansion of off-farm employment opportunities. By 2007 all African countries should allocate least 5 percent of the national budget to agriculture, with donor support. By 2010 this should reach 10 percent.

Build developing country capacity to achieve the hunger Goal	Invest in education, including community-level literacy and nutrition education; primary and secondary school curricula on nutrition, and university programs on nutrition, agriculture, business, and rural development. Build skills in planning, policy analysis and advocacy, implementation, and monitoring—including the community level. Strengthen basic education and skills at the community level, particularly among women and girls. Invest in broad-scale on-the-job training of staff at existing institutions. Create a corps of paraprofessional extension workers in agriculture, nutrition and health, based in hunger-intensive areas. Conduct public awareness campaigns on nutrition, agriculture, and gender equality. Ensure independent media and freedom of expression.
Link nutritional and agricultural interventions	Create institutional structures to integrate agriculture and nutrition policy at all levels (from ministries to community levels) and encourage cross-sectoral coordination at legislative and executive levels. Formulate agricultural policies and investments to bring nutritional benefits, and assure that nutritional interventions are fully funded parts of the country's agricultural development strategy. Formulate nutritional policies and programs to stimulate agricultural production (such as school feeding with locally produced foods and home gardens). Reinstate "home science" primary and secondary school curricula addressing nutrition, health, and sustainable livelihoods.
Increase poor people's access to productive resources	Provide clear ownership of land to all farmers and urban dwellers, with a special focus on securing the land rights of women. Create legislation to establish private land titles, access or rights to community property. Use affirmative legislation to help marginalized people gain property rights or access. Provide innovative tenure arrangements for wise use of shared resources. Ensure that women have the legal right to inherit, retain, and trade property. Ensure effective enforcement of contracts, property laws, and rights to redress, and monitor progress through regular national assessments of land ownership.
Empower women and girls	Empower women as farmers and food producers by assuring their property rights to land, water, trees, and fisheries through enforcement of constitutional rights and increasing their access to credit, extension services, and information. Empower women as caregivers and family nutritional managers by assuring their access to nutrition, hygiene, and healthcare information. Empower women as household income earners by ensuring primary education of all girls, providing numeracy and literacy programs for adult women, and assuring women's access to information on finance and productive assets.

Empower women as decisionmakers and leaders in the household, community, and political arenas by encouraging the formation of women's self-help groups to initiate community-level actions.

Strengthen agricultural and nutrition research	Increase public investments in national research systems to at least 2 percent of agricultural GDP in developing countries. Research should include nutrition, with a focus on marginal lands. Research funding should be increased and diversified to include public, private, and community support. CGIAR donors should increase their investments in the international agricultural research system from $400 million to $1 billion a year within five years, assuring the inclusion of nutrition research, and focusing at least half of total funding on addressing the needs of poor farmers on marginal lands. Research agencies, the private sector, universities, donors, and civil society groups should participate in national priority-setting and implementation, under the overall coordination of the ministry of agriculture. Increase the accountability of research institutions for disseminating their innovations to target communities, and measure results by impact.
Remove internal and regional barriers to agricultural trade	Facilitate the unhindered transport of agricultural inputs and products, within a country and between neighboring countries. This requires policy, legal, and administrative reforms, training and enforcement to reduce corruption, and investment in transport and storage infrastructure. OECD countries should reform policies that reduce access to their markets. The primary actors—national governments working through the World Trade Organization and regional organizations like the Economic Community of West African States, Economic Growth and Agriculture Development, the Common Market of Eastern and Southern Africa, and the Association of Southeast Asian Nations—should make these commitments and take responsibility for their implementation.
Increase the effectiveness of donor agencies' hunger-related programming	Measure donor agency performance based on impact (or progress toward the Millennium Development Goals or other goals), and report it annually to each country where they operate. Donors should enhance complementarity and coordinate their country-level investments to meet the hunger Goal through country-led "basket funding," using the poverty reduction strategy and other planning instruments to set priorities. Donors should also reduce administrative costs. Milestones include a doubling of donor investments by 2015.

Create vibrant partnerships to ensure effective policy implementation	Link public accountability, performance and funding of hunger reduction efforts among developing country governments, civil society, the UN system, and donors. Create a forum of annual meetings to coordinate efforts and monitor progress toward the Goals. Strengthen international networks of stakeholders (including NGOs, the private sector, and international research centers) around the Goals. Key ingredient for success include creating a climate of trust and fora for collaboration between government, NGOs, donor agencies, national governments, civil society, Bretton Woods institutions, the UN system, and donor agencies.

Recommendation three

Increase the agricultural productivity of food-insecure farmers

The world faces a major conundrum: food has never been more abundant, yet 852 million people go hungry. Highly productive agriculture in the developed countries has ensured that the world has plenty of cheap food. This has led some people to question the need to increase the productivity of smallholder farming in developing countries. They argue that the solution to world hunger lies simply in the global redistribution of food from food surplus countries to deficit areas in developing countries.

But the mass transfer of world surpluses to the poor will not solve the problem in the long term. Transportation and distribution costs, along with the cultural values attached to food, would be some of the major constraints. The mass transfer of surpluses could seriously affect local production, reduce income-earning opportunities for the poor, and affect the potential of rural developing economies to prosper. A much more tenable long-term solution to hunger is better distribution of assets and opportunities for improving the productive livelihoods and reducing the vulnerability of poor and food-insecure communities. This would complement growth in commercial agriculture and rural-urban linkages, stimulated by the private sector and trade.

The interventions described here will empower poor farming communities to increase their food production, so that they produce enough for themselves and have a surplus for sale on the market. These interventions are closely linked with those in the proceeding chapters to enhance access to markets and strengthen service providers and institutions. A major focus here will be the crop, tree, and livestock systems of resource-poor, food-insecure farmers in marginal lands, mostly in subhumid and semiarid tropical areas, at both low and high elevations, where the bulk of food-insecure smallholders are located. The UN Millennium Project considers raising agricultural productivity as a priority investment area necessary for Africa (UN Millennium Project 2005).

Raising agricultural productivity is a priority investment area for Africa

But improving the productivity of agriculture, broadly defined, is an important objective in all countries where there are significant numbers of poor rural people, especially in landlocked countries and remote areas where people have poor access to markets. The Task Force on Hunger recommends five interventions as the most important in increasing agricultural productivity for the food-insecure:

- Improve soil health.
- Improve and expand small-scale water management.
- Improve access to better seeds and other planting materials.
- Diversify on-farm enterprises with high-value products.
- Establish effective agricultural extension services.

Background

Over the past 50 years very few countries have tackled mass poverty and hunger without strong economic growth based on increasing agricultural productivity. Statistics show that undernourishment has fallen where food production has risen, at least at the early stages of growth. Between 1990 and 1999 per capita food production grew by only 0.4 percent a year in countries where the number of undernourished increased significantly. But it grew by 3.8 percent in countries where the number of undernourished decreased significantly (FAO 2001a). Raising agricultural productivity where yields are low has the potential to reduce hunger and poverty by directly increasing access to food for producer households and communities. As the Green Revolution demonstrated in parts of Asia and Latin America, raising productivity also increases the supply of food for nonfarming families (the rural landless and urban), stimulates the local and national economy by creating demand for consumer goods and farming inputs, and creates nonfarm jobs in the rural economy.

Today's glut of food is largely the result of market distortion—of the rich world offering subsidies that create surpluses. The hungry poor are isolated from the markets where this food is available, and have little money to pay for it. Small farming families represent half of the hungry worldwide. These producers are offered no subsidies to support their efforts to grow food (Scherr 2003). They have neither the technology nor the inputs to make their efforts more productive. So they remain hungry. Moreover, their coping strategies often lead to the depletion of natural resources, deepening the poverty trap and losing valuable ecosystem services.

Hunger tends to be concentrated in remote rural areas, often where rainfall is poor or erratic and where soils are susceptible to degradation. People living in these areas have been neglected by policymakers in the mistaken belief that they are few in numbers, that the natural resource base cannot support more intensive use, and that land will inevitably degrade as the population, whether of people or animals, rises.

Tree cover on small farms increased with higher human population density

For example, it is commonly believed that increasing production in the drylands will lead to degradation and desertification. But more than 70 empirical studies found that local population growth in hills and mountains of developing countries did not necessarily threaten forest production, agriculture, livestock production, or watershed stability (Templeton and Scherr 1999). Tiffen, Mortimore, and Gichuki (1995) have shown that land degradation can actually decrease as population increases. As population growth raises the value of land and resources, people often change their methods of managing economic plants and animals and make land improvements—individually and collectively—to offset initial declines in productivity and resource quality that result from more intensive use of resources (Templeton and Scherr 1999).

Holmgren, Masakhad, and Sjoholm (1994) also reported a positive correlation between the volume of deliberately planted trees on farm and human population density in 30 districts of Kenya. They found that tree cover on small African farms increased with higher human population density. As long as farmers had secure land tenure, they planted more trees when they no longer had access to nearby forests for tree products. If people have access to markets, they will invest more in their land and increase production and income while conserving the soils they depend on for their future income.

The number of people living in marginal areas is high. The world's drylands (arid, semiarid, and dry subhumid zones) constitute more than 40 percent of its potentially productive land (UNDP and WRI 1997) (figure 6.1). Best estimates are that between 800 million and 1 billion people depend on the natural resources of these lands (Dobie 2001). For example, 11 percent of the world's people live in mountainous areas, 40 percent of them food-insecure (Huddleston and others 2003). Some hunger hotspots nevertheless occur in humid and subhumid areas with favorable topography, usually with high rural population densities. Many of these areas are considered high-potential areas, but soil nutrient depletion and erosion have made them no longer favored lands.

Figure 6.1

About two-fifths of the world is arid or semiarid—three-fifths of Africa

Source: UNDP 2004a.

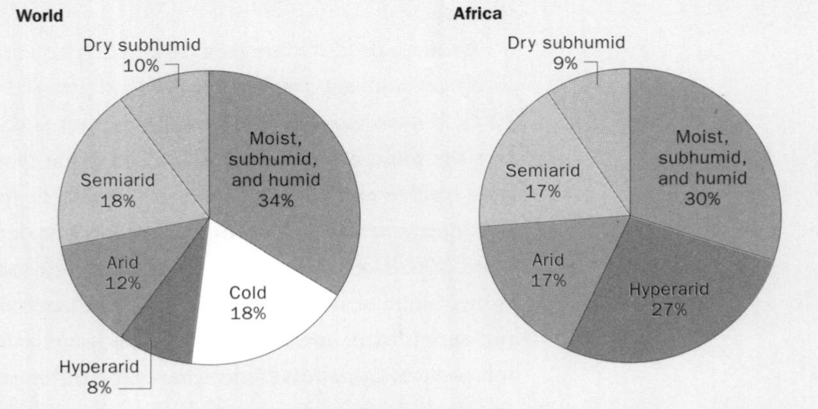

The main development pathway for hungry smallholder farmers is to increase their productivity

Evidence is accumulating that greater returns can now be achieved by investing in marginal lands than in high-potential lands. Results from India and China suggest that government investments in the less favored areas have greater poverty-reducing effects, as well as greater productivity effects, than investments in the better endowed areas. This may reflect past high investment in the more favored areas in these two countries, leaving plenty of neglected investment opportunities in marginal lands.

It has recently been shown that mobile pastoralists living in the drylands have greater economic potential under modern conditions than has long been assumed. Pastoralists are experts at maximizing the benefits from pasture and water resources while minimizing the environmental damage (UNDP 2003). Making development work in more marginal areas will be more challenging than in high-potential areas, but evidence from both developed and developing countries shows that it can be done. To ignore marginal lands would consign millions to poverty and hunger—and abandon vast areas with genuine potential for increased productivity.

The two ways of increasing food production from settled agriculture are to increase the area of land under cultivation and to increase the productivity of land and farm labor. Smallholders have few opportunities to increase the size of their farms, because additional land is not available. Moreover, there are often shortages of labor at peak periods of land preparation, weeding, and harvesting due to a lack of appropriate tools and animal power, the rural exodus of household members to seek income, and the impacts of HIV/AIDS.

The main development pathway for hungry smallholder farmers, then, is to increase their productivity—defined as the yield per hectare per year of crops, livestock, trees, and aquaculture—by intensifying their enterprises. Proven technologies can double or triple yields, even in remote smallholder farms on marginal lands. The most important constraints to achieving yield gains are soils depleted of nutrients, shortages of water, lack of access to improved crop varieties, failure to diversify farm enterprises, poor control of pests and diseases, and extension services that are weak or moribund and divorced from research.

Women produce between 60 and 80 percent of the food in most developing countries and are responsible for half the world's food production (Hayzer 2003). Given women's heavy workload on and off the farm, technologies that ease the burden on women should be made more broadly available. Improved farm implements for poor women farmers, to replace the antiquated hand hoe and machete, will ease labor and improve agricultural processing and productivity. Woodlots and agroforestry techniques can provide firewood closer to the home. Small-scale water harvesting can improve access to water for domestic and agricultural use. In semiarid areas, grass and fodder trees planted in fenced compounds can allow high-value dairy and meat production close to the home and open up numerous sources of income—if markets are accessible. Dissemi-

Many of the food-insecure farmers in the developing world are farming on severely degraded soils

nating these technologies will be facilitated if the number of women extension agents rises. Targeted public policy and investment programs can facilitate all these initiatives.

Improve soil health

Many soils in Asia, Latin America, and especially in tropical parts of Africa have become so degraded that they have greatly reduced productivity. Others, such as those in the Sahel, are inherently infertile. Small-scale farmers over decades have removed large quantities of nutrients from the soils without replacing them with manure or fertilizer in sufficient quantities. This has resulted in a high average annual depletion rate of 22 kilograms of nitrogen, 2.5 kilograms of phosphorus, and 15 kilograms of potassium per hectare of cultivated land over the last 30 years in 37 African countries—an annual loss of nutrients the equivalent of $4 billion in fertilizers (Sanchez 2002).

Many of the food-insecure farmers in the developing world are farming on severely degraded soils, which lack nutrients and organic matter, have poor structure, and often suffer from unchecked erosion. Nutrient imbalances in the soil and pollution by excess nutrients can create unhealthy soils in previously healthy soils, as is now happening in the cradle of the original Green Revolution. Because of the magnitude of soil degradation, restoring its health is often the first entry point for increasing agricultural productivity in many hunger hotspots. This section examines five major soil health interventions, to be used simultaneously: increasing soil nutrients through the appropriate combination of mineral and organic fertilizers, using green manure to improve soil fertility, planting fertilizer trees on farms, returning crop residues to the soil, and using better methods of soil erosion control and water conservation.

Mineral and organic fertilizers

The soil nutrients needed by crop plants can be provided by either organic inputs or inorganic and mineral fertilizers. In environments with a high production potential that are well integrated into commercial markets, mineral fertilizers, supplemented by organic inputs, are the dominant practice. In marginal or remote areas, internally generated organic sources of nutrients from animal manures and nitrogen-fixing leguminous plant species may be the best-bet technologies, though mineral fertilizers (particularly phosphorus and sometimes potassium) are often needed.

Both mineral and organic technologies can be cost-effective, especially for smallholders who face cash constraints, as long as the soils have not been so extensively degraded that most of the organic content is lost (Omamo 2002). The arguments for or against mineral versus organic fertilizers are often debated in development circles (box 6.1). The Task Force on Hunger believes that the soil fertility debate should focus on economic issues, such as cost and risk, since either mineral or organic nutrients can safely supply needed plant nutrients

Farmers and herders need a basket of options to choose from

when used in appropriate amounts. We recommend the combined use of both, accompanied by other measures needed to restore soil health.

Adaptive, integrated soil fertility, crop, and livestock management research, in collaboration with farmers, is needed to develop options suitable for different agro-ecologies and socioeconomic circumstances at the hotspot level. The ways organic and mineral sources of nutrients can be combined with available water and integrated pest management systems can be identified to produce sustainable increases in agricultural productivity.

Much of this site-specific adaptive research should be carried out with farmers in their fields. It is especially important for farmers and extension workers to understand the basic principles of soil fertility management, rather than simply be given prescriptive solutions. Farmers and herders need a basket of options to choose from. Through farmer field schools and participatory technology development approaches, farmers worldwide have proven capable and motivated to test, compare, and adapt technological options, combining their own knowledge and innovations with modern scientific solutions to suit their specific situations.

The farmer's perception of the risk of crop failure and the cash and other resources available are very important considerations in developing recommendations. While it may be important for farmers to have a sense of what is bio-

Box 6.1

Mineral versus organic fertilizers

Source: Sanchez 2002.

Unlike other agricultural inputs, nutrient inputs are essential in all forms of agriculture. They come mainly from inorganic (mineral) and organic fertilizers. Agronomists know that the plant does not care whether the nitrate, phosphate, or potassium ions it absorbs come from a bag of fertilizer, a piece of manure, or a decomposing leaf. There is nothing wrong with mineral fertilizers when properly used. Correctly applied and ensuring a balanced supply of required nutrients for plant growth, they produce high yield increases and good economic returns.

Organic inputs include livestock manure, compost and biomass transfers from plants outside the field, green manure, cover crops and fertilizer trees. They have a low concentration of plant nutrients, are bulky, and in the case of manures, composts, and biomass transfers are labor-intensive to transport. Derived from plants, organic inputs add all 16 essential elements to the soil, including potassium, calcium, magnesium, and micronutrients. Mineral fertilizers usually add only the three major elements—nitrogen, phosphorus, and potassium (though more recent bulk blended products allow the addition of secondary and micronutrients).

Although the plant doesn't care where its nutrients come from, the soil cares about the level of organic carbon it receives. Organic fertilizers add carbon, which improves the soil's water-holding capacities and the energy source for the microorganisms that enhance nutrient cycling.

Virtually all sustainable crop production systems combine the use of mineral fertilizers with organic inputs. The sole application of nitrogen fertilizers accompanied by total crop residue removal is doomed to fail—and is not recommended.

A major challenge is to find ways of making fertilizer available to smallholders at affordable prices

logically possible on their fields, in most cases yield maximization is unlikely to be the most desirable way to go, given risk and financial considerations. Intermediate solutions will generally be more appropriate. Where the cost of mineral fertilizers is high, as in Africa, it is especially important to focus on achieving maximum efficiency in the use of purchased fertilizers. This entails timely application of inorganic and organic fertilizers in ways that minimize the nutrient losses associated with broadcast surface applications.

While nutrient depletion and erosion are the most pervasive soil productivity problems in food-insecure areas, there are growing sustainability problems in many intensive production systems, such as the irrigated rice-wheat farming system in the Indo-Gangetic plains of South Asia and in irrigated areas of China. Excessive use of cheap, subsidized nitrogen fertilizer has led to a decline in organic matter—and in soil health (box 6.2). Unless these issues are addressed, food security in Asia could be undermined through the decline of food production in intensively farmed areas.

A major challenge facing the development community is to find ways of making fertilizer available to smallholders at affordable prices. Many resource-poor farmers use very little fertilizer, especially in Sub-Saharan Africa. High cost to price ratios (fertilizer to crop yield) and difficulties in getting the right fertilizers when needed are the main reasons. Fertilizers cost from two to four times more at the farmgate in Sub-Saharan Africa than in Europe, North America, or Asia.

The prescriptions for economic adjustment that donors have imposed on Africa have led to the elimination of the subsidies that mineral fertilizers used to enjoy. The significantly higher prices after market liberalization led to the collapse of fertilizer imports into most countries. The result is that the prices of mineral fertilizers are now too high for most small farmers, especially if applied to basic food crops. This is especially true in remote marginal areas, where input costs are even higher and the risk of crop failure greater.

The notion of reintroducing fertilizer subsidies to benefit food-insecure farmers is controversial, since subsidies are costly, have often failed to reach the poorest farmers, and have inhibited private sector development. Moreover, the few small-scale farmers who buy fertilizers often apply them to cash rather than food crops. Even so, the Task Force on Hunger considers that it is vital for food-insecure farmers to use increased quantities of mineral fertilizers combined with organic fertilizers in their struggle to improve food security and restore soil health.

As an emergency, relatively short-term intervention, we believe that targeted subsidy programs should be designed to supply both mineral and organic fertilizer as an investment to improve the status of highly food-insecure farmers. One promising strategy is the use of nontransferable certificates of entitlement or tamper-proof "smart cards" redeemable at private agrodealers,

Box 6.2

Unhealthy soils in the cradle of the Green Revolution

Source: Lal and Dawswell 2004.

Irrigated rice and wheat are grown on 23.5 million hectares in India, Pakistan, Bangladesh, Nepal, and China—supporting more than 1 billion people in the Indo-Gangetic plains and other fertile valleys of Asia. This system was the backbone of the original Green Revolution, which saved hundreds of millions of people from starvation. Rice production in South Asia increased from 67 million tons in 1960 to 178 million tons in 2000—wheat production from 15 to 90 million tons.

But yields in the rice-wheat system have reached a plateau, largely because of declining soil health. Farmers apply too much nitrogen fertilizer and too little organic matter and other sources of essential nutrients. Because of high prices, phosphorous and potash fertilizers are not used, and there is a strong nutrient imbalance. The fertilizer response of crops to nitrogen is declining because of the severe deficit of phosphorus and potassium. Micronutrient deficiencies are widespread, precipitating similar deficiencies in people.

Too low a proportion of crop residues is incorporated back into the soil, and topsoil organic matter contents have drastically declined. Farmers remove the wheat stover to feed livestock. Rice straw is burned. The remaining wheat stubble is heavily grazed. Excessive tillage is practiced for weed control. And instead of returning cattle manure to the soil, dung is used as fuel for cooking since there are no trees. Little or no green manure, cover crops, or agroforestry technologies are used.

Nutrient mining is being exacerbated by the use of topsoil for brick making. Landowners in India sell topsoil down to a depth of 1 meter for about $3,000 a hectare. Crops are then grown in the subsoil, which is essentially devoid of organic matter, has low inherent fertility and yields very little. Another problem affecting soil health is that groundwater levels are rising in areas irrigated by canals. Rising water tables are invariably accompanied by increased salinization. Vast areas of once-productive lands are now barren and encrusted by salts.

The degradation of soil and water resources severely affects human health. Many parts of South Asia that depend on the rice-wheat system are now hunger hotspots. In addition to calorie and protein undernutrition, iron and zinc deficiencies are pervasive, particularly among nursing mothers and infants.

Agricultural productivity in the intensively cultivated irrigated areas of Asia will only be sustained if soil and water resources are restored and maintained. On a promising note, improvements in crop management are now spreading in these high-potential areas, including conservation tillage and planting on raised beds. Conservation tillage is now used on about 1.3 million hectares of irrigated wheat land, where the crop residues left as mulch have begun to rebuild organic matter.

which would support input market development (see chapter 11). Countries that have demonstrated a willingness to improve governance and fight corruption should be assisted in establishing such systems.

The task force also advocates supplying food-insecure farmers with nutrients, whatever their source, at the lowest possible cost. But we also recognize that for high-value crops, organic farming may be an attractive option. Whether certified as organic or not, it may be an alternative as long as sufficient organic material can be produced or accessed. The task force acknowledges that this may be difficult in nutrient-depleted soils.

Green manure and cover crop systems that improve soil fertility are well proven

Phosphorus deficiency exists in parts of East Africa, the Sahel, and some highland regions of Asia and Latin America. While the task force believes that improved systems of agroforestry, and green manure and cover crops can increase the availability of nitrogen for crop production, other essential plant nutrients cannot be supplied in sufficient amounts by organic means (Palm, Myers, and Nandwa 1997). Phosphorus will have to be supplied mainly through mineral fertilizers. But in some areas of Africa, where phosphate rock is abundant and of the right quality, there is scope for developing local rock phosphate industries for direct application. Research has shown that indigenous rock phosphate deposits can provide a cost-effective alternative to imported super-phosphates (Jama, Swinkels, and Buresh 1997).

Green manures and cover crops

Green manure and cover crop systems that improve soil fertility are well proven. More than 145 different systems have been identified and adopted with few or no subsidies needed (Bunch 2001a, b). On poor land, farmers typically achieve grain yields of around one ton per hectare. With appropriate biological systems, this can be raised to three to four tons per hectare within three or four years. Some green manures and cover crops can also produce high-protein food, feed, and medicines. Smallholder farmers around the world currently use some 70 species of green manure and cover crops. Conventional production systems on poor land often require that land be left fallow to restore its fertility. With improved techniques, land can be cultivated every year, and total production can be increased to six or eight times that of the traditional system.

Other technologies that improve soil fertility without fallowing include intercropped green manure, cover crops, mulching, conservation tillage, and zero tillage. These technologies have spread across southern South America over the past decade and are now used by about 2 million farmers, both large and small. Yields of food crops have risen by between 50 and 200 percent, with only moderate added costs. These technologies also greatly reduce erosion, increase soil organic matter content, and reduce the amount of mineral fertilizer needed per unit of yield. Even herbicide use for weed control can be reduced if green manure and cover crops are used.

Fertilizer trees (nitrogen-fixing tree fallows)

Trees on farms provide numerous benefits. One of their most valuable services is to increase the fertility of the soil. Leguminous trees of the genera *Sesbania, Tephrosia, Crotalaria, Glyricidia,* and *Cajanus* can be interplanted into a young maize crop and allowed to grow as fallows during the dry seasons, accumulating 50–100 kilograms of nitrogen per hectare in 6–12 months in subhumid East and Southern Africa (Kwesiga and others 1999). After harvesting the wood from the tree fallows, nitrogen-rich leaves, pods, and green branches

Tree fallows are economically and ecologically sound

are hoed into the soil before planting maize at the start of a subsequent rainy season. This above-ground litter and the tree roots then decompose, releasing further nitrogen and other nutrients to the soil.

Farmers are now establishing tree fallow-crop rotations spontaneously in some parts of Africa. These rotations consist of one year of trees followed by one crop of maize in bimodal rainfall areas of East Africa, or two years of trees followed by two or three maize crops in unimodal rainfall areas of Southern Africa. Tree fallows are economically and ecologically sound. And they fit well with farmers' customs and work calendars, in part because the technology was developed with farmers (Kwesiga and others 1999; Sanchez and Jama 2002). *Glyricidia* can also be considered as a permanent intercrop with cereals, allowed to grow during the dry season and subsequently cut back before the next planting, when the nitrogen-rich pods, foliage, and branches are incorporated into the soil.

Crop residue return

Crop residues (stalks, leaves, husks) are valued for a number of uses. They constitute an important source of feed for animals. They are sometimes used as fuel. And they are even used as building materials. Taking the residues out of the field robs the soil of nutrients and affects the porosity and water-holding capacity of the soil. In principle, good soil management should involve the return of all plant residues, by ploughing them in, leaving them on the surface as mulch, or composting them. In most of the farming systems managed by food-insecure smallholders, a substitute for their other uses would be necessary, especially other sources of animal feed. Grasses, multipurpose trees, and various shrubs are potential substitutes.

In parts of the Sahel nomadic pastoralists have traditionally been granted the right to graze their animals in the fields of settled farmers after harvest. The animals feed on the crop residues, but this does not deplete soil nutrients because their dung falls on the field and is rapidly assimilated into the soil.

The main limitation in using compost is the lack of plant material to make enough compost for use on anything but high-value crops. Composting is also labor-intensive.

Soil and water conservation

Also important for soil health is effective soil and water conservation. Conservation agriculture combines no tillage with the maintenance of a protective vegetation cover, crop rotations, and reduced traffic. The damaging effects to tropical soil structure and soil biological activity through conventional tillage with a plough, or even a hoe, have only recently been well understood. The development and adoption of no tillage practices to overcome erosion and productivity decline has been driven by smallholder farmers largely in South and Central America, covering millions of hectares.

Many of the world's hungriest farmers are in the seasonal subhumid and semiarid tropics

The accelerating adoption process by a wide range of farmer types and situations, and its more recent successful testing and adaptation in many agro-ecological zones, counties and regions, is testimony to its success. Conservation agriculture is a win-win technology in many senses. It restores a healthy functioning soil. It saves labor. It captures rainwater in areas prone to drought. And it has beneficial effects on the wider hydrological regime and nutrient and carbon cycles.

Contour terraces, necessary on sloping lands, can serve several purposes when furnished with grasses and trees. The bunds can grow grasses and leguminous fodder trees for livestock, alleviating the pressure on crop residues. They can also grow timber and fruit trees that do not compete with the crops in the terrace, as well as nutrient-accumulating shrubs like the Mexican sunflower *(Tithonia diversifolia)* for biomass transfers to adjacent crop fields. In totally deforested places, like much of Tigray, Ethiopia, soil conservation structures are being built with stones. Once the soil has stabilized, they can be clothed with grasses and trees. Since much soil erosion in food-insecure regions occurs on communally held land, such as grazing areas, roadsides, and riparian zones, similar practices need to be put in place there.

Many challenges remain in replenishing soil health. Mineral fertilizers are expensive, and farmers who face high risks from drought and fluctuations in market prices will be reluctant to invest in them. There will be little advantage to provide mineral fertilizer in places that lose three of every five crops to drought, unless water management practices described in the next section can reduce this risk. Improved tree fallows have yet to prove their worth in the Sahel, where the much longer dry season limits their growth and their potential to fix nitrogen. Fallows also do not perform well on shallow or poorly drained soils—or in frost-prone areas. The availability of high-reactivity rock phosphate is limited by poor market development, but demand is growing. Many of the rock phosphate deposits in Africa are of low reactivity and have limited potential for direct application.

Despite these limitations, various soil improvement techniques have proved highly effective throughout the developing world. They remain the basis for improving agricultural productivity in food-insecure farming communities.

Improve and expand small-scale water management

Many of the world's hungriest farmers are in the seasonal subhumid and semiarid tropics. While soil health remains an issue in these zones, water availability is critical and in many places even more central. Various techniques of water harvesting and small-scale irrigation, combined with efficient water use, should be used to transform crop and livestock production. Building effective technical backstopping capacity in water harvesting, small-scale irrigation, and efficient water use is critical to achieving impact through scaling up.

Various forms of water harvesting can be employed in drier areas

Over the next 10 years rainfed agricultural systems are likely to come under more pressure to increase crop and livestock production. Many food-insecure smallholder farmers are unlikely to benefit from increased large-scale irrigation for technical and environmental reasons. Water is expected to become scarcer as farmers compete with domestic users. Climate change may worsen the situation (Rosegrant and others 2002). Many hunger hotspots are in areas of irregular or inadequate rainfall. Improved small-scale water management has more potential to increase yields than any other intervention in such areas.

The first requirement of water harvesting is to replenish soil moisture by increasing the infiltration of rainfall. Water infiltrates best when the topsoil is porous, contains adequate organic matter, and is covered by a layer of live or dead vegetation. Infiltration is reduced when the soil is crusted and compacted by raindrops, animals, or agricultural machinery, particularly when crop residues are removed from the field. Various management practices can improve infiltration by slowing the runoff of rainwater. These include grass bunds, terracing, tied ridges, zai holes, and many other techniques that also have other advantages, notably protecting against soil erosion (Hillel 2004). Maximizing infiltration is vital in semiarid areas, but it may also be necessary to ensure supplementary watering if crop yields are to increase substantially. For grass production, however, good results can be achieved by improving infiltration alone, without supplementary water.

Various forms of water harvesting can be employed in drier areas. All involve intercepting rainwater as it runs off slopes. The water is typically led to microcatchments—where the land has been shaped to hold the water until it penetrates the soil—or to small impoundments (usually behind a dam), or into cisterns for domestic use or for watering livestock. Water can be caught and channeled using techniques ranging from simply clearing slopes to building channels that bring water to pipes. Considerable amounts of water can be retrieved from apparently dry riverbeds using small dams, walls, and pits, even replenishing wells, as the task force members saw in Rajasthan, India.

Large-scale irrigation is unlikely to bring substantial additional benefits to many small-scale farmers over the next decade. Many large-scale irrigation schemes in developing countries have proved to be uneconomic because output markets are weak. Lately, concern has grown over the environmental effects of such schemes and the effects on people who are displaced when they are built. But there is considerable scope for increasing the use of small-scale irrigation. Traditional irrigation methods have involved periodic flooding of the fields—often with water harvested from slopes, which is not very efficient. Newly developed "micro-irrigation" techniques aim to apply just the right amount of water to plant roots (Hillel 2004). The most advanced systems deliver water through flexible plastic pipes, dripping it through tiny nozzles or porous materials.

The main challenges to increasing the use of water management methods are social and managerial, not technical

Other micro-irrigation systems include micro-sprayers (fine jets fanning from small nozzles) and bubblers, where water "bubbles" slowly flow from the top of a vertical tube set in the soil. Where this technology is too expensive to install throughout whole farming communities, human or animal labor can carry the water to where it is needed. These techniques can make land previously unsuited to irrigation irrigable. The water is constantly supplied to the plant roots, and it becomes less important to store the water in the soil. Thus porous sandy and rocky soils can be irrigated. Small-scale irrigation is, however, technically exacting, and considerable skill is needed to ensure the correct growing conditions for the plants. If the supply is interrupted, total crop failure is likely. Farmers often improvise—say, by punching holes in plastic tubing.

In wetter areas, digging drainage ditches and using gates or siphons to control water flow is common. These techniques require little capital and are easily managed. In places with high water tables, hand-dug wells can ensure access to water for either domestic or agricultural use. It is important to recognize that wells tap a common water resource, so local management is needed to ensure that not too many are sunk, while still ensuring the equity of access to water. Wells commonly proliferate where water is scarce, leading quickly to all of them drying up simultaneously. Extracting water from wells for agricultural use is laborious. Animal traction is often used, though the modern preference is to use mechanical pumps. This draws attention to the need for improved rural energy supplies.

The main challenges to increasing the use of small-scale water management methods are social and managerial, not technical. Although individual farmers can apply basic water infiltration techniques, water harvesting and most forms of irrigation require community effort and a willingness to share resources. Efforts to improve water management have often failed because they were driven only by technology. In the future, the emphasis must be placed on developing the social capital needed to ensure effective community action, and on ensuring that people have access to the information they need. Water user associations, with appropriate training and clear roles and responsibilities, have proven to be extremely capable of managing small-scale water resources management systems.

But funding water management has been a particular problem. Centralized governments find it difficult to fund small, scattered investments that have to be locally conceived, designed, built, and managed. The decentralization of planning and funding will be imperative. Communities will often need compensation for the effort they dedicate to communal construction work, and carefully designed food-for-work programs can be instrumental in that regard.

Better small-scale water management can make almost every other operation on a farm more productive and less risky. In some communities in India, for example, a combination of water harvesting and the rehabilitation of

Genetically superior crop, pasture, and tree varieties can increase the productivity of farms

degraded land has boosted farmers' incomes by more than 600 percent (FAO 2002b).

Improve access to better seeds and other planting materials

If soil and water problems are brought under control, the provision of genetically superior crop, pasture, and tree varieties can enormously increase the productivity of farms in food-insecure areas. Indeed, the interaction between improved germplasm and improved soil fertility is very strong. Often, improved varieties are the catalyst for a range of other improvements, yet there is usually no magic in a variety alone. Only for a serious pest or disease problem, such as downy mildew in Southeast Asia, does developing a resistant variety make sense without other innovations.

The high-yielding fertilizer-responsive semi-dwarf wheat and rice varieties of the original Green Revolution—combined with improved soil fertility, water management, markets, and infrastructure—were responsible for rapid and sweeping changes in agricultural production in parts of Asia and Latin America. It shifted countries from recurrent famine to a level of production that enabled them not only to meet their domestic needs but also to export a surplus. International and national plant breeding research institutes have continued to improve varieties of these and other crops for medium to high-potential areas, and the private sector is heavily involved in plant breeding research and seed marketing for these areas.

But as described in chapter 4, the successes of the Green Revolution have not been replicated where hunger still persists, especially in Sub-Saharan Africa. The rainfed agriculture of Africa is far more complex than the irrigated systems of Asia, requiring improved plant varieties with markedly different traits (such as early maturity, multiple food and fodder uses, and tolerance to drought and low nitrogen). Maintaining and, where possible, enhancing the diversity of these systems is essential to their stability and sustainability. Higher value crops, trees, and livestock are the most important options for diversification open to poor smallholder farmers.

Much has been achieved through global research to improve basic food crops. But there has been a bias toward the crops grown in more favored areas, with less attention to those suitable for more difficult environments, such as millet, sorghum, root crops, bananas, and the pulses. Despite the expansion of the international research system to cover these commodities, there is still an inadequate allocation of resources to the traditional food crops grown in marginal lands by resource-poor farmers—and, at the other end of the spectrum, to the high-value crops, including oil seeds, horticultural crops, and tree crops needed to allow small-scale farmers to diversify.

Resistance or tolerance to such stresses as drought, salinity, low soil fertility, pests, and diseases are important genetic improvements that will benefit the food-insecure. Some exciting developments are occurring in stress tolerance

Greater diffusion of early-maturing varieties will be especially beneficial

research and development. One is unfolding in southern Africa, where at least 20,000 tons of improved seed of new stress-tolerant open-pollinated maize varieties were available for planting in the 2003–04 cropping season, enough to plant 1 million hectares. These varieties have markedly higher yield potential under conditions of drought and low nitrogen levels in the soil—two problems that frequently affect food-insecure farmers in marginal areas. Another is the 400,000 hectares of quality protein maize varieties that are now planted in Sub-Saharan Africa, a figure that could easily double by 2007. Quality protein maize has much higher levels of lysine and tryptophan than normal maize.

Greater diffusion of early-maturing varieties will be especially beneficial to resource-poor farmers in drought-prone areas. Extra-early improved varieties of maize, wheat, rice, sorghum, millet, cowpea, and cassava are now available in West Africa, and may prove adaptable to lowland tropical areas of Eastern and Southern Africa. Early-maturing varieties give farmers added flexibility in managing their cropping systems, by expanding the "planting window."

Progress has been made in developing dual-purpose food-feed varieties of a number of crops, such as sorghum and cowpea. These varieties should be widely tested with farmers and, where results merit, aggressively promoted. Biotechnology can do much to improve the efficiency of planting-breeding and dissemination of improved planting materials (box 6.3).

Once researchers have developed useful varieties, significant challenges remain in multiplying and distributing the seed, especially to resource-poor farmers located in remote or marginal farming areas. There is a need for a considerable expansion of privately funded seed multiplication to address marginal areas and resource-poor farmers. In the long run the private sector is likely to dominate seed production and distribution for favored areas and for high-value seed products such as F1 hybrid varieties. Given appropriate incentives and well organized partnerships with governments and NGOs, private seed growers and companies can also be persuaded to produce seeds for poor people. An essential ingredient of such partnerships is to offer growers a guaranteed price for seed that meets various important pro-poor criteria.

Informal seed delivery systems, involving NGOs and farmer organizations, will be needed to complement more formal seed delivery systems. Effective seed distribution will depend on establishing rural markets and developing much better rural road systems. The task force recommends that countries aim to develop seed and livestock production and distribution systems (through agrodealers and other channels) that can achieve 50 percent adoption rates by food-insecure farmers of key staple food crops, trees, grasses, fodder crops, and livestock breeds.

Diversify on-farm enterprises with high-value products

After soil and water constraints have been largely overcome and smallholder farmers are using improved varieties of basic food crops, many farmers become

Box 6.3
Plant biotechnology

Source: Adapted from FAO 2004b.

A common question following a Task Force on Hunger presentation is our stance on biotechnology. We do not support either extreme in the biotechnology debate—that biotechnology is the key to eliminating world hunger, or that it is a major threat to the environment, food safety, or poor farmers. Some forms of biotechnology, such as tissue culture, are uncontroversial. The contentious debate focuses on gene transfers among plant species and between plants and other phyla. For example, the advent of genomics took plant breeding out of the realm of intuition and keen observation by plant breeders into a world in which it is possible to manipulate genes directly. This allows genetic improvements in a more quantifiable and predictable manner.

We believe that it is important for biotechnology to focus on traits that are important to poor and hungry farmers in the basic staple foods of the poor such as cassava, millets, rice, wheat, and white maize (FAO 2004b). There are already examples among poor farmers in South Africa of cotton bearing the Bt gene from a bacterium reducing the need for insecticide applications, lowering costs, and reducing the threat of insecticide toxicity to the environment and human health. Agricultural researchers are also developing "Golden Rice," inserting dandelion genes that encode the precursors of vitamin A into high-yielding rice, perhaps to reduce this key micronutrient deficiency from millions of rice eating people.

Poor farmers need improved varieties that are tolerant to major fungal, bacterial and viral diseases as well as insects, more tolerant to drought and salinity, and more able to take up nutrients from the soil with larger root systems, as well as those with better protein quality and micronutrients (FAO 2004b). Biotechnology research on soil microorganisms may result in major advances in soil health.

Transgenic research must be done with adequate safeguards under scientifically based protocols approved by each developing country. Reviews of many scientific bodies of genetically modified crops recognize the potential of biotechnology to address critical problems in agricultural productivity and nutrition. We believe that agricultural research must continue to explore the potential benefits of biotechnology to safely and equitably address the needs of the poor and is more responsive to societal needs.

food-secure enough to take the next step of diversification into livestock, vegetable crops, fisheries, and trees that produce high-value products. Diversification increases farmer incomes, addresses nutritional deficiencies, and is the first step out of poverty. Diversification not only generates income for individual farmers—it also enhances the whole rural economy.

For African women, combining the production of food and agricultural cash crops with nonfarm income-earning activities has long been a survival strategy which allows them to reduce the risk of starvation for themselves and their families during periods of chronic or transitory food insecurity (Devereux 1993; Maxwell and Frankenburger 1992). Due to the smaller plot sizes of poor rural female-headed households, increasing yields of food crops will not be sufficient to cover the yearly food consumption requirements of the family. The policy solution for female-headed households is therefore to diversify land use—and take some small amount of land out of the subsistence crop and

Box 6.4

Cash cropping for women farmers

Source: Gladwin and others 2001.

Intensification, diversification of food production, and cash cropping by women farmers are interdependent, requiring a complex strategy. Constraints to immediate expansion of women's cash cropping—such as women's roles as food provisioners in the household and the problem of cash crops as culturally part of the male domain—need to be overcome. Programs should ensure the following elements:

- Encouraging women's cropping of very profitable cash crops, nonfarm microenterprises, and agricultural labor that will bring in cash to the household. Cash cropping on a small portion of women's land devoted to subsistence can be encouraged by women's clubs, which give credit to women for fertilizer for both food and cash crops, to be repaid from proceeds of the cash crop. Government can encourage women's earning cash income by expanding microcredit programs for women.
- Aiming agricultural research programs at increasing women's returns to their land as part of the overall package. The goal is to discover sustainable and affordable agricultural technologies while taking into account the diversity of livelihood systems needed by women farmers.
- Provide "fertilizer safety nets" or "fertilizer-for-work" programs targeted at the chronically food-insecure. In the short term, public works programs will improve the food security of participating households if the time spent on them does not conflict with food production activities. Such programs could possibly lead to improvements in longer term food security, depending on how the additional income is used within the household.

plant it to a cash crop. Yet cash and food crop production by African women farmers are interdependent (see box 6.4).

In this section we outline four methods for diversification with high-value products through raising livestock, planting farm trees, investing in fisheries and aquaculture, and planting vegetables.

Livestock

Livestock production provides an important opportunity for smallholders to diversify their diets and sources of income, while generating manure that can improve soil health. In many African countries the livestock sector contributes 20–30 percent of agricultural GDP, yet the continent has a large trade deficit in livestock and livestock products. The InterAcademy Council (IAC 2004) urged special attention to the role of livestock in African farming systems. The InterAcademy Panel report identifies poor nutrition, diseases, and poor genetic potential as the major constraints to the intensification of smallholder crop-livestock systems.

Increases in milk production can reduce hunger, malnutrition, and food insecurity in both rural and urban settings, at both household and national levels. The protein and micronutrients contained in milk, eggs, and meat are especially needed by the most severely affected food-insecure groups—women and children in poor households. The dilemma has always been that these

Farm communities must have opportunities for moving beyond subsistence agriculture

groups are the least able to secure livestock, because they lack the cash to buy them or the assets needed to raise livestock.

In mixed crop-livestock systems, significant gains can be achieved—even for the semi-landless and especially for vulnerable household members—through improvements in productivity and livestock herd or flock size. Small intensive production systems with dairy products, eggs, and poultry for income are the most suitable (Heifer International 2004). Programs modeled on Heifer International have disseminated such animals to poor farmers and communities, achieving sustainability by the simple requirement of having recipients repay the program with the female offspring of the initial animal.

It is more difficult to improve the systems of nomadic pastoralists. Levels of hunger are high among herders, but many of the proposed solutions to their problems have proved wrong. Pastoralists are highly efficient users of grazing and water resources, and if allowed to continue with their mobile lifestyle, they can exceed the efficiency of any comparable ranched or sedentary system (UNDP 2003). For them, improved breeds are usually not the solution to their challenges. Pastoralists are constrained by competition for land as cropping expands, by a lack of veterinary services, and by the remoteness of markets. In all cases access to veterinary products is extremely important, because of the large role livestock products play in human nutrition.

Farm trees

Given rapid urbanization in developing countries, farm communities must have opportunities for moving beyond subsistence agriculture to supply products demanded by urban dwellers. The sale of tree products—such as timber, fruit, fuel, fiber, fodder, and medicine—can raise the cash incomes of poor households, providing a platform for greater food security and prosperity.

Unsustainable harvesting from natural forest, the biodiversity concerns about large-scale monoculture, and smaller farm sizes have increased interest in smallholder timber production throughout the world. Although climate, markets, and grower profiles differ between tropical and temperate regions, developing countries in the tropics have often failed to recognize the potential of the small independent producer. In several countries, this group is emerging as the largest supplier of timber products for national consumption and export.

In India, where the High Court banned the extraction of timber from state-owned forests to reduce deforestation, farmers are now supplying the bulk of the nation's domestically produced timber products. The agroforestry sector in Haryana and Punjab states, where poplar and eucalyptus grown for timber are intercropped with cereals and fruit trees such as mango, is now part of a $500 million domestic industry poised to compete with annual imports valued at $2 billion. Indeed, most of the timber produced in the tropics is now grown on small to medium farms, not on large commercial plantations. This

Women are likely to be the hardest hit by declining stocks of fish and other aquatic resources

trend is likely to accelerate, with smallholders emerging as the timber suppliers of the twenty-first century. The domestication of indigenous fruit trees, done throughout tropical Africa, can lead to new sources of farm income and rural jobs, as it has in parts of Asia and Latin America.

For diverse farming systems the establishment of trees on the farm enhances the natural assets of poor farmers. Trees may be grown for a wide range of purposes including soil fertility and conservation, the fencing of gardens and livestock paddocks, home garden development with fruit trees, shrubs and palms, riparian re-vegetation for the protection of water sources, and timber to be harvested to meet long-term needs, such as children's education. Tree species can also be used to restore degraded areas—a win-win proposition since both farmers and the environment gain. There is a critical shortage of tree seed in most poor rural areas, so the most important priority for increasing the use of trees is to start tree nurseries—small enterprises that can create employment opportunities for women and youth.

Fisheries and aquaculture

Those involved in fisheries are among the poorest in the developing world. The WorldFish Center (ICLARM) estimates that more than 30 million people are directly employed in primary capture fisheries and aquaculture, while another 200 million depend on fishing as part of their livelihood. Fish are a healthy source of protein, calcium, vitamin A, and essential fatty acids. But given declining catches and rising demand in urban areas, many of the poor cannot afford to eat the fish they catch. For many of the urban poor, fish is the only source of animal protein, so increasing the supply of low-cost fish will contribute significantly to their diets.

Women play a key role in fisheries and aquaculture, especially in processing and marketing. They are likely to be the hardest hit by declining stocks of fish and other aquatic resources. They are also likely to benefit most from efforts to improve the productivity of this sector. Small aquaculture can also diversify livelihood options for poor farmers, increasing income while reducing risk and vulnerability. Technical impediments include the lack of high-quality fingerlings, the lack of high-quality low-cost feed, diseases, and competition for water (IAC 2004).

Vegetables

Vegetables are vital for healthy diets. They provide a rich source of many essential micronutrients, including vitamins C and K, folate, thiamine, carotenes, several minerals, and dietary fiber. More than 2 billion of the world's people—mostly women and children in the tropics—do not have adequate access to vegetables. In some parts of the world, this situation is due to lack of awareness about the benefits of vegetables. Elsewhere, vegetable production is constrained by pests and diseases and the availability of well adapted varieties.

To be effective, extension usually requires considerable public investment

The Task Force on Hunger sees the incorporation of vegetables into farming systems, feeding programs, and household diets as an important dimension of nutritional improvement. Efforts should be stepped up to extend knowledge about the production and preparation of vegetables. Well adapted germplasm, of indigenous as well as exogenous species, is needed. The World Vegetable Center, the International Plant Genetic Resources Institute, and national partners should be supported in their efforts to develop and disseminate suitable vegetable production systems in low-income countries.

Establish effective agricultural extension services

The major role of extension services is to provide information and training to farmers. Yet smallholder farmers, especially food-insecure ones in remote areas of poor countries, frequently lack access to extension services—or to most of the other services that support agriculture. To be effective, extension usually requires considerable public investment. Its high cost has inhibited most developing countries from investing adequately in it. This has led to a dependency on donor projects and NGOs, which may also lack the resources and often the technical know-how to do the job properly.

Much technical support has focused on more favored production areas and larger scale farmers. It has often been delivered in a top-down fashion by advisors who have had scant and inappropriate formal training and whose in-service training is little better. In addition, operational support has often been woefully inadequate, preventing extension workers to visit poor farmers.

Problems often begin with the selection and training of extension staff. Many agricultural graduates in developing countries do not have farming backgrounds, and most have sought education to launch them on career paths that do not include difficult and arduous work with farmers in the field. Once qualified, there are few incentives—financial and otherwise—to attract the best graduates into extension work. Those who do end up in extension may not be the best people to advise farmers. For example, most extension workers are men, whereas most farmers are women. According to the FAO, only 5 percent of extension services have been addressed to rural women, while no more than 15 percent of the world's extension agents are women (FAO 1997). In addition, most of the extension services are focused on cash crops rather than food and subsistence crops, the primary concern of women farmers and the key to food security (FAO 1997).

Centralized, top-down organizational models have tended to give extension workers technological recipes rather than develop their diagnostic skills. Many of them seem to lack respect for the knowledge and skills of the farmers they are there to serve—and so are unable to work with them effectively. Finally, agricultural research is often poorly linked with extension services, and as a result extension workers lack knowledge of new technologies, while researchers remain ignorant of the real needs of farmers.

It is important that innovations address the special requirements of women farmers

Despite these shortcomings, there are good agricultural extension practices and practitioners. These have promoted such innovations as farmer-to-farmer extension, local learning networks, the participation of farmers in trials and demonstrations, the training of farmer-researchers, the integration of local and traditional knowledge into research and development efforts, the deployment of locally recruited agricultural advisors, and "farmer first" extension and research. Much more attention has been placed on strengthening the capacity of service providers to respond to and support a farmer-driven agricultural development process. With the large number of women farmers in developing countries, it is important that these innovations address the special requirements of women farmers—requirements that may differ from those of their male counterparts.

Another bold and innovative approach is that of Ethiopia, where the government is seeking to reinvent extension by training 45,000 secondary school graduates to serve as paraprofessional extension workers. Each of the 15,000 villages covered in the first phase of this initiative will have a residential team of three agents, specializing in crops, livestock, and natural resources. These agents will interact with the professional ranks of the formal extension service. This admirable initiative could be further improved if trained nutritionists and healthcare and engineering workers were to join the teams.

The Task Force on Hunger strongly supports actions that involve and mobilize the farming community, specifically women, in improving extension services. Instead of relying on outside experts, selected farmers can be employed at a fraction of the cost to work with extension officials and deliver extension messages to other farmers. In this way the ideas and innovations of farmers can be combined with technological advice to ensure that the solutions proposed are the most appropriate. It is crucial these programs ensure that women farmers have equal access and participation in these programs.

Facilitators and intermediaries from NGOs, who have a proven track record as partners in participatory community processes, can provide support to such efforts. So can the general public. Successful models that could be scaled up or replicated include landcare association groups in the Philippines and South Africa and soil and water conservation groups in Kenya. One of the most impressive track records is that of farmer field schools in Southeast Asia, which have successfully promoted integrated pest management practices (FAO 2001c). The schools' estimated 2 million graduates have cut pesticide use in half with no decline in yield. Progress is being made in developing the farmer field school approach to promote soil and water management, enhance the sustainability of crop and livestock farming systems, and address such socioeconomic issues as nutrition, HIV/AIDS, microfinance, business management, and financial sustainability through income-generating activities. Similar institutions are needed to address the technical needs of herders, fishers, and forest dwellers.

Extension should give priority to participatory processes that enhance local decisionmaking and support the interventions recommended by the Task Force on Hunger. These are the key entry points for increasing agricultural productivity and natural resource management—and thus for reducing hunger and poverty. Subject matter specialists, well versed in the range of options related to these factors of production (including farmer-based innovations), will be critical to training frontline extension workers and farmers. Links to other vital agricultural services—especially input delivery, seed multiplication and distribution, grain storage and agro-processing, and marketing—will also be critical.

Actions needed to implement recommendation three

Improve soil health

Facilitate expanded access to inorganic fertilizers through public investments, including short-term targeted subsidies. Use innovative strategies, such as "smart cards." Expand the use of agroforestry, green manures, cover crops, and other biological methods to improve soil fertility, weed control, and moisture conservation. Stimulate the development of private distribution networks for these inputs, focusing on rural agrodealers. Scale up training and information provision to teach farmers how to use soil fertility restoration techniques effectively.

Relevant government ministries should lead these efforts, with others (the private sector, civil society, research agencies, and donors) providing supportive mechanisms. By 2015, 25 million additional smallholder farmers should be using organic or inorganic fertilizer and improved soil and water conservation methods.

Improve and expand small-scale water management

Stimulate the adoption of water conservation and management techniques, matching appropriate technology with local conditions. Provide training and extension services, and support organizing efforts of community groups, to facilitate technology adoption and community resource management. Investment in decentralized planning, funding, and management is key to effectively scaling up these techniques. A broad range of stakeholders should support these efforts, including national and local government authorities, civil society and community groups, research organizations, donors, and local financial institutions. The goal should be to extend these technologies to 10 million smallholder farms worldwide by 2015, with need and cost-efficiency guiding the priorities.

Improve access to better seeds and other planting materials

Strengthen the capacity of national research systems to develop improved crop varieties with traits needed by hungry farmers in marginal lands. Promote public-private partnerships to develop and produce quality seeds by increasing incentives.

Promote community-based production of seeds. Encourage farmers to preserve traditional seeds while adopting new ones. Encourage the responsible use of biotech seeds, together with effective biosafety standards. Develop seed and livestock production and distribution systems (through agrodealers and other channels) that can achieve 50 percent adoption rates nationally in key staple food crops (maize, rice, wheat, barley, sorghum, millet, pulses, cassava, potatoes) and livestock breeds by poor, food-insecure farmers. Achieve comparable results in the improvement of trees, grasses, and fodder crops. Promote rural business development and training, and devise market-based incentives for distribution and adoption of seeds that benefit food-insecure farmers.

Involve public research institutions, private companies, NGOs, and local farmers' associations as well as farmers and extension workers. Target 20 million households for adoption of improved varieties by 2015.

Diversify on-farm enterprises with high-value products

Increase livestock production in food-insecure communities to expand access to milk, eggs, and meat and raise incomes. Assist in establishing small-scale intensive production systems for dairy products, eggs, and poultry. Promote small-scale aquaculture to provide low-cost fish for food-insecure communities.

Establish tree nurseries, using small enterprises to fill critical shortages of tree seed in rural areas. Promote tree-growing to supply timber, fruit, fuel, fiber, fodder, and medicine for household use or sale, or for land conservation purposes. Promote the incorporation of vegetables and fruits into farming systems, to generate micronutrient and economic benefits. Conduct public education and training on vegetable production and preparation.

Establish effective agricultural extension services

Train and deploy 100,000 new village extension workers in food-insecure areas (75 percent in Africa) by 2010. Increase the proportion of women extensionists to 50 percent by 2015.

Expand extension services in marginal areas, and sharpen the focus on women farmers. Emphasize participatory technology development, and high-impact, high-value innovations—particularly in soil health, water management, and improved varieties. Expand farmer-to-farmer extension, deploy locally recruited agricultural advisors, increase farmer participation in research, field trials, and demonstrations, and integrate local and traditional knowledge into research and development efforts, and "farmer first" extension. Use information technologies to improve effectiveness of extension programs. Do independent, quantitative evaluations of impact.

Facilitate and increase the accountability for coordination between research, extension services, and community farmers' organizations.

Recommendation four

Improve nutrition for the chronically hungry and vulnerable

Adequate nutrition lies at the heart of the fight against hunger. According to the International Conference on Nutrition, household food security, health services and a healthy environment, and care for women and young children are the underlying determinants of sound nutrition (FAO and WHO 1992). None is sufficient by itself, and all three are necessary for improving nutrition outcomes (Sethuraman, Shekar, and Kurz 2003).

The Task Force on Hunger recommendations in this chapter focus on improving the nutrition of vulnerable groups facing chronic hunger and micronutrient deficiencies. The interventions constitute a targeted life-cycle approach designed to reduce the prevalence of underweight children, reduce stunting, and ensure adequate micronutrients for those suffering from vitamin and mineral deficiencies (UN ACC/SCN 2000). We place special emphasis on reducing malnutrition among children under two years of age and among pregnant and lactating women. We also emphasize the need to address other nutritionally vulnerable groups, such as children between two and five, school-age children and adolescents, and those affected by HIV/AIDS.

Few of the interventions are new in themselves. What is new is the priority attention accorded them in this global development agenda. While best practices in targeted nutrition interventions are well established, poor implementation in nutrition programs remains a key constraint. This is in large part because nutrition is a multi-sectoral concern that needs to be addressed by more than one line ministry and at more than one level. As mentioned in chapter 2, at least 38 countries are unlikely to achieve the hunger Goal. To reach the hunger target, these countries must reduce malnutrition.

Nutrition must thus be placed at the heart of national poverty reduction strategies, which implies finding a central place in those strategies and, where

A life-cycle approach emphasizes critical "windows of vulnerability"

applicable, in poverty reduction strategies and poverty reduction credits. Nutrition should also be a priority in policy statements and investment strategies. This needs to be reflected in targeted activities on the ground at community level. All these elements are critical to ensuring satisfactory progress.

This chapter puts forward five interventions to improve nutrition among vulnerable groups:

1. Promote mother and infant nutrition.
2. Reduce malnutrition among children under five years of age.
3. Reduce malnutrition among school-age children and adolescents.
4. Reduce vitamin and mineral deficiencies.
5. Reduce the prevalence of infectious diseases that contribute to malnutrition.

In all cases, much depends on increasing local capacity to improve nutrition and health at the community level, including both formal networks of paraprofessional nutrition extension workers and informal self-help and mother-to-mother groups of nutrition and health volunteers. Much depends, too, on the ability of governments to pay greater attention to quality nutrition education (through media campaigns and school curricula) that gives parents information on locally feasible but internationally recognized best practices in achieving maternal and child well-being.[1]

Background

Sound nutrition underlies the achievement of all the Millennium Development Goals, not just halving hunger. Levels of malnutrition continue to be high throughout most of the developing world and nutritional interventions are required almost everywhere, but especially where significant numbers of poor and vulnerable people live. These interventions will vary from place to place, depending on geography, socioeconomic status, cultural practices, and the stage in life of those most affected. A life-cycle approach emphasizes critical "windows of vulnerability"—times in life when the prevalence of malnutrition tends to be higher and the consequences more severe (see figure 7.1).

Pregnancy, lactation, and early childhood (up to two years) are periods of rapid physical and cognitive development that require higher nutrient requirements than other stages of life. Ill-timed pregnancies, specifically short birth intervals, place even greater stress on women and their newborns during these critical years. Women giving birth at shorter intervals are more likely to experience anemia, third-trimester bleeding, and possibly death. Likewise, their children are more likely to suffer low birthweights and are at higher risk of dying by the age of five. These same women often have less opportunity to breastfeed their children, further worsening the poor nutritional status of newborns (Johns Hopkins University 2002). Inadequate feeding and care practices at an early age contribute to immature immune systems that increase the incidence

Figure 7.1

The life-cycle of malnourishment

Source: UN ACC/SCN 2000.

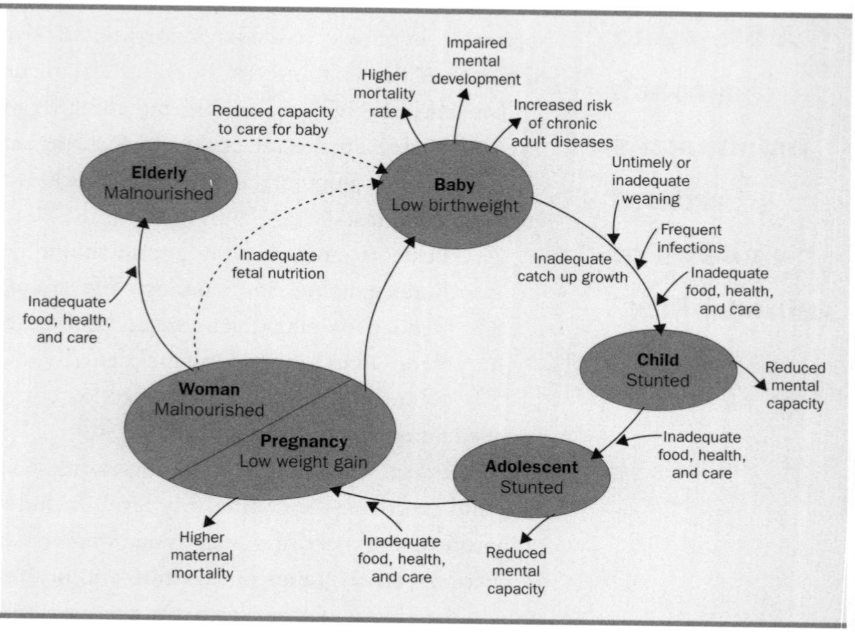

and severity of infection throughout life. For most of the children who are underweight and stunted today, the majority of the damage was done before they reached the age of two.

Malnutrition has multiple causes and is related to the abnormal physiological condition caused by deficiencies, excesses, or imbalances in energy, protein, and other nutrients. It involves both undernutrition (insufficient food intake to meet continuous dietary energy requirements) and overnutrition (excess food intake to meet continuous dietary energy requirements). Although obesity is becoming a major health risk in many rich and some poor countries, the Task Force on Hunger's primary focus is on undernutrition, which has devastating social as well as economic impacts at both the individual and national levels (see chapter 1).

For children under five, malnutrition is often caused by the interaction between a lack of nutritious food, the prevalence of common childhood illnesses such as diarrhea and pneumonia, and the impaired ability of parents to nurture their children because of resource or knowledge constraints. Goiter, scurvy, anemia, and xerophthalmia are forms of malnutrition caused by inadequate intake of iodine, vitamin C, iron, and vitamin A respectively (FAO 2003). And when siblings are close in age, they compete for these constrained resources as well as for maternal care, further increasing the likelihood of malnutrition in this high-risk group (Johns Hopkins University 2002). In 2005, despite abundant global food supplies, at least 130 million children under five will suffer various forms of malnutrition. The devastating results include underweight children, stunted growth, more severe infections, physical and

The key to long-term nutritional improvement lies in family and community action

cognitive disabilities, and the premature death of nearly 6 million children each year.

Malnutrition is also closely linked with HIV, tuberculosis, and malaria. For example, nearly 57 percent of malaria deaths are attributable to malnutrition (Pelletier and others 1995; UN SCN 2004). Research also shows a clear link between malnutrition and poor cognitive function (Gratham-McGregor and Ani 2001). Links between anemia, cognitive function, and school performance are becoming more evident. Iodine-deficient children have been shown to have, on average, 13 fewer IQ points than iodine-sufficient children (Sethuraman, Shekar, and Kurz 2003).

Promote mother and infant nutrition

The key to long-term nutritional improvement lies in family and community action to prevent malnutrition. This requires harnessing the resources of governments, civil society, and the private sector to empower individuals, families, and communities with knowledge and to support them with services, including universal access to reproductive health services. It also requires much greater emphasis on enhancing nutrition knowledge at the household level. This means increasing people's access to both formal and informal sources of nutrition information. It also means standardizing messages based on best practice, tailoring the communication method to local cultural norms, investing in the measurement of impacts, and systematizing the use of information across all aspects of nutrition programming. Public action should include strong community initiatives to support breastfeeding and specific action by employers.

As the primary care providers for children and families, women can improve nutrition outcomes and break the cycle of malnutrition. A focus on pregnant women and infants under two is critical for reducing child malnutrition, child mortality, and maternal mortality. And as the Task Force on Education and Gender Equality points out, recent research is also pointing to the preconception period, because women who are underweight prior to pregnancy have as much risk of a poor pregnancy outcome as those who are underweight during pregnancy (Allen and Gillespie 2001).

Ensuring universal access to reproductive health services is essential to improving the nutritional status of pregnant women and their children. Malnourished women have weaker immune systems and are more susceptible to infection during pregnancy. Likewise, poor reproductive health, especially closely spaced births, leads to the worsening nutritional status of women and their children.

Increasing women's income and their control over family assets is also extremely important for improving nutrition outcomes in their children (Engle 1993). When women are involved in household decisionmaking, they are better able to care for themselves and their children. Protecting women's and

Box 7.1

The South Asian enigma—high rates of child malnutrition despite economic and agricultural gains

Source: Ramalingaswami, Jonsson, and Rohde 1996; UNICEF 2004; UN Millennium Project 2003a.

South Asians have higher levels of economic growth, agricultural production, infrastructure, and public services than those who live in Sub-Saharan Africa. Yet South Asia has by far the highest prevalence of underweight children of any region as a whole. In 2002 nearly half (47 percent) of South Asian children under five were underweight, compared with 31 percent in Sub-Saharan Africa. The question of why this region has the world's highest rates and numbers of underweight children, despite a growing economy and food supply, has been called the South Asian enigma (Ramalingaswami, Jonsson, and Rohde 1996). One factor that may explain the differing status between poor women in Sub-Saharan Africa and those in South Asia is one of social inequalities. Poor women in Sub-Saharan Africa have greater opportunities and freedoms than poor women in South Asia. The exceptionally high rates of malnutrition in South Asia are thought to be deeply rooted in the inequality between men and women. These social inequalities affect mothers and children's nutrition in several ways:

High rates of low birthweight. South Asian women's health status is lower than that of Sub-Saharan women on a number of counts, including anemia rates, average weight gains during pregnancy, and life expectancy in relation to men. The result: 30 percent of babies in South Asia were born with low birthweight, compared with 14 percent in Sub-Saharan Africa during 1998–2002 (UNICEF 2004). Low birthweight indicates that a baby's mother was malnourished before or during pregnancy.

Differences in infant and child feeding. In South Asia the health of infants receiving exclusive breastfeeding often falters at four months, possibly due to suboptimal breastfeeding practices or conditions. The quality of child care in South Asia is reduced by women's lack of education, economic opportunity, and freedom outside the home—all restricting knowledge transmission, self-esteem, and income generation.

Poor sanitation and hygiene. A lack of adequate sanitation facilities affects 66 percent of South Asia's population, compared with 47 percent of Sub-Saharan Africa's (UN Millennium Project 2003a). The combination of poor hygiene and overcrowding greatly heightens the incidence of infectious disease—creating a vicious cycle of malnutrition and illness among young children.

These factors, among others, present a series of setbacks to children's health status from gestation through the first crucial years of development. Actions to address them include increasing girls' education, promoting the rights and opportunities of women, expanding adequate sanitation facilities, and empowering communities by taking a rights approach to nutrition.

girl's rights, including their access to education and productive assets, is also critical for the sustainable elimination of malnutrition (box 7.1).[2]

But to support the empowerment of families, particularly women, it is clear that greater capacity—knowledge, institutions, resources, and motivation—needs to be built and sustained at the local level. The task force recommends increasing the number of community nutrition extension workers in villages. Without additional workers in the community—serving as a conduit for nutrition information, the distribution of micronutrient supplements, the referral of serious cases (of malnutrition or ill health), and the training of trainers—it will remain extremely difficult to reach all the Goals. Close

There is now a broad consensus on the fundamental need for achieving interventions together rather than separately

collaboration is required between government and networks of communities; neither will succeed alone.

Establish prenatal nutrition and supplementary feeding programs

Many low-income women have been malnourished from childhood. They tend to marry early, typically having their first child in adolescence, and have closely spaced births. Malnourished girls become malnourished mothers and give birth to low birthweight babies (less than 2.5 kilograms at birth) who fail to thrive as infants. To break this cycle of malnutrition, the task force recommends direct actions focused on supplemental feeding for underweight pregnant and nursing mothers—in conjunction with synergistic actions to promote education, improve health, and reduce the prevalence of intestinal worms. Priority should go to improving the nutritional quality as well as increasing the quantity and diversity of food consumed during pregnancy. The following points from the literature highlight the importance of programs for pregnant women (Allen and Gillespie 2001; LoPriore, Webb, and Van Nieuwenhuyse 2004):

- Maternal supplementation can increase maternal weight gain—and when there is a serious food energy shortage, the length of the newborn infant.
- Undernourished women can improve their pregnancy outcomes by eating more of their normal diet and appropriate energy-containing supplements.
- When the normal diet is low in protein or micronutrients, it is important to ensure that they are provided as supplements or in micronutrient-fortified foods.
- Young maternal age at conception is a risk factor for poor pregnancy outcome, so encouraging later and well spaced pregnancies is important.
- In areas of endemic iodine deficiency, adequate maternal iodine status is critical to prevent neonatal deaths, low birthweight, and cognitive or physical abnormalities.
- Other interventions that improve pregnancy outcomes include reducing physical energy expenditure, reducing teenage pregnancies, protecting against malaria, enhancing health and nutrition knowledge, and not smoking.

Interventions for overcoming low birthweight

The main interventions recommended for addressing low birthweight include breastfeeding and, where necessary, complementary feeding promotion, supplementary feeding, and micronutrient supplementation. None of this is new—but there is now a broad consensus on the fundamental need for achieving these interventions together rather than separately. In other words, sound nutrition depends on reaching the most vulnerable demographic groups

Exclusive breastfeeding is strongly recommended for the first six months of life

(pregnant women and infants under two years) with all the essential inputs and services they need, not just some of them.

Children born with low birthweight face increased risk of mortality and morbidity and are more likely to become malnourished in childhood.[3] They may also be more susceptible to chronic diseases in adulthood. Factors underlying low birthweight are high workloads for pregnant women, closely spaced births, infections during pregnancy (such as malaria), and inadequate pregnancy weight-gain. These conditions are created by inadequate food consumption, inequitable patterns of food and care allocation within the household, inadequate access to reproductive health services, a lack of knowledge about promoting the nutrition of adolescent girls, and feeding behavior during pregnancy (eating less, due to cultural factors or in response to inadequate birthing facilities—smaller babies are easier to deliver without complications). The risk of low birthweight is compounded if pregnant women themselves are stunted or undernourished at the time of conception—or if their first pregnancy occurs before they are fully grown.

For optimum nutrition, babies up to the age of six months should only be breastfed. Breastfeeding should then be continued up to the age of two years, during which time the child is gradually weaned onto solid foods. Currently, only about 40 percent of infants worldwide are exclusively breastfed, signaling the need for more information dissemination, nutrition education, and direct support to mothers from community-level nutrition extension workers.

Exclusive breastfeeding is inhibited due to lack of knowledge of its importance, poor nutrition status of the mother, and a lack of time or opportunity. Systems therefore need to be in place (through public education and community-level nutrition extension workers) to communicate the following key points:

- Exclusive breastfeeding is strongly recommended for the first six months of life.
- Breastfeeding should be continued as other foods are added to the diet, since the quality of complementary foods is often poorer than breast milk.
- Encouraging the consumption of animal products by young children can also improve micronutrient intake. The consumption of animal milk, for example, was associated with better growth and micronutrient status in several studies.
- Even where breast milk intake is relatively low, the amount of protein in complementary foods will, in most situations, be more than adequate. Adding protein alone or improving protein quality will seldom improve growth.
- Micronutrient fortification of cereal staples is especially important where these are major constituents of complementary foods.

Micronutrient fortification of cereal staples is especially important

Box 7.2 describes improvements in maternal and infant health by enhancing the nutritional content of food rations in Nepal.

The links between breastfeeding and the transmission of HIV from mother to infant have been the subject of considerable research over the past decade. On average, 63 percent of children of HIV-positive mothers will not be infected by HIV, while 7 percent will be infected during pregnancy, 15 percent during delivery, and 15 percent during the first two years of breastfeeding (WHO 2001). The risk of transmitting HIV through breast milk seriously complicates the options that women have to ensure good nutrition for their young babies.

A large proportion of infant deaths have been associated with poor infant feeding (Caulfield and others 2002). Shifting from a regime of breastfeeding because of the risk of HIV infection thus incurs other risks. WHO (2001) recommends that HIV-positive mothers should give up breastfeeding only when replacement feeding is acceptable, feasible, affordable, sustainable, and safe. This is rarely the case. Indeed, replacement feeding in developing countries carries such risks for young children that it might be less risky for HIV-positive mothers to breastfeed (Coutsoudis and Rollins 2003). The decision remains difficult.

A global strategy on infant and young child feeding was developed jointly by the United Nations Children's Fund and WHO and approved by

Box 7.2

Improved birthweight among refugees in Nepal

Source: Shrimpton, Tripp, and Thorne-Lynn 2002.

In 2003 birthweight data collected at antenatal clinics in Bhutanese refugee camps in Nepal revealed that the incidence of low birthweight had fallen from about 18 percent in 1995 to as low as 8 percent in 1998—a lower rate than the 30 percent observed in hospitals in Nepal. The average birthweight in the camps significantly improved from 2.8 kilograms in 1996 to 3.0 kilograms in 1998, a period that coincided with improvements in the nutritional content of the general ration, including the addition of fortified blended foods.

Figure 1 The average birthweight in refugee camps in Nepal has increased over time

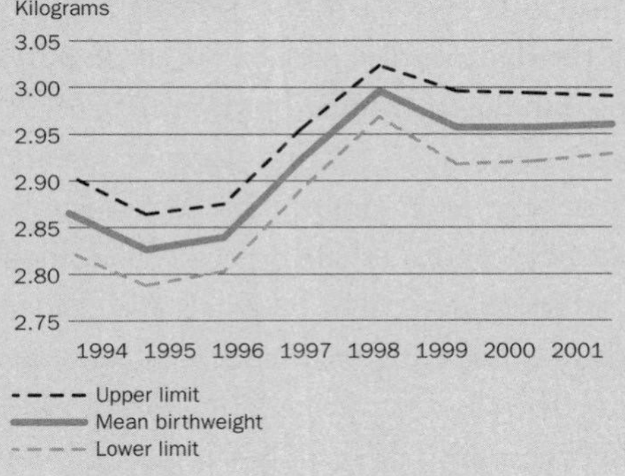

It is important not to treat malnourished individuals in isolation

the World Health Assembly in May 2002. All developing countries should develop national policies in line with this strategy. It is also essential to ensure implementation and monitoring of the International Code for Marketing of Breast Milk Substitutes (WHO 1981).

Reduce malnutrition among children under age five

Childhood malnutrition is in part the outcome of low birthweight. But many children with low or normal birthweights become malnourished in infancy for reasons that include the lack of health services, clean water, good sanitation, or nutritious foods. Once past 18 to 24 months, the opportunities for children to catch up are greatly diminished. The one-time loss in physical and cognitive development becomes a permanent burden carried throughout life.

To reduce malnutrition among children under five years of age, the task force recommends the following three actions: complementary feeding at home, with continued breastfeeding until two years of age; providing malnourished children with appropriate complementary foods, including fortified and blended foods; and providing necessary therapeutic care to all seriously malnourished children and women, especially in remote rural areas.

For more details on infant and young child feeding, see the *Global Strategy for Infant and Young Child Feeding* (UNICEF and WHO 2003). In addition to improving feeding practices directly, more attention should go to controlling infections and providing a healthy environment, safe water, and adequate sanitation, since these measures indirectly improve the nutritional status of preschool children, especially in the first two years of life.[4] This includes immunizations, de-worming, healthcare, and nutritional education.

In dealing with chronic malnutrition, it is important to consider better links with actions to overcome acute malnutrition, usually in the context of major humanitarian crises. Paradoxically, humanitarian work to treat acute malnutrition is often more successful than development work focused on preventing long-term chronic conditions. For example, refugees settled in camps sometimes enjoy better nutritional status than surrounding host communities—mainly because of the professionalism of relief agencies and partly because of the sharp focus and concentration of resources on a clearly defined, usually geographically confined problem (WFP 2004a).

A major challenge is to find ways of scaling up these successes so that best practices can be maintained in emergency situations and replicated in post-emergency contexts. Curing acute conditions and resolving underlying chronic conditions need to be better coordinated as mutually reinforcing aims. All too often, therapeutic feeding centers close down once a crisis has passed, even though the processes that led to widespread malnutrition and loss of life have not substantially changed. It is important not to treat malnourished individuals in isolation from the rest of the population.

Direct access to nutritious food should be increased among today's school-age children and adolescents

One novel approach to bringing knowledge and responsibility to mothers at home is "community therapeutic care," originally developed by Valid International and now piloted in a dozen countries by Concern and other NGOs (Grobler-Tanner and Collins 2004). This approach offers a potential bridge between curative and preventive approaches. It aims to mobilize communities, support local health systems where they exist, and manage severe malnutrition by treating the majority of acutely malnourished children at home rather than taking them away to rehabilitation centers.

Moving children to rehabilitation centers usually requires the mother to spend significant amounts of time away from home, work, and the family's other children. Community therapeutic care instead emphasizes outreach and community mobilization to promote participation, self-identification of problems, and longer term behavioral change. Also central to the approach is the use of appropriate therapeutic foods containing appropriate mixes of nutrients needed to aid treatment and rehabilitation.

This and other innovative approaches that seek to raise survival rates by expanding the coverage of services—and maximizing the impact of treatment by transferring major responsibility to the mother and to community support systems—should be explored and extended wherever possible. Local nutrition programs should always seek to enhance community-level institutional capacity and establish systems that can persist into the recovery and development period (Webb and Rogers 2003).

Reduce malnutrition among school-age children and adolescents

The chances of survival increase for children after they reach the age of five. But their diet continues to be inadequate right up to the adolescent years, when there are increased nutritional needs to support the growth spurt (Nestel 2000). What is essential for school-age children and adolescents is adequate diet rich in energy and micronutrients in both quantity and quality, as well as frequent deworming and if necessary micronutrient supplementation. In addition, the links between anemia, cognitive functions, and school performance are becoming more evident (Sethuraman, Shekar, and Kurz 2003). The task force recommends that direct access to nutritious food, combined with health and nutrition interventions, should be increased among today's school-age children and adolescents.

To do this, we place a high priority on nutrient-rich meal programs offered through schools to eliminate short-term hunger and increase children's attentiveness at school. This should be linked with other school-based health and nutrition interventions, such as water and sanitary latrines, deworming, health, hygiene, and nutrition education, HIV/AIDS prevention and awareness, and school gardens (Del Rosso and Marek 1996). A comprehensive school-based health and feeding program can also serve as a community-based vehicle for reaching preschool children (under five) and pregnant and lactating mothers with similar resources and services.

Although the task force does not view school feeding as a direct nutritional intervention, it can reduce a child's hunger during the school day. A comprehensive food-for-schooling program can also ensure that children who attend school are given food rations to bring home, offering economic incentives for poor families to release children from household or labor obligations so that they can attend school (WFP 2004b). Such programs broaden the reach of feeding programs to the entire family, using the school as the epicenter of community nutrition (box 7.3).

Combining school feeding programs with health interventions can have a strong synergistic impact. For example, new research by the World Bank on the effects of de-worming demonstrates a 15 percent reduction in underweight among Ugandan children receiving two doses per year of the drug Albenzadole compared with a control group who received none (Behrman, Alderman, and

Box 7.3

School-based feeding reduces short-term hunger and improves education in Mexico

Source: ECLAC 2004.

The Programa de Educación, Salud, y Alimentación (Progresa) in Mexico, targeted directly to rural people living in extreme poverty, provides monetary and in-kind benefits to mothers who keep their children in school. The program offers nutritional supplements for children under five and for pregnant and lactating women—plus monetary incentives tied to mandatory healthcare visits to public clinics. Its main intent is to induce households to make more intensive use of educational and health facilities.

Operational since 1997, Progresa covered about 2.6 million families, or 40 percent of all rural families in Mexico, in 50,000 localities by the end of 1999, with an annual budget of $77 million, or 0.2 percent of Mexico's GDP. Now covering urban households as well, under the name Oportunidades, it is a model for other Latin American countries, including Honduras, Nicaragua, and Argentina.

Box 7.4

School-based systems for systematic deworming

Source: Stoltzfus and others 1997; WHO 2002.

Intestinal parasitic helminth infections are a major public health problem throughout the world. The infection is long term and chronic, leading to malnutrition, greater vulnerability to other infections and decreased mental capacity, as well as retarded growth. School-age children are the most heavily infected group for many helminthes infections, both in terms of prevalence and intensity of infection. Helminth infections (particularly hookworm) have been shown to cause iron deficiency anemia, reduce growth, and may negatively affect cognition (Stoltzfus and others 1997).

Highly effective drugs, safe and easily administered, are available. The prices of drugs that control schistosomiasis and soil-transmitted helminthes have plummeted in the last three to four years. By using the school system as a platform for delivery, the cost of treating a school-age child is usually less than $0.50 a year for both schistosomiasis and common intestinal worms. For only worms, the cost is $0.20 a year. This price covers the cost of the drugs, their delivery, equipment, health education materials, training for implementing personnel (teachers), and monitoring and evaluation (WHO 2002).

Hoddinott 2004). In other words, de-worming through school programs can have a significant effect not only on reducing anemia but also on improving child growth, as manifest in their weight-for-age (box 7.4).

The Task Force on Hunger recommends locally produced foods rather than imported food aid for school feeding programs, based ideally on locally produced staple crops, complemented by fortified blended foods, vitamin, and mineral supplements. This will ensure the provision of meals that are culturally acceptable as well as nutritionally balanced (see chapter 11 for a more detailed description of a "homegrown school feeding program").

The treatment of micronutrient deficiencies is one of the most cost-effective nutritional interventions

Reduce vitamin and mineral deficiencies

Deficiencies of vitamins and minerals are the world's most common form of malnutrition, affecting more than 2 billion people worldwide (MI and UNICEF 2004). Over half these people consume adequate amounts of calories and protein and so do not fall into the category of food-insecure. Deficiencies usually occur when the habitual diet lacks diversity and does not include sufficient quantities of the fruits, vegetables, dairy products, meat, and fish, the best sources of micronutrients. But deficiencies are also associated with low caloric intakes. Micronutrient deficiencies can reduce productivity, health, and life expectancy—and lead to significant mortality. Inadequate infant and young child feeding practices and infectious diseases also cause micronutrient malnutrition. Each year, about 1 million children under five lose their lives to vitamin A deficiency, and more than 60,000 women die from severe anemia during pregnancy (MI and UNICEF 2004).

The treatment of micronutrient deficiencies is one of the most cost-effective nutritional interventions available (Copenhagen Consensus 2004). To increase vitamin and mineral intake, the task force recommends three actions: increase the consumption of micronutrient-rich foods, improve food fortification, and increase micronutrient supplementation when necessary. Although these options are mutually reinforcing, we advocate the use of all three to address chronic hunger and micronutrient deficiencies. And we urge that they should be promoted vigorously by village nutrition and agricultural extension services—and through social marketing campaigns at national and district scales.

All countries should place a high priority on promoting the local production and consumption of affordable and culturally appropriate foods rich in micronutrients, such as local fruits and vegetables. Overcoming vitamin A, iron, and zinc deficiencies can readily be accomplished at the village level by consuming fruits high in vitamin A, such as mangoes, and vegetables high in iron, such as kale *(Brassica oleracea cv acephala),* as well as indigenous vegetables, such as amaranths. Where adequate distribution systems exist, it is fairly easy and highly cost-effective to add micronutrients to staple foods such as flour, salt, sugar, and milk. The private sector can play an important role in this (box 7.5).

Box 7.5

The private sector and food fortification

Source: Unilever Health Institute Symposium, Vlaardingen, April 21–22, 2003.

Private companies are becoming partners in the fight against hunger. Unilever created the *Annapurna* brand of iodized salt to address the serious problem of iodine deficiency disorder (IDD), which affects 50 million children worldwide. IDD is the most common cause of preventable mental retardation. Children born to iodine-deficient mothers often have a lower than average IQ. In Ghana Unilever forged a partnership with the United Nations Children's Fund and the Ghana Health Service to promote Annapurna iodized salt through advertising and education. Advertisements were needed to raise awareness of the importance of iodine in the diet, but did not refer to any specific brand of salt.

Teams then went into schools to educate children about the need to raise their iodine levels. Children were invited to bring salt in from home, which was then tested with a special kit to find out if it was iodized. Iodized salt consumption by Ghanaians now stands at 50 percent, up from just 28 percent in 1998. The program has been extended to cover consumption of vitamin A, zinc, and protein as well. Unilever's fortified foods business in Ghana is being extended to Mozambique, Malawi, and Kenya. The company has announced that it is at an advanced stage of negotiations with the United Nations Children's Fund on a global partnership to reduce child mortality.

The Ghana experience and the global partnership are examples of how the private sector can, through its own commercial programs, deliver the kinds of food needed to improve nutrition.

The cost of fortified foods need not be high. Iodized salt, for example, costs as little as $0.05 per person a year, while iodine supplementation costs about $0.50 per household a year.

Local production of fortified foods is highly cost-effective and can have considerable impact (box 7.6). The task force recommends that governments encourage private sector capacity to produce local fortified blended foods, which should then be bought and distributed under government contracts, through schools and other community-based programs. Successful models exist in India, Zambia, and Senegal. Over time the aim would be for such industries to become fully self-sustaining.

Agriculture and nutrition extension workers should work in tandem to provide information to small farmers on the crop and quality requirements of food fortification industries—as well as technical support to help them meet quality and reliability standards.

To allow farmers to fortify foods locally, suppliers of fortification ingredients to farmers will need to work with governments to reduce the cost of premixes or even subsidize their use. There is also a need for simple mixing equipment at the local level that will guarantee homogenous distribution and dosing of micronutrients in the finished product.

Another option is the biofortification of food crops through research. This involves breeding food crop varieties to increase their micronutrient content (see chapter 6). Biofortified crops can provide higher levels of micronutrients in the foods that the poorest people grow and consume daily. It can also comple-

Box 7.6

Village-level fortification of wheat flour in Bangladesh

Source: USAID/MOST 2003; Rahman and others 2002.

The Vulnerable Group Development program run by NGOs in Bangladesh reaches more than 500,000 very poor women. In 2002 a pilot project to fortify whole-meal wheat flour *(atta)* was introduced to tackle micronutrient deficiencies, while reducing milling costs to beneficiaries and providing new employment opportunities. Working on a "no-loss and no-profit" basis, the NGOs, with the help of the United Nations World Food Programme, set in place four small hammer mills, each equipped with novel "fail-safe" devices that prevent overfortification, and each staffed by beneficiaries. The four units provide 28,000 families with 25 kilograms of milled, fortified flour each month at a total processing cost of less than $20 per metric ton, around half the cost previously paid for unfortified flour.

Studies by USAID/MOST (2003) show that beneficiaries recognize this cost saving, and a study by Rahman and others (2002) confirms the beneficial impact on their vitamin A status. According to the second, "Six months after the start of the study, mean serum retinol in the fortified group [villagers consuming the fortified *atta* flour] was significantly higher than in the control group. Separate analyses showed that membership in the fortified group substantially reduced children's risk of having inadequate retinol. Overall the study provides clear evidence that the use of even modest amounts of fortified wheat flour markedly improves vitamin A status in a period as short as six months." The project is to expand to 20 units in 2006.

ment other approaches by reducing the number of people requiring treatment through supplementation and commercial fortification (CGIAR 2002).

The task force thus recommends giving more attention to the emerging field of biofortification. The CGIAR system is making major investments in biofortification through an international, interdisciplinary research program that will cover such crops as rice, sweet potato, cassava, and maize. Similar research is being done to develop a variety of oil palm that produces vegetable oil rich in vitamin A. In all cases, appropriate public education (social marketing) will be essential to the effective dissemination of fortified products.

Reduce infectious diseases that contribute to malnutrition

The protection and promotion of health is an essential complement to food security strategies in preventing malnutrition. The task force recommends that governments ensure that all children are fully immunized and receive prompt treatment for common infections such as diarrhea, pneumonia, malaria, and helminths. School-age children are particularly vulnerable to intestinal parasites and, in endemic areas, should receive de-worming medications. In addition, malaria is a leading cause of low birthweight, and innovative measures to combat it need to be considered. These include distributing insecticide-treated bed-nets in the course of antenatal care.

Also of growing importance are the links between nutrition, food security, and HIV/AIDS. Projections are that AIDS will claim 20 percent of the agricultural labor force in Sub-Saharan Africa by the year 2020, with devastating consequences for food security and nutrition. Today, there are 11 million

The task force recommends the increased coverage and quality of HIV/AIDS prevention and treatment programs

orphans in the region (UNICEF 2003), and millions more vulnerable children are caring for infected family members, dropping out of school due to a lack of financial support, and going hungry (Kadiyala and Gillespie 2003).

Interventions that enhance the immune function may reduce both the transmission of HIV/AIDS and prenatal mortality caused by a range of diseases. Micronutrient supplements, when given to HIV-positive women, improve their health and the health of their children—and can reduce the incidence of life-threatening conditions associated with the disease (Kumwenda and others 2002; Fawzi and others 1998; Fawzi 2003). In general, however, there is little hard evidence that vitamins reduce mother-to-child transmission of HIV before or during childbirth (Kumwenda and others 2002). In Tanzania, supplementation with vitamins B, C, and E provided to breastfeeding mothers modestly reduced transmission of the virus through breastfeeding. In addition, HIV-free survival was significantly prolonged among children born to HIV-infected mothers, even when the women already had compromised immune systems (Fawzi and others 2000).

Good nutrition does have the potential to prolong the asymptomatic phase of HIV infection, to forestall the onset of opportunistic diseases, and so to prolong life (WHO 2003a). Offering vitamin B, C, and E supplements to HIV-positive pregnant women in Tanzania increased lymphocyte (cells associated with immune responses) and hemoglobin levels (Fawzi and others 1998). An enhanced regime of vitamin A over one year led to average height and weight increases of one inch and two pounds among children in Tanzania, particularly among those who were HIV-positive (Villamor and others 2002).

The use of antiretroviral drugs on a large scale is only beginning in developing countries. Evidence from developed countries shows a high level of interaction between nutrition and drug efficacy. Children undergoing antiretroviral drug therapy show weight gain, linear growth, and less anaemia (Verweel and others 2002; Semba and others 2001). There is not yet much experience of interactions between antiretroviral drugs and nutrition in the developing world, but it is certain that, unaided, poor people will be unable to get the quality and quantity of food needed to combat the effects of HIV.

The Task Force on Hunger fully supports the recommendations of the Task Force on HIV/AIDS and recommends the increased coverage and quality of HIV/AIDS prevention and treatment programs, which should be combined with measures to ensure appropriate nutritional care for people living with (or affected by) HIV/AIDS.

Actions needed to implement recommendation four

Promote mother and infant nutrition

Focus nutrition interventions on young women, pregnant and nursing mothers, and children under two years of age, creating "mother and baby-friendly communities." Empower communities with knowledge about the benefits of birth spacing, delaying first pregnancy, antenatal and postnatal care, good birth outcomes, and relevant nutrition knowledge. Empower women through access to universal access to reproductive health services, increased control over productive and family assets, and increased decision-making power in the home.

Offer supplementary feeding for underweight pregnant and nursing women, distribute iron and folic acid through community health workers to all pregnant and lactating women, and promote additional fortification of cereals with folic acid. Markets and dealers should supply and distribute locally produced supplements, while adhering to international policies on breast milk substitutes.

Create education programs on the benefits of exclusive breastfeeding for the first six months, followed by complementary feeding at home, with continued breastfeeding after until two years of age.

Train and assign paraprofessional nutrition extension workers at the village level; train local community groups and local women to become nutrition knowledge workers. By 2010, 50 percent of communities with high hunger prevalence should be formally recognized as mother and baby-friendly communities; and existing international commitments on raising rates of exclusive breastfeeding should be achieved.

Reduce malnutrition among children under five years of age

Provide undernourished children with appropriate complementary foods, including fortified and blended foods. Provide necessary therapeutic care to all seriously undernourished children and women, particularly in remote areas, with the goal of extending care to 25 percent of them by 2008.

Strengthen the nutritional status of small children by providing access to sanitation and clean water through investments in rural infrastructure. Provide regular deworming, appropriate immunizations, and access to healthcare and nutrition education services. Support the creation of community-based growth promotion programs.

Train nutrition extension workers and extend health services into remote areas, where they can support home-based therapeutic care programs. Work with all stakeholders, including all levels of government, national and international experts on nutrition, and community-based groups. Encourage local production of fortified and blended foods, with the goal of 50 percent being bought locally by 2010.

Reduce malnutrition among school-age children and adolescents	Provide nutritionally balanced and micronutrient-fortified school meals to all elementary and secondary school children by 2010. Source from locally produced foods as much as possible, to stimulate local agricultural production and incomes. Provide take-home rations as an incentive for school attendance. Combine with other school-based interventions including deworming, education on nutrition, hygiene, and health including HIV/AIDS prevention, and provision of safe drinking water and sanitary latrines. Programs should include outreach and nutritional education to adolescent girls and mothers in the community, monitored by local health facilitators.
Reduce vitamin and mineral deficiencies	Increase consumption of micronutrient-rich foods by expanding local production of affordable and culturally appropriate micronutrient-rich foods, particularly local fruits and vegetables. Promote their consumption through village nutrition and agricultural extension services, as well as local and national educational campaigns. Where possible, combine outreach on supplementation with existing programs for immunization, antenatal care, schools, literacy, and income generation programs. Improve food fortification by supporting local private industry to produce fortified foods, including informational and technical support to producers to assist them in meeting quality standards. Foster coalitions of government, the private sector, and civil society to conduct public awareness campaigns and ensure that fortified foods are affordable and widely available to food-insecure households. Provide direct micronutrient supplements to young children, adolescents, and pregnant and lactating women as appropriate.
Reduce the prevalence of infectious diseases that contribute to malnutrition	Ensure that all children are fully immunized. Increase the coverage and quality of health services, particularly in areas with high prevalence of malnutrition, to prevent and treat common childhood illnesses such as diarrhea, pneumonia and malaria. Provide semiannual deworming medications in areas where helminth infections are endemic. Link these programs to antenatal care, preschool, and school programs wherever possible. In areas where malaria is endemic, integrate malaria prevention and control activities with antenatal care. Ensure appropriate nutritional care for people living with or affected by HIV/AIDS, including orphans. The ministry of health should coordinate these interventions with district health officers, nutrition extension workers, NGOs, and schools.

Recommendation five

Reduce the vulnerability of the acutely hungry through productive safety nets

People who are hungry and prone to undernutrition are vulnerable to events and influences that they are unable to control. These range from natural disasters, to sudden fluctuations in commodity prices, to catastrophic illness. Droughts, floods, armed conflicts, and political and economic instability aggravate the risks facing food-insecure communities, particularly for people already malnourished. While investing in agricultural productivity, education, and health remains critical to achieving long-term food security, past gains can be threatened if people's vulnerability to short-term disasters and shocks is not tackled head on.

The Task Force on Hunger recommends the following interventions to protect vulnerable people made acutely hungry by natural disasters and economic shocks:

1. Build and strengthen national and local early warning systems.
2. Build and strengthen the capacity to respond to emergencies.
3. Invest in productive safety nets to protect the poorest from short-term shocks and to reduce longer term food insecurity.

Background

Vulnerability to shocks and disasters is a cross-cutting issue that affects all efforts to reduce poverty and hunger. Vulnerability makes people risk-averse, leading to low investment and low output. Under these circumstances it is difficult for people to accumulate assets and climb out of poverty. Resilience cannot be achieved by reducing exposure to shocks and disasters. Most naturally occurring disasters (earthquakes, floods, and droughts) cannot be prevented, and many experts argue that their frequency is increasing as climate changes. Reducing vulnerability rests on helping communities better predict

"Shock-spots" will overlap with hotspots in some countries

and manage the risks they face—and on enhancing their nutritional status so that they can better resist shocks and disasters when they occur.

Households are most vulnerable when they have few options for earning a living. A family that has members earning an income off the farm, or that receives income through remittances and public safety nets, is more likely to survive a shock than households that depend entirely on farm income. The communities most at risk are those having most people involved in identical livelihood activities.

A prime responsibility of government, therefore, is to formulate and implement policies that reduce the effects of catastrophic shocks and disasters, as well as longer term threats such as HIV/AIDS. In the short term, poor and hungry communities will remain highly vulnerable. And even in the longer term, shocks and disasters will still occur, but their effects should be felt less keenly, and it should become easier to recover from them quickly. It is necessary not only to focus on the needs of vulnerable people in defined hunger hotspots, but also to enhance the analysis of risks, and the preparation of contingency plans, in places prone to periodic disasters—what might be called "shock-spots." These will overlap with hotspots in some countries, but they are not necessarily coincident, and they require focused attention in their own right.

For malnourished, vulnerable people, the risk of shocks and disasters, and their long-lasting effects, curb their efforts to escape food insecurity and mire them in hunger and poverty (Webb and Harinarayan 1999). Development policies and actions need to be reframed so that the vulnerability of food-insecure households and communities is addressed more directly. As individual and family coping capacities become stretched, there will be greater need for broad-based, locally managed social security systems. Carefully targeted interventions, including safety nets, can reduce the susceptibility of people to infection by HIV by making it unnecessary to adopt risky behavior to earn money (Kadiyala and Gillespie 2003).

This calls for operations that not only enhance farm productivity, reduce the risks of crop failure, or offer succor during crises. It also calls for enabling food-insecure households to withstand shocks better, enhancing people's capacity to grow out of insecurity, by investing in the assets they need to enhance their labor productivity, and empowering people to make better informed choices.

In sum, mainstreaming the management of vulnerability to shocks and disasters will allow governments to protect and perhaps even enhance their investments in long-term development. That means increasing the ability to predict shocks and disasters—and to respond to them quickly when they occur. It also means managing post-crisis investments better. These should maintain the stability of consumption and generate assets that will take the population beyond where they were before the crisis—that is, they should buffer them from future shocks and disasters. Even emergency nutrition interventions, such

The scale of humanitarian action needed continues to grow

as therapeutic feeding to rehabilitate severely malnourished children, should whenever possible be linked with ongoing community outreach and home-based care systems (as in the community therapeutic care activities described in chapter 7). Marginal communities stand to benefit greatly from development investments that have a "risk dimension" embedded in them.

Build and strengthen national and local early warning systems

Recurring food crises in poor countries are among the most formidable challenges facing the world community today. Extreme weather conditions, armed conflict, failed economic policies, and the devastating impacts of HIV/AIDS have combined to create massive needs requiring urgent action. It is not necessarily that there are more extreme events today, compared with previous decades—though this may well be the case. It is that the scale of humanitarian action needed today is considerably higher and continues to grow. The reason is that vulnerable people are increasingly concentrated in places where a single disruptive event can affect huge numbers of them, causing massive disruption.

The task force recommends that governments build on existing data collection and analysis efforts to identify at-risk groups in defined shock-spots, with a view to enhancing their capacity to build early warning systems against shocks.[1] Early warning systems already exist in some developing countries, but not all regions of these countries are covered (often a country's hotspot locations have the least coverage). More effective nutritional surveillance would provide critical information in "normal" years and early warning in times of impending crisis. A relatively small investment would allow national governments to establish and maintain nutritional surveillance, with reputable national institutes and universities as potential collaborators.

Early warning systems need to be fairly sophisticated to be effective. Capacities need to be developed for strong central and district coordination—while strong local capacities are needed to identify and monitor local parameters. Field monitoring can provide regular flows of information on water availability, crop production, livestock sales, and market prices. Remote sensing can complement field monitoring and help meteorologists and others to predict weather and its likely effects on vegetation and livelihoods. With more understanding of global atmospherics, especially El Niño phenomena, longer term prediction of weather is becoming possible (Hansen and others 2004).

Early warning of crop and livestock failure needs to be carried out within an understanding of the livelihood systems used by the people affected. Some communities may have sophisticated coping strategies that allow them to ride out a drought of moderate severity, while others may have less well developed strategies or strategies that have been weakened by past disasters. In other cases, the disaster—again taking drought as an example—may be so severe or prolonged that external assistance suddenly becomes necessary. Pastoralists often

There is an urgent need to strengthen early warning systems

suffer considerably during droughts of two years or more, and early warning systems seldom serve their needs (box 8.1).

There is an urgent need to strengthen early warning systems—and to build capacities at all levels to understand the interactions between disaster onset, disaster preparedness, and the socioeconomic measures that can transform vulnerable societies into resilient ones (Barrett, Reardon, and Webb 2001). Only through detailed contextual analysis will programs be able to identify both the potentials and the limitations of humanitarian aid. Relief programming will always have an impact on prospects for recovery (for example, ISDR 2003). Just as good warnings are not always met with rapid responses, so effective relief is not invariably followed by effective transition into reconstruction and development. Part of the disconnect is due to a lack of attention to contingency planning, and part to a continuing lack of knowledge of best practices for when and how to make the transition. More investment is needed to review recent experience in this area.

Some interagency efforts currently under way merit further support. The Food Insecurity and Vulnerability Information and Mapping Systems is an international network of UN agencies, Bretton Woods organizations, OECD governments, international NGOs, and relief agencies. It works at the international level to improve awareness and understanding, together with the quality of information related to food security, and helps countries to strengthen their early warning capacities (FIVIMS 2004). The progressive adoption of standards for humanitarian responses to early warnings and crises has also been a positive development of the 1990s (Sphere 2004).[2] Further developments

Box 8.1

Early warning systems—knowing when to intervene

Source: Buchanan-Smith and Davies 1995; Sommer 1998; Toulmin 1995.

The first early warning systems were established to assist the planning of donors and relief agencies. Most still monitor trends in food crop production with a view to identifying probable shortfalls that will need to be covered through commercial imports and food aid. Few extend to the rangeland areas that lie beyond cropland, where droughts are most serious.

Pastoralists respond to drought in a number of ways. They move animals to areas where forage is available. They sell and slaughter animals. They take advantage of kin and family ties by lodging animals with other pastoralists. And they supplement their incomes and diets through hunting, gathering, or selling their labor. All these coping strategies can significantly reduce the need for food aid, even during a moderately serious drought.

But if the drought is prolonged or recurrent, people's capacity for recovery can be fatally impaired. Families that have sold their animals are often unable to build up their herds and recover their livelihoods, even when rainfall improves. Poorer households may have to continue to sell their assets. Under these conditions, they can sink into destitution.

There is thus a need not only to extend early warning systems so that these cover pastoral areas but also to refine understanding of the dynamics of pastoral systems under stress—to know when and how to intervene.

Developing countries need to build their own humanitarian relief institutions

include the Standardized Monitoring and Assessment of Relief and Transitions initiative, which seeks to standardize methods and approaches for measuring and documenting the effectiveness of humanitarian responses by measuring child malnutrition and mortality, as well as food security indicators, against benchmarks. Such initiatives, aimed at raising transparency and enhancing the effectiveness of international action, should similarly inform and assist national action.

Build and strengthen the capacity to respond to emergencies

Developing countries need to build their own humanitarian relief institutions and networks to protect against extreme hunger in timely, effective, and professional ways. Some countries and regions (Ethiopia and southern Africa) have established reasonably efficient early warning systems for famine, while others (Bangladesh, Indonesia, and Thailand) possess good nutrition surveillance systems. Some NGOs (as in Sudan and Ethiopia) have made strides toward developing community-based early warning systems. But these need to be better linked with contingency planning and with multiyear budgeting of national resources for immediate use during times of crisis.

Multiyear budgeting is also needed at the international level to ensure that major emergency needs are met as quickly as possible. The task force recommends that funding for organizations such as the UN's Immediate Response Account, which sets aside cash for rapid response to major emergencies, should be increased to a level more consistent with the growing humanitarian needs of recent years.

While there has recently been progress in mobilizing resources for humanitarian responses to crises through the Consolidated Appeals Process, problems remain.[3] Although food aid appeals have (by and large) been met, nonfood requirements remain substantially underfunded. And emergency resources, while large and significantly greater than 10 years ago, are still insufficient to meet demand. Huge amounts of direct food aid are still needed every year. In 2003 the United Nations World Food Programme delivered 10.2 million tons of food, of which 8.9 million tons were cereals. Emergency food deliveries reached a record level of 6.8 million tons (67 percent of total deliveries).

Too many emergencies still seem to take national and international institutions by surprise. More investment in the assessment of risks is needed, particularly in areas of high hunger prevalence. This should be supported by:

- Precrisis investments in community planning for local disaster response.
- Insurance functions of microfinance programs (flexibility in repayment, savings, support for consumption credit).
- Community-level buffers (such as emergency grain reserves maintained as revolving credit funds).
- Identifying and protecting emergency grazing reserves.

More flexibility is needed to allow for the rapid release of funds

- Crop insurance.
- Employment guarantee schemes (building labor-intensive assets).
- Financing humanitarian resources for rapid distribution in times of urgent need.

As much targeted food assistance as possible should come from local or at least regional purchases, again supporting local or regional agricultural and marketing systems. In 2003 the United Nations World Food Programme purchased almost 2 million tons of food from developing countries and transition countries. But there are difficulties in doing this. Developing country markets are often unstable or unable to provide the required food every year. Food must also be delivered at international quality standards, and local markets often cannot do that.

The debate on food aid is often contentious, ranging from disputes on trade, issues over genetically modified foods, and determining the effects on local agricultural production and market functions. In the absence of adequate local insurance, food assistance can act as an insurance policy, giving communities time to invest and recover. During acute emergencies, when local food production and commercial imports are insufficient, food aid can fill an important gap in food availability. And if used properly, it can contribute to economic development and the protection of basic human rights (Barrett and Maxwell 2004). But if used inappropriately or managed poorly, it can undermine agricultural production, market development, and international trade, thus countering the benefits.

Food aid dependency is most likely to build when food is continually delivered as part of bilateral government-to-government assistance. Used inappropriately, program food aid can substitute for local production and remove incentives from the local economy, although the proof of this remains contentious. It is argued that such negative effects can be avoided through carefully targeting low-income or acutely food-insecure people—in ways that would enhance food demand in addition to increasing supplies (Barrett and Maxwell 2004). Indeed, former regular recipients of food aid over many decades (such as India, Viet Nam, and Bangladesh) have now become food exporters. Used appropriately, food aid has the potential benefit of providing targeted assistance in instances of acute shock where food is insufficient and markets cannot deliver food reliably and quickly enough to protect the vulnerable.

More flexibility is needed to allow for the rapid release of funds to launch rescue efforts rapidly. This would require policy changes by the donor governments and by the agencies that distribute the aid. This involves situating food aid within agricultural and development policies and programs—and ascertaining when and where food aid can become an effective instrument to promote income and productivity as well as humanitarian preparedness and response (Barrett and Maxwell 2004). Implementing such a strategy will

The task force recommends the substitution of cash for program food aid

require concerted efforts to restrict the abuse of food aid and to concentrate its use on the most effective procurement and distribution modes.

The task force recommends the substitution of cash for program food aid, so that governments can invest more flexibly in reducing hunger among people at risk. As previously stated, the UN funding mechanisms for emergency hunger response should be increased to a level more consistent with the growing humanitarian needs of recent years—to roughly 10 percent of total humanitarian relief over the previous three years, on a rolling average basis. The most significant current UN fund for this purpose—the World Food Programme's $70 million Immediate Response Account—would cover only four weeks worth of food in a large operation, such as the response to the southern Africa drought in 2002–03, which reached more than 10 million people. A fund of $300 million would be more appropriate, providing fast access to cash at the outset of food crises. This would vastly increase the response time of humanitarian agencies, allowing more food to be purchased locally or regionally, local transport to be hired, communication lines to be set up, and breaks in food aid pipelines to be filled. New or existing funding mechanisms could also be expanded to cover certain immediate nonfood needs, such as medicines or seeds, for which funding tends to materialize at an even slower rate than for food.

The task force recommends that the additional resources to reduce vulnerability to shocks must not draw funds away from support for long-term development. Instead, an increase in overall official development aid is required. A relatively new idea is to twin donor resources with those of developing countries—to make both more effective. The G8 and other donors could help developing countries become donors by establishing a fund that would match commodity contributions from India, China, or South Africa, for example, with cash to cover transportation, storage, distribution, and management in such countries as Nepal, Afghanistan, or Haiti.

Cash contributions made this way could attract considerably more assistance for hungry people through relationships among developing countries—supported by donor countries. For example, a cash contribution of $20 million in 2002 attracted a donation of 100,000 metric tons of food from South Africa—destined for drought victims in Zambia. The same transaction through developed countries alone would have cost around $40 million.

Invest in productive social safety nets to protect the poorest from short-term shocks

More developing countries are building pension and other social security schemes to protect the elderly and the unemployed (often only in urban areas) from destitution or temporary economic setbacks. These countries also have traditional community-based systems of social solidarity. But in the poorest, these systems are already stretched by the progressive erosion of livelihoods and

Synergistic interventions are a guiding principle in the design of productive safety nets

by multiple shocks. In areas of high and growing HIV prevalence, people are unable to earn a living and have become dependent on other families or the state for survival.

Today most developed countries, and a growing number of developing ones, have accepted the political duty to protect vulnerable citizens. Public opinion no longer tolerates government inaction in the face of widespread humanitarian need. But if the lives and livelihoods of poor people are to be effectively safeguarded during times of crisis, investments in safety nets must be made before crises occur.

The benefits delivered through regular safety nets can make the difference between life and death when shocks or disasters occur. Timely humanitarian response often depends on a prior institutional presence in rural regions and the pretargeting of risky communities and demographic groups. In other words, public action should seek to combine longer term economic growth with initiatives that protect the assets of hungry people—to achieve larger net reductions in aggregate poverty. Making safety nets effective during shocks and more economically productive during noncrisis years is the goal. In other words, safety nets should be a means to protect multidimensional assets, to ensure that the vulnerable are not faced with a choice of selling off livestock, land, or even themselves or their children (through high-risk occupations such as prostitution).

This involves investing in community activities that reduce vulnerability while increasing productive potential. Such activities include operating community food banks, rehabilitating degraded environments (through food-for-work or cash-for-work schemes), and protecting natural assets. Other interventions include employment guarantees (regular public works with a stronger employment guarantee element), rural financial systems that offer consumption credit, microfinance schemes that focus on the hungry, the protection of livestock-based livelihoods, and seasonal food market interventions to stabilize prices.

Synergistic interventions are a guiding principle in the design of productive safety nets. For example, food-for-work schemes, which increase immediate food access through interventions in the labor market, can simultaneously raise productivity and income flows through such activities as road building and watershed management. And new income-generating activities and microfinance schemes help smooth short-term consumption while supporting longer term income flows through the accumulation of productive assets.

In other words, there are upstream and downstream complementarities associated with the individual parts of productive safety nets. For example, village food banks work best when there is a regular rotation of stocks—with drawdown and replenishment carefully monitored. This can be facilitated if stored food is used as part of a local food-for-work activity that creates food banks or rural roads.

Donations of food or cash should be used as an investment in future development

Rural roads can help improve access to markets for new or value-added food products. Such products generated through local food processing industries (such as drying fruits or making blended foods or biscuits) can be stimulated in the early start-up stages with rural microcredit schemes. Locally blended micronutrient-fortified foods can support community-level maternal and preschool nutrition activities. Schools and clinics can be constructed as part of food-for-work schemes using food on rotation from the village food bank.

The key here is to identify mutually supportive interventions that enhance many sectors of economic activity for many groups of local people—and to ensure that no one falls through the cracks.

Whenever possible, donations of food or cash should be used as an investment in future development. For example, food-for-work schemes pay people in food for work on infrastructure development, either to restore lost assets or to build new ones. But any large injection of food or cash into a region in which markets are malfunctioning can have a distorting effect on the local economy. There is also a risk that benefits may not flow to the communities' neediest people but will rather be diverted by those who do the actual work. There is, however, a considerable body of knowledge about how food-for-work schemes can function, and agencies have drawn up strict guidelines for their design.

Actions needed to implement recommendation five

Build and strengthen national and local early warning systems

Ensure that every country has effective systems in place to monitor food insecurity and identify the most appropriate national and international responses to evolving crises. Monitor and analyze conditions in areas of high hunger prevalence to identify potential shocks and risks that will compromise other hunger reduction actions.

Increased development, dissemination, and uptake of standardized monitoring techniques, and greater integration with monitoring of nutrition indicators. Governments should work with Food Insecurity and Vulnerability Information and Mapping Systems to strengthen their early warning capacity, in coordination with national and international groups undertaking relief and rehabilitation programs.

Build and strengthen the capacity to respond to emergencies

Governments, local stakeholders, and international partners should establish contingency plans, technical capacity, logistical capacity, and funds to ensure timely and effective national response to food crises. Improved risk assessment is needed, together with precrisis investments in community planning, insurance, buffers (such as grain or grazing reserves), and prelocating or financing humanitarian resources.

Resources needed for emergency responses should be available as needed. The UN's Immediate Response Account should be consistently funded at

	the level of 10 percent of total humanitarian assistance, or $300 million a year. Food aid should be used only in emergencies, not in an ongoing manner that can undermine local economies. Donor countries should facilitate assistance among developing countries in the form of food donations. Appropriate transitions should be provided from emergency relief to long-term development assistance. Improve ongoing and transparent monitoring of relief operations, including their appropriateness, timeliness, and effectiveness. Strengthen capacity among all responders including governments, UN agencies, NGOs, donors, and communities.
Invest in productive safety nets to protect the poorest from short-term shocks and to reduce longer term food insecurity	Invest in community activities to reduce vulnerability through improved credit and savings arrangements, diversified livelihoods, and shared community action. Create the enabling conditions for community ownership. Invest in developing safety nets during times of noncrisis. This includes restoring degraded environments, creating community food banks, and protecting community assets. Use food-for-work schemes to build community assets while providing immediate relief. Establish new income-generating activities and microfinance schemes to smooth short-term consumption while supportive long-term income and asset accumulation. When possible, use emergency food or cash donations as investments in future development. National and local governments should partner with civil society and community groups to plan for and provide relief during crises.

Recommendation six

Increase incomes and make markets work for the poor

The food-insecure suffer from the inaccessibility of food, either because they cannot produce enough themselves or because they cannot afford to buy or equitably exchange for it in markets. Rural populations in many developing countries—especially poor smallholder farmers in remote areas and in landlocked countries—are often inadequately served by input and output markets. As a result, farm-gate prices are higher for inputs and lower for outputs than they would be if markets operated efficiently. Well functioning markets can ensure that people earn an income, sell their products and services at fair prices, and have reliable access to affordable, nutritious food to feed their families.

The sources of income to purchase food in the poorest households can be surprisingly varied: off-farm work, sales of natural or processed products, and remittances. To earn an income, food-insecure people must have access to input and output markets and financial and labor markets. Input markets are needed so that farmers can buy fertilizer, seeds, tools, and other necessities. Output markets are vital to allow farmers to sell their harvest and earn income. A lack of functioning markets is one of the main reasons that agricultural productivity for the poor smallholder farmer may stagnate or decline, reducing income and increasing the food insecurity of millions of poor people.

This chapter addresses a major dimension of food insecurity—the lack of income to buy food. The following eight interventions deal with strengthening input, output, labor, and financial markets in ways that will increase income for the food-insecure:

1. Invest in and maintain market-related infrastructure.
2. Develop networks of small rural input traders.
3. Improve access to financial services for the poor and food-insecure.

Well functioning markets can create a significant increase in real incomes

4. Provide and enforce a sound legal and regulatory framework.
5. Strengthen the bargaining power of rural and urban poor in the labor market.
6. Ensure access to market information for the poor.
7. Promote and strengthen farmer and community associations.
8. Promote alternative sources of employment and income.

Background

It is estimated that close to 75 percent of the world's poor live in rural areas, with agriculture making up their largest economic activity (Majid 2004). A growing rural economy is vital to provide employment opportunities for the landless poor and for food-insecure farming households. A thriving agricultural sector can be the engine of economic growth, generating on-farm and off-farm employment for the rural landless and creating opportunities for smallholder farmers to get into other economic activities. But if markets do not work efficiently for the poor, they can become a major obstacle for rural economic growth.

Many food-insecure regions experience a "hungry season," when farm food stocks are depleted and families lack the income or savings that would enable them to buy food from elsewhere. Such seasonal hunger is most common in small rainfed farming systems that are poorly linked to markets and that require people to maintain home-grown food stocks through the dry season and into the next growing season, until the new harvest becomes available. Increased productivity, improved connections to markets, and community-based safety nets such as food banks can help overcome this seasonal hunger.

The links between increased production, income, and food security are complex. But increased production and functioning markets are fundamental for food-insecure farm households. Increasing agricultural productivity and linking producers to markets are practical ways of enabling poor rural families to enter the broader economy and so break their dependence on seasonally produced food. Well functioning markets can also create a significant increase in real incomes if surpluses produced in rural areas are delivered quickly and efficiently to urban areas. Linking poor producers to efficient marketing systems can also reduce food prices for the urban food-insecure, who spend a large part of their income on food.

There are three explanations for why markets may not "work for the poor."

First, markets may not exist or do not function properly due to lack of infrastructure, leaving few opportunities for the poor to gain from voluntary exchanges of goods and services. For example, in many parts of Africa, input and output markets fail to exist or operate effectively because of poor transportation and communication infrastructure, undefined property rights, and inadequate storage facilities. In this stage investments should focus on developing

Markets will not develop without adequate public investment in transport and other infrastructure

better transportation, communication, and storage infrastructure—as well as creating innovative marketing arrangements for the poor, such as networks of small rural traders for fertilizers, seeds, and other inputs.

Second, markets might exist but the poor are shut out of participating due to lack of productive assets and collateral. In most of Sub-Saharan Africa, smallholder farmers cannot use land, machinery, or property as collateral because legally recognized titles to land and housing do not exist (de Soto 2000). The poor may also be shut out of markets because they lack the capital required to enter transactions (for example, licenses to trade in grain often require the licensee to provide a deposit), or because social attitudes may bar women from controlling assets and from participating in lucrative markets. In this stage interventions should focus on improving access to financial services for the poor, advancing gender-focused policies and measures that empower women's access to and control of assets, and providing a sound legal and regulatory environment.

Third, markets exist and the poor can participate but suffer from unfavorable terms of trade in the marketplace. In South Asia it is difficult for laborers to demand higher wages because they do not have assets or savings to fall back on if they should reject a wage offer (Lanjouw and Stern 1998; Ravallion and Datt 1999). In this stage interventions should focus on increasing access to market information, building farmer and community associations and cooperatives, strengthening labor markets and unions, increasing access to financial markets, and promoting alternative sources of rural employment and income.

Barriers to functioning markets for the poor and food-insecure include the low density of dispersed rural households, poor rural roads, lack of market information, weak financial markets, gender inequalities, weak application of contract law, formal and informal barriers to regional trade, restricted access to markets in both OECD and other developing countries, and subsidized production by OECD farmers, especially in the European Union, Japan, and the United States. Policy responses that remove these barriers are very much needed and must be suited to the specific conditions of the local food-insecure people.

But integrated policies alone are not sufficient to bring about competitive markets that are accessible to the food-insecure and that quickly and efficiently transmit economic signals of relative scarcity. Supporting institutions and policies that enable the poor to gain access to markets—plus investments in technical and educational training and physical infrastructure—are equally important. The appropriate sequencing of market reforms is important to ensure pro-poor market development.

Invest in and maintain market-related infrastructure

Markets will not develop without adequate public investment in transport and other infrastructure. The low density and quality of road and rail systems in

Road building is needed in many remote areas where the density of hunger is high

many developing countries greatly increases the transport costs in both input and output markets. This reduces farmer competitiveness and greatly increases urban food prices.

Major efforts in road building are needed in many remote areas where the density of hunger is high. Improving rural roads would break the isolation of the rural poor from markets, reduce the time spent by the poor in getting to markets, lower the cost of supplying agricultural inputs to rural areas, and improve opportunities for migration and the development of rural nonfarm sectors. Government should give much higher budgetary priority to the construction and maintenance of primary and secondary roads, and in some instances should revisit the cost-effectiveness of upgrading or building rail systems, particularly in Africa (box 9.1).

The task force recommends that road networks should be developed to enable farmers, pastoralists, fishers, rural entrepreneurs, and traders to gain access to markets. The task force further recommends that, in addition to roads, programs be put in place to ensure that each village of roughly 5,000 people has access to vehicles to transport inputs and outputs to and from markets, as well as provide important services such as taking sick people to the hospital.

Box 9.1

The challenge of rural infrastructure in Africa

Source: World Bank 2003; Spencer 1994.

Africa's lack of rural infrastructure severely constrains not only access to markets but also the ability to engage in production in the first place. Much of the region is landlocked, with very poor road and rail infrastructure, resulting in extremely high transport costs. The lack of transport, energy, water supply, sanitation, and telecommunications infrastructure is a substantial barrier to development, which if left unaddressed will constrain regional growth for decades. By contrast, improved infrastructure can be a springboard for growth: India's road density after independence, for example, was significantly higher than Africa's is now (see table). A massive program of investment over several decades will be needed to close the gap.

Table 1. Road density comparisons

	Road density (kilometers/ 1,000 square kilometers), early 1990s	Density required to match India in 1950
Benin	36	291
Cameroon	38	168
Côte d'Ivoire	94	258
Ghana	17	429
Mozambique	17	135
Nigeria	97	718
Sierra Leone	80	391
Tanzania	66	181
Zambia	36	110
Madagascar	67	137

Local governments and the private sector should develop essential market infrastructure

To minimize environmental damage, new roads should be planned jointly by agricultural and environment ministries through a transparent and participatory process involving all stakeholders, in accordance with international standards for environmental and social impact evaluation and compensation. Special emphasis should go to road building in areas where agricultural extension and other investments are also being introduced. Evidence from the International Food Policy Research Institute suggests that road building in China and India has been the single most effective public investment for poverty reduction. In China, $1 million spent on roads moves 7,000 people out of poverty (IFPRI 2002b). Roads and market infrastructure are not only necessary public investments but are also essential to attract private-sector investment.

In addition to roads, local governments and the private sector should jointly develop other essential market infrastructure, including local storage facilities for crop surpluses. A common problem facing smallholders is their inability to sell their produce at a fair price. The lack of local storage capacity often means that farmers must sell at harvest time, when prices are low, only to have to buy food back later in the season, when prices are high. Investment is needed in storage facilities for farms, cooperatives, and marketing centers. Special attention must ensure that these storage capacities are equally accessible by men and women farmers.

Storage has implications for the profitability of farming and the marketability and safety of farm produce for consumers. Owing to poor storage facilities, high proportions of farm harvests are lost to fungi, rats, and other pests. The losses vary depending on the product. Losses of properly dried durable products such as grains and pulses can be quite low, but they may reach 20 percent or more if insect infestation becomes severe. Poorly dried grain can suffer devastating fungal damage. And even where visible damage is light, highly dangerous toxins can build up as a result of infection by certain fungi. Perishable commodities can suffer a total loss if they do not get to market quickly enough or if there are no cold or cool facilities to preserve them.

The strategic value of stored food to a family often leads each household to store and protect its own grain. This increases unit costs and reduces the cost-effectiveness of introducing better storage technology in communities. But community storage produces economies of scale and becomes feasible where strong community or trading associations and cooperatives exist.

Investment is needed in small processing facilities, to allow value to be added to produce before sale. These investments should quickly yield benefits in greater employment opportunities at the local level. Access to electricity is pivotal in spurring a viable and growing rural nonfarm sector. It is also vital to engage the rural poor in processing. Because establishing a rural electric infrastructure is capital-intensive, small community-managed power units should be considered whenever feasible.

Three-way partnerships among communities, traders, and companies accelerate the supply of inputs

Develop networks of small rural input traders

Across the length and breadth of rural Africa, it is possible to buy Coca-Cola, yet in many places poor farmers cannot find the seeds and fertilizers they need for their survival. If rural shops have provided the basis for market penetration by Coca-Cola, efforts should be made to use them as the keys for opening up rural markets for the supply of seeds, fertilizers, and other inputs.

Unlike selling soft drinks, selling agricultural inputs requires knowledge of what inputs are available, of farmers' needs at different stages of the cropping season, and of how to store and handle chemicals safely. Storekeepers should also be able to advise buyers on how to use products. Private suppliers often lack working capital to buy and store large quantities of a commodity with a largely seasonal demand, such as fertilizers. They also lack technical knowledge about the proper use of fertilizers. Yet with proper training and support on the proper use of fertilizers and other agricultural inputs, many rural entrepreneurs could become the means of reaching the remotest parts of Africa with agricultural inputs. The Rockefeller Foundation has carried out a project on the feasibility of supplying fertilizer, seeds, and agrochemicals through small rural traders who stock small quantities of these agricultural inputs and sell them along with other articles of daily use (box 9.2).

Through this innovative approach, three-way partnerships among communities, traders, and companies have emerged to accelerate the supply of inputs to poor farmers in rural areas of Malawi, Zimbabwe, Uganda, and Kenya. So far, about 300 agrodealers have been trained across Malawi. All the major seed, fertilizer, and agrochemical companies in the country are working with these agrodealers, using them to channel inputs into rural areas. In less than two years, the agrodealers have become the major suppliers of hybrid seed, chemical fertilizer, and pesticides to the rural poor. Along with these approaches, various interventions have reduced the costs of inputs to poor farmers, including targeted voucher schemes to subsidize inputs to the most needy without risking the corruption and excesses of early subsidy schemes (see chapter 11).

The task force recommends that governments, donors, the World Bank, and the regional development banks—in partnership with private sector companies dealing with agricultural inputs—develop networks of small input dealers by:

- Establishing mechanisms to link agrodealers with input supply companies and accelerate the access of the rural poor to agricultural inputs.
- Training small input suppliers about seeds for food and cover crops, agroforestry trees, and green manures, as well as chemical fertilizers, rainfall harvesters, drip irrigation, and agrochemicals. These suppliers can then serve as extension nodes to provide vital information on new technologies and products.

Box 9.2
Creating agrodealers in Africa

Source: Adesina 2004.

The Rockefeller Foundation has used an innovative approach to develop a network of rural input traders, or "agrodealers." The approach tackles five constraints that hinder the development of viable input markets in rural areas.

- The storekeepers are trained to improve their knowledge of improved seeds and other planting materials—at the end of which they qualify as certified "agrodealers."
- The agrodealers are linked with the commercial input supply companies using a credit guarantee scheme to lower their marketing risks.
- Commercial trust is gradually developed between the agrodealers, the farmers, and the companies, with all participants trained to respect normal terms of trade and contracts between buyers and sellers.
- National Input Credit Guarantee Funds are established to accelerate the access of the rural poor to agricultural inputs.
- Extension services use the agrodealers as extension nodes to reach poor farmers with vital information on new technologies.

Three problems have to be solved for this approach to succeed. First, these traders require working capital to carry stocks of agricultural inputs, as there can be a gap between the time they are acquired by the trader and the time they are sold. One possibility is to set up a risk-sharing fund. For example, prospective dealers in agricultural inputs might be asked to put up 30 percent of the value of the stock of inputs, receiving a loan from a commercial bank for the remaining 70 percent using warehouse collateral. The other 30 percent could come from the risk-sharing fund.

Second, input buyers need credit and may not be in a position to provide collateral if they are small farmers. Solutions include promoting well functioning rural financial markets, a system of vouchers to be used for buying fertilizers which would be targeted to small farmers, and information sharing (and thus necessarily some collusion) among traders to ensure repayment of loans. As the latter conflicts with the need to promote competition, it brings up once again the central importance of well functioning rural financial markets that provide savings, credit, and insurance services.

Third, poor farmers may lack technical skills. Since it is in the interests of the lender to ensure that the credit they provide is put to good use, one would expect the lender to provide this technical assistance. There is little evidence that this is generally provided by private dealers for whom the opportunity cost of acquiring and passing on these skills may easily exceed the expected benefit from a higher probability of repayment since these skills are relevant to only a small part of their inventory of goods and services. In this situation, good extension services assume particular importance.

Improve access to financial services for the poor and food-insecure

Market failure often leads to a lack of credit for food-insecure farmers, who incur high interest-bearing debts to meet their minimum consumption requirements between production cycles. Barriers to these markets for the rural poor include:

- Information asymmetries in financial markets that create a demand for collateral since lenders have a limited ability to assess a borrower's creditworthiness.

Loan guarantees could provide an incentive for poor people to take the risk of borrowing

- The large transaction costs associated with sparsely populated or remote rural communities.
- The transaction costs associated with the risks of rural production, notably natural calamities that can strike a large number of borrowers simultaneously in a particular area.

Women face specific barriers to obtaining access to financial services, including lack of collateral, low levels of literacy, and less time to make the journey to a credit institution. Due to existing social bias, banks and moneylenders are hesitant to lend to women. Rural banking needs to be reoriented to meet their needs through awareness campaigns and the design of new programs that target women borrowers. Banks should be encouraged to establish microcredit programs for groups of women farmers. And governments should create environments that encourage women farmers to establish cooperatives, giving them greater power in negotiations with middlemen and greater access to credit.

Collective action or community associations can substitute to some extent for the missing collateral. The loan is made to the group, which decides which of its members will receive it, thus performing a screening function on behalf of the lender. If that individual defaults, the group will be held collectively responsible. Self-help groups and other mutual insurance mechanisms are prime examples of substitutes for markets in financial services, including savings, credit, and insurance (Zeller and Meyer 2002). Such community-based microfinance programs allow poor people to substitute their social capital (good reputation and connections to others) for more tangible forms of assets (land or jewelry) as a form of collateral. In such cases, collective action can have the double benefit of substituting for a missing market and allowing poor people to build assets through access to credit. But even here, care must be taken to ensure that extremely poor people who are thought to be a "bad risk" are not excluded (Morduch 1999).

Access to credit is particularly problematic for small food-insecure farmers, as they are perceived to be more vulnerable to shocks caused by poor weather or fluctuating prices. A system of loan guarantees could provide an incentive for poor people to take the risk of borrowing and for financial institutions to lend to poor people. Community groups that take on loans on behalf of their members can mitigate risk and make lending more attractive to financial institutions. The Grameen Bank in Bangladesh, self-help groups in India, and the rotating savings and credit associations in West Africa have demonstrated the feasibility of group borrowing schemes, especially when combined with saving schemes. To move beyond microloans, strengthening of landownership and property rights are essential.

Microfinance, still used mainly for short-term investments, is generally too expensive to allow borrowing over a whole cropping season. Yet other forms of finance are seldom available, again because poor borrowers are perceived as

Ensuring a high level of impact from loans is indispensable for scaling up finance schemes

risky, despite evidence from microfinance experiences throughout the developing world that poor households do repay their loans. A promising possibility is to integrate loans with saving services, which allow members to save in small amounts every day or every week. Not only are these savings available to members to serve as collateral when they apply for a loan, but members will also be more willing to undertake risky but profitable investments because they no longer fear becoming destitute if the investments should fail.

Ensuring a high level of impact from loans is, therefore, indispensable for scaling up finance schemes in developing countries. If returns to investments are low or negative, this will almost certainly result in unstable repayments. Like other investments, those in microfinance have the greatest returns only when there are also investments in complementary sectors. Public investments in communications infrastructure, roads, and storage can reduce transaction costs and increase the returns and repayment rates on loans. Transaction costs can be reduced by attaining some economies of scale, by focusing on high volumes of loans and using standardized procedures to lend products. It is now recognized that the high returns on loans in Bangladesh (compared with neighboring countries) reflect complementary investments in rural infrastructure. This is an important lesson to bear in mind when planning to launch or scale up microfinance schemes.

An effective means of increasing the availability of credit for farmers and others is for borrowing groups to take on loans on behalf of their members. A group can negotiate for larger loans than those available to the individual and provide management and accounting services.

Agrodealers are another source of credit for communities. Local storekeepers often extend credit to their customers. They know them, so the need for reliability is mutually accepted, and they can lend with minimum formality. Linking agrodealers with financial institutions could provide them with a source of funds for lending on to the community. NGOs and community groups are other principal actors in ensuring credit availability.

Measures to reduce the riskiness of agricultural production by making investments in complementary sectors will assist in overcoming the barriers to financial institutions by poor farmers. Public investments in irrigation infrastructure that reduce the likelihood of a crop failure—or investments in roads that reduce transportation costs—will increase the returns and repayment rates on loans. Well functioning financial markets will allow individuals to borrow and save to smooth consumption and make productive investments—and to insure themselves against unanticipated shocks such as drought or illness.

Provide and enforce a sound legal and regulatory framework

Markets for smallholders require an enabling environment, with a sound, honest judicial system in which the sanctity of contracts is protected—and private invest-

Government control over markets should be relaxed

ment promoted. Eliminating the barriers that prevent producers from entering markets could have a profound impact on poor consumers as well as producers. Reducing the excessive regulatory burden on entrepreneurs in relation to permits, inspections, and environmental protection among others is essential to reduce the risks and increase the returns to small farms and agribusinesses. Smallholders should be free to sell their products to any buyers at the best price—and to sell directly to any consumers without being threatened. Simplifying the procedures for obtaining import and export licenses and dropping minimum volume rules would greatly encourage small production for external markets.

Contract law, vital for markets to function well, should be enforced, preferably at the community level with community mediation and arbitration. Although contract laws exist in most developing countries, they are often not well adapted to the needs of poorly educated rural populations—and for group transactions they are often applied inequitably. Unequal bargaining power between producers and traders, exploitative behavior by traders and companies, and uncertainties over the quality standards required of farmers complicate the transition from subsistence to commercial farming for small producers. A properly enforced grades and standards system, particularly for such major food grains as maize and rice and for other staples, is especially important for reducing transaction costs while ensuring quality for the consumer. Most transactions involving poor farmers are conducted in spot markets on a cash and carry basis, leaving farmers vulnerable. Poorly organized farmers generally have to absorb the high risks in commercial markets.

The government's primary responsibility is to provide a business-friendly legal and regulatory framework together with the public goods that will create the incentives for private traders and businesses to establish and operate. The task force recommends that government investments in developing markets be made in ways that do not directly involve the government in the supply of goods and services that can be more efficiently supplied by the private sector. Short-term market responses by government have undermined long-run market development and have led to continuing dependence on government intervention. Government control over markets should be relaxed, allowing more competition among suppliers and encouraging the movement of food from surplus to deficit areas. To be retained, however, is the necessary degree of regulation to ensure food safety and access to regional and global markets.

Strengthen the bargaining power of the rural and urban poor in labor markets

Large numbers of landless hungry people depend on labor markets to earn their livelihoods. Yet labor markets often function poorly in rural areas, where alternatives to farming may be scarce and the poor have limited education and training. Many more opportunities to earn income are needed. The large numbers of landless laborers in South Asia, for example, lack productive assets and

Governments should strengthen the position of the poor in labor markets

alternative decent employment opportunities—and are thus obliged to take on farm work at low wage rates.

The Task Force on Hunger recommends that programs and organizations that empower the rural landless and urban poor in labor markets be strengthened and promote the freedom to organize. For example, the creation of labor organizations is one way for the hungry to increase their bargaining power in the labor market. Certainly the case with large urban trade unions, this could also apply at the local level within rural villages. Labor cooperatives may be able to negotiate higher wages, particularly when they are needed to perform time-critical jobs, such as harvesting, and can save farmers the time and trouble they would have to take to recruit many individual laborers.

Both the rural and urban poor usually lack tradable skills. A variety of interventions, such as training, capacity building, and providing access to productive resources, will be required to promote the nonfarm sector, each tailored to specific local conditions (Lanjouw 1999). Primary education and skills training focused on men and women are vital for preparing community members to join the competitive labor market. Yet there are other household labor constraints—ill health, premature death, or other causes that preclude entry into the labor market or new programs intended to benefit the poor. So, policies must also address the health and welfare of poor laborers to break this cycle of hunger, poverty, and lost productivity. Laws that regulate the labor market are also important and should be reinforced. For instance, government should regulate overtime compensation and ensure safety in the workplace.

The Task Force on Hunger recommends that governments strengthen the position of the poor in labor markets by investing in education and vocational training as well as by enacting legislation that permits workers to organize and allows for the movement of labor across borders

Ensure access to market information for the poor

All farmers require access to price information to make good decisions about what to grow and when and where to sell it. Remote rural dwellers are at a major disadvantage if they do not know what price their produce will fetch in urban centers. Lack of market information reduces the terms of trade for poor farmers and raises market transaction costs. A common problem facing smallholders is that they cannot sell their produce at a fair price. They typically lack information on prices beyond their own communities, and as a result often sell at much lower than market value. Middlemen (and women) typically control the terms of trade, leaving farmers with little opportunity but to sell at harvest when prices are low (box 9.3).

Farmers can be enabled to participate in markets on more equal terms. Improving infrastructure, particularly roads, can reduce the isolation of many farms and allow farmers to get their produce to areas where it will be in demand. In addition, the provision of market information, now more possible

Box 9.3

Farmers who must sell low and buy high

Source: Earth Institute 2004.

Chronically hungry farmers in the Bar Sauri village of western Kenya usually harvest their maize crop at the end of the rainy season, in August. Lack of information and storage facilities, weak local markets, and the urgent need for cash force them to sell most of the crop to middlemen at about $120 a ton. When these same poor farmers have eaten the maize they have retained for personal consumption, they must then buy back their maize from the market at $264 a ton, more than twice the price they received for it. Although the cost of stored grain normally rises with time, poor farmers are placed at a severe disadvantage due to their weak bargaining power, lack of information, and insufficient access to more distant markets.

Box 9.4

Reaching the unreached—rural knowledge centers in India

Source: M.S. Swaminathan 2004.

The M.S. Swaminathan Research Foundation has linked 10 villages in India in a network consisting of personal computers, telephones, VHF radio, dial-up email, satellite communications, public address systems, and community newspapers. The network enables information to be passed to all villagers—and for local information to be generated, stored, and disseminated. It has significantly increased the exchange of information on such subjects as daily market prices, women's health, how to protect crops from diseases, and local weather forecasts. The project has yielded significant success. For example, fishermen now use mobile phones to seek the best prices from dealers before deciding where to sell their catch.

using mobile telephones and radios, can improve the ability of smallholders and small traders to respond quickly to new opportunities.

Farmers who have access to timely and accurate information can respond to price signals, resulting in more efficient and profitable farming systems. Market information also reduces farmers' risks by improving their knowledge of market prices and alternative buyers, enabling them to store grain to sell when prices are higher, and allowing them to organize with fellow farmers to buy inputs and sell outputs.

Smallholders seldom have access to modern information technology. Even if they have a radio, and can afford the batteries to run it, the programs they can tune into seldom meet their needs. Internet technology barely penetrates most rural areas. But things are changing rapidly: new technology is making wireless digital connectivity a reality in rural areas. Solar power can keep a radio going all day. A wind-up radio generates its own electricity.

Governments and donors are investing in Internet technology and making it available to rural communities. Brazil, for example, has begun to pursue innovative polices to address this need with very positive results, even in the remotest regions of the country. Combinations of technology—mobile telephone, landline telephone, radio, and Internet—can be assembled to bring valuable information to farmers (box 9.4). It is important that extension services become major users and suppliers of rural information services, helping farmers get the information they need.[1] The task force recommends that

Making markets work for the poor must be seen as a long-term goal

partnerships among governments, the private sector, and NGOs be created to improve radio, cellphone, and Internet access for poor people.

Promote and strengthen community and farmer associations

Making markets work for the poor must be seen as a long-term goal that depends greatly on building capacity among individual farmers, farmer associations, NGOs, researchers, and policy analysts. Associations, like individuals, also need capacity and skills development if they are to function effectively. People who are remote from markets lack knowledge of how markets work, especially finance and credit. They may need training in contract negotiation and technical assistance to meet quality standards. They may also require technical training in handling, storing, and processing food. Increased investment is needed in vocational skills training at the local level and for the adaptation of training to local needs.

By forming groups and associations, the poor can gain a stronger voice in market transactions. Investment is needed to promote and strengthen farmers' associations, women's groups, and traders' associations. Groups can pool their resources, bargain for better prices, hire transport and equipment, and borrow money with better protection against losses. Governments need to encourage the formation of groups by devolving decisionmaking and financial authority to the local level and providing support for the basic establishment costs.

Another method to gain a stronger voice is to establish savings schemes, including "cereal banks," managed by groups that undertake collective storage, safeguard grain quality, negotiate prices, and seek out new markets (Adesina 2004). Cereal banks are proving effective in raising the prices of crops such as maize—in the districts where food-insecure farmers live. Governments should support such initiatives at the local level and scale them up, linking them to marketing parastatals.

Marketing cooperatives have provided inputs and credit to farmers and purchased and aggregated the output of many farms. There have been notable successes, such as milk cooperatives in India, which have stimulated substantial increases in the production and availability of dairy products throughout the country—collecting milk from more than 10 million producers, 60 percent of them small-scale farmers or landless laborers. A three-tiered cooperative structure employing professional staff links local collection with processing plants and marketing channels to distribute the milk to consumers, returning the profits to the cooperative members rather than middlemen (Candler and Kumar 1998). Dairy cooperatives in Kenya have achieved similar results, if on a smaller scale (Staal, Delgado, and Nicholson 1997). But political interference in both India and Kenya has been associated with less efficient outcomes than would otherwise have been the case.

The Task Force on Hunger recommends that governments put in place policies that encourage the formation of community and farmer groups, devolve decisionmaking and financial authority to the local level, and provide support for the basic costs of organizing associations, for example by providing publicly funded meeting places with essential equipment. Ministries of education, local governments, and NGOs should be active in these efforts.

Smallholder farmers can compete successfully with large producers

Promote alternative sources of employment and income

Since most of the world's poor and hungry people live in rural areas and are already engaged in agriculture, there are significant opportunities for increasing their income by encouraging them to diversify food crops into higher value outputs such as livestock products—and by adding value to their produce through processing. Processing activities range from simple procedures such as cleaning, grading, and bagging through to fairly complex agro-industries that process and distribute fruits, vegetables, and livestock products.

Many poor smallholder farmers face daunting challenges when they try to shift to high-value outputs. First, they have to learn how to grow the new crop or feed the new animal. They may not get much help in this from the extension system, which is likely to be underresourced and largely ineffective. Second, they have to enter a market that assures them adequate returns. Third, they may face competition from larger producers who are often better equipped to meet the quality demands of the high-value market.

A further set of challenges faces poor farmers seeking to enter export markets. Yet numerous schemes around the world have demonstrated that smallholder farmers can compete successfully with large producers in these markets, if they can obtain the knowledge and skills and gain access to the necessary specialized services. For example, the Kenyan tea industry is controlled by a parastatal organization that permits smallholders to deliver tea for processing at local centers. Tea that has been carefully tended by Kenyan smallholders consistently fetches premium prices at auction because of its high quality.

There are numerous out-grower schemes around the world whereby farmers grow crops for large-scale producers. Often, the large-scale producers find it more cost-effective to increase output by contracting smallholders than by expanding their own capacities. In these cases, the large producer provides inputs and technical advice—and pockets most of the proceeds. In other out-grower models, however, associations of smallholders have created the critical mass of production capacity and knowledge to enter the high-value market without working under contract to a large producer. These agro-industries can increase the share of the final price obtained by small-scale farmers. Even if owned and operated externally, out-grower schemes can provide important employment opportunities for the poor by using labor-intensive techniques in poor rural areas.

Governments have an important role in creating the enabling environment for smallholders to enter high-value markets. They should ensure the provision of inputs, processing capacity, and technical assistance through the private

Cooperatives can help smallholders meet quality standards

sector, with the collaboration of marketing bodies. They should also ensure the provision of information and technical support. High-value production is extremely knowledge-intensive. For example, EU phytosanitary regulations have recently expanded and are now very complex. Farmers need considerable advice on how to achieve the standards to enter the European market.

Supermarkets are also becoming dominant buyers in many parts of the world. Governments must provide a sound regulatory system that ensures and stimulates competition, prevents the formation of monopolies, and ensures socially responsible policies. With the growing penetration of supermarkets in developing countries, smallholders are excluded because of difficulties in meeting the quality standards set by supermarket purchasers (Reardon and Berdegué 2002). Small-scale farmers face additional difficulties in producing for supermarket chains due to their inability to guarantee the year-round supply of produce. As for milk marketing, cooperatives can help smallholders meet quality standards.

Diversifying into high-value production and ensuring quality standards becomes even more important when one considers that between now and 2015, the number of people living in cities in the developing world will likely rise by 50 percent or more. Urban demand for food will rise rapidly, requiring increased investment not merely in the infrastructure needed to produce and deliver primary produce but also in the capacity to add value through processing under hygienic conditions. City and local authorities should rely on four strategic principles when formulating policies to provide an enabling environment for such developments:

- Adopt an approach that is participatory, alliance-seeking, and technically sound.
- Promote competition and reduce the influence of a few large intermediaries.
- Involve the private sector in the provision of facilities and services that can be run as businesses.
- Encourage development that lowers the cost of living and stimulates employment growth in the city.

Beyond just meeting the standards set by companies, farmer associations should initiate a dialogue with the government and with traders over such issues as grades and standards, the provision of market information, and the institutional culture in regulatory bodies—to make sure that small-scale farmers' voices are heard and they are taken seriously as market participants (Kherालla and others 2000). National farmers' unions in such countries as Kenya, Uganda, and India provide farmers with a voice in national policymaking. The International Federation of Agricultural Producers (IFAP) even represents farmers in such international forums as the World Trade Organization (www.ifap.org).

Key ingredients for increasing employment and income through diversification include good market intelligence, increased skills training, switching to appropriate high-value crops, having access to credit, providing roads and other infrastructure, and observing contractual obligations. Extension services, farmers, agrodealers, ministries of commerce, and the private sector all have a role.

Actions needed to implement recommendation six

Invest in and maintain market-related infrastructure	Build, upgrade, and maintain transport infrastructure (ports, railways, feeder and other roads), transportation services, and storage facilities. Build and operate electricity grids and alternative or renewable generating systems. Build and operate communication systems (phone, radio, Internet). Develop small processing facilities for agricultural products. Governments should use competitive and transparent bidding systems; donors should not tie aid.
Develop networks of small rural input traders	Train and certify agrodealers in business management skills and in the handling and use of such inputs as seeds and fertilizers. Use agrodealers as extension nodes to provide vital information on new technologies. Investments and policies for establishing agrodealer networks should be coordinated by national governments, in coordination with the private sector (input suppliers, banks), donors, NGOs, and extension agencies. Establish input credit guarantee funds, enforceable contracts, and transportation and communication networks to help link agrodealers with input supply companies and customers. Use "targeted vouchers" and microcredit to assist poor farmers—particularly women—in purchasing inputs at local agrodealer stores. Vouchers should have a built-in "sunset clause," reducing the subsidy level after five years and eliminating it entirely after 10 years.
Improve access to financial services for the poor and food-insecure	Encourage microfinance institutions to provide credit to agrodealers, who then lend to farmers. Establish group lending programs, allowing the food-insecure and poor to increase credit access through self-selected groups. Link group lending with complementary interventions made in rural infrastructure, health, and education. Ensure that women are fully included and target at least 50 percent of credit to them. Encourage well managed community groups to take out loans on behalf of their members, and facilitate group savings schemes. Governments can help scale up group lending programs by providing a legal framework for farmer associations and women's groups, investing in infrastructure to reduce transaction costs, and building group capacity.

Provide and enforce a sound legal and regulatory framework	Establish an enabling environment for the development of markets, including contract enforcement and private investment. Reform contract laws and define and enforce product grades and standards. Reduce barriers to market entry, including relaxing and simplifying regulatory requirements where possible—without compromising safety or quality standards.
Strengthen the bargaining power of rural and urban poor in the labor market	Invest in building skilled labor, including universal primary education and vocational training. Form labor cooperatives and placement agencies to aid in job placement, strengthen bargaining power, and improve working conditions. Enact legislation that allows for organizing labor. Establish government agreements allowing the movement of labor across borders. Invest in regional economic zones. The ministries of education, labor, and foreign affairs will have a role in these interventions, as will local governments, NGOs, and workers' unions.
Ensure access to market information for the poor	Establish rural market information points in open air markets, where market price information for crops, livestock, and agricultural inputs is provided daily for farmers, processors, middlemen, and traders. Develop and test radio-based market information systems. The goal of these programs will be to transition into a self-sustaining pay-per-use system. Invest in communications infrastructure, organizing information around groups with common interests, and maintaining a profit motive for service suppliers. Partnerships to achieve this are needed among governments, the private sector, and NGOs. Community groups can assist villages in obtaining access and sharing information. Extension services should become major suppliers and users of rural information services, helping farmers to get the information they need.
Promote and strengthen farmer and community associations	Governments should support farmer and community associations by providing legal status to farmer associations, training group members in business management and internal governance, and devolving decisionmaking and financial authority to the local level. They can support the basic costs of organizing associations—for example, by providing publicly funded meeting places with essential equipment. NGOs can facilitate the formation and training of farmer groups.
Promote alternative sources of employment and income	Diversify crop mixes to include high-value crops in the farming system and links to reliable market channels (such as supermarkets or export markets). Encourage the formation of associations of smallholders to contract with and supply goods to large producers, often using labor-intensive techniques that create employment.

Governments should encourage supermarkets to adopt socially responsible practices and contract with smallholder cooperatives. Invest in urban processing and delivery systems and in expanded urban employment. Create the necessary incentives to train and maintain skilled people at the community level. Creating opportunities for nonfarm employment on a broad scale will require research to develop locally adapted high value crops, good market information, and adequate infrastructure as well as the necessary legal and regulatory frameworks, skills training, and access to credit.

Recommendation seven

Restore and conserve the natural resources essential for food security

The rural poor depend heavily on agro-ecosystems and natural ecosystems for their food and livelihood security. A high proportion of the food-insecure are rural smallholders who rely on natural resources to sustain food production, provide supplemental food and income, and serve as food safety nets. An estimated one-tenth of chronically food-insecure people globally, and roughly one-fifth of those in Africa, depend primarily on forests, fisheries, and rangelands for their food (Scherr 2003). Restoring and improving ecosystem functions and the services they provide are therefore key to building food security in rural areas.

The Task Force on Hunger emphasizes raising agricultural productivity in ways that protect and restore soil resources and minimize the tradeoffs with environmental protection. Our recommendation for agricultural production thus includes investing in soil conservation, agroforestry, and green manure and cover crop technologies, conservation tillage, integrated pest management, and natural pest control, among others. Because these technologies are described elsewhere in this report, they will not be presented as new interventions here. In this chapter, the task force recommends four interventions to secure and enhance other components of natural capital of the food-insecure while restoring and increasing their productive capacity. These include fields, forests, grasslands, wetlands, and water resources. The interventions are to:

1. Help communities and households restore or enhance natural resources.
2. Secure local ownership, access, and management rights to forests, fisheries, and rangelands.
3. Develop natural resource-based "green enterprises."
4. Pay poor farmers for environmental services.

The focus of investments in natural resources should be on food-insecure rural communities

The priority focus of investments in natural resources should be on food-insecure rural communities that lack the means for restoring or improving their landscape. These investments should form a part of each nation's poverty reduction strategy, reflecting inputs from rural stakeholders. They should be designed to reduce both chronic and acute hunger, but at the same time meet other Goals. Special attention should go to working with low-income women to identify the resources and investments of greatest importance to them—and to mechanisms ensuring their greater access and management control.

To achieve maximum early impact, the task force recommends targeting investments to highly degraded areas where hungry people are most densely concentrated. Critical areas of this kind include:

- Highly populated semiarid highland environments (such as Tigray and Amhara in Ethiopia, parts of the African Rift Valley, northeast India, the dry Andes, and the Mesoamerican highlands).
- Highly populated semiarid agricultural and pastoral regions (such as the Sahel).
- Highly populated forest regions, where low-income households rely for their food and income on degraded forests (such as those in the Himalayan foothills, Mesoamerica, southwestern China, and Southeast Asia).
- Inland and coastal fisheries that are overfished, degraded, or polluted (such as the Caribbean, African coastlines and great lakes, and insular Southeast Asia).
- Dryland regions experiencing large-scale aquifer or surface water depletion (such as much of South Asia and southern Mexico).

Background

Degraded natural resources and reduced biodiversity directly threaten the food supplies and income of food-insecure people, leading to a vicious circle of poverty, environmental degradation, and hunger (DFID, EC, UNDP, and World Bank 2002). Some agricultural practices have negative effects on soil health, water resources, and biodiversity. Inefficient irrigation leads to salinization of the soil. Agrochemicals used in large-scale agriculture can cause pollution. Land-clearing and mono-cropping reduce biodiversity. As ecosystems become badly degraded due to pollution, poor management practices, or overuse, the productive capacity of the land becomes seriously compromised. Half of all agricultural land is considered to be significantly degraded. A fifth of irrigated lands are affected by salinization. Degraded rangelands threaten not only the livelihood of pastoralists, but also wildlife habitat, and dryland degradation can lead to desertification (Wood, Sebastian, and Scherr 2000).

Poverty, food scarcity, and population pressures fuel deforestation and the overharvesting of vegetation, stripping landscapes of their forest and plant

Communities have considerable potential to manage their own resources

cover and destroying riparian vegetation. The loss of soil cover and nutrients and the compaction of soil make it difficult for plants to reestablish themselves. The resulting decline in biodiversity and water retention increases the risks of drought, flooding, and erosion. It also results in reduced domestic and agricultural water supplies, falling water tables, dried-up springs and rivers, and deteriorating water quality (Penning de Vries and others 2003; Bridges and others 2001). Water scarcity already affects nutritional status, agricultural production, and livelihoods in many rural areas. It is predicted to increase sharply in dry areas in coming decades, especially in low-income countries where rural populations continue to rise.

More than a billion people around the world depend on fish as their primary source of animal protein. Freshwater and coastal pollution, destruction of mangroves that serve as marine nurseries, overfishing (particularly by large-scale commercial fishers), and unsustainable aquaculture practices are resulting in dramatic declines in fisheries and lost livelihoods and reduced protein consumption for the poor.

Environmental degradation increases the vulnerability of the poor and hungry. Natural systems are critical safety nets for poor and hungry people when disaster strikes. For example, more than a fifth of the household income of poor rural communities comes from forest products (Vedeld and others 2004). And this dependence increases in years when harvests fail or in times of economic crisis. Environmental degradation increases the vulnerability of people to hunger by reducing their access to food and farm inputs, fisheries, wild game and foods (including famine foods), and nontimber forest products for medicines. Women's domestic responsibilities for providing food, healthcare, water, and fuel depend directly on the quality and availability of natural resources. As a result, they are often severely affected by resource degradation.

Communities do have considerable potential to manage their own resources, and local organization has been found essential for sustainable natural resource management. For example, at least 360 million hectares of forest are under some level of conservation management by communities—more land than is in formal protected areas (Molnar, Scherr, and Khare 2004). But the cost of restoring degraded land, forest, and water resources is frequently beyond the capacity of chronically poor communities. Reversing the trend toward degradation requires both community and national interventions, supported by the international community.

The international community has begun to recognize the human, economic, and environmental costs of land and resource degradation. Recent initiatives to address degradation include the Sustainable Land Management program of the Global Environment Facility, the UN Convention to Combat Desertification, resource rehabilitation projects of the International Fund for Agricultural Development, the United Nations Development Programme's Drylands Program, and the newly launched TerrAfrica program of the World

More explicit attention needs to go to reducing hunger and malnutrition directly

Bank. Both China and India are undertaking national "greening" programs, while South Africa has large ecosystem rehabilitation programs.

Many development, relief, and conservation NGOs now integrate elements of land restoration, while farmer federations and community groups in places experiencing rapid degradation—such as parts of South Asia, East Africa, the Philippines, and the Andes—have organized themselves to restore key resources, as in the International Landcare movement. In most of these initiatives, the involvement of poor local communities is now recognized to be essential (Bridges and others 2001; Katon, Knox, and Meinzen-Dick 2001).

Even so, the funding for most of these programs remains grossly inadequate relative to the scale of the problem. Few poverty reduction strategies in low-income countries address natural resource restoration (Bojö and Reddy 2003). And in the design of these projects, more explicit attention needs to go to reducing hunger and malnutrition directly, by integrating elements of production, conservation, and nutrition (Bridges and others 2001).

Help communities and households restore or enhance natural resources

Each nation's poverty reduction strategy and other poverty reduction programs should help local communities plan, implement, manage, and monitor investments to conserve and restore the degraded natural resources they depend on for their food and livelihoods. Plans should include strategies for coping with risks and disasters.

Community initiatives for environmental restoration may include strategies for rangeland rehabilitation, such as replanting, building windbreaks, stabilizing gullies, and managing common grazing lands (box 10.1). Water resources can be improved and recovered through watershed restoration, micro-watershed rehabilitation, village ponds, stream bank revegetation, and building vegetative filters and barriers to protect water quality. Biodiversity can be protected by establishing reserves, reforesting degraded areas, managing communal forests, and establishing fisheries. Communities can reduce disaster risks through forest fire control, dry-season fodder reserves, and cultivating famine foods.

Investing in natural resources essential to food security offers important synergies with other actions to reduce hunger—and with other Goals. Natural resource investments can increase agricultural productivity by increasing the supply of natural inputs, protecting crop pollinators, and providing domestic water and fuel for cooking. Such investments can increase the availability of micronutrients, proteins, and calories from wild sources, while reducing the impact of natural climatic risks and disasters on food security. Watershed protection increases the availability and quality of water, and health benefits stemming from that. By reducing time required for collecting water, fuel, and food,

Box 10.1
Restoring degraded grasslands in Kenya

Source: Meyerhoff 1991.

The Rehabilitation of Arid Environments Charitable Trust in Kenya has worked for more than 20 years on the rehabilitation of grasslands in the watershed of Lake Baringo. This Rift Valley lake is rapidly becoming an environmental disaster area. The lake has always been fairly shallow, and the land around it sparse grassland and savannah, best suited to nomadic pastoralism and wildlife. While nomadic land use was practiced in the past, the catchment is now used continually. As a result, overgrazing has severely affected the grass and trees, soil erosion has intensified, and silt is rapidly filling the lake, which is projected to become a swamp within two decades. The resulting decline in water quality has led to the collapse of the local fishing industry and threatens the local hippopotami.

The Trust has pioneered private and communal fields protected from grazing animals by electric or live fences. Local communities have recognized that intensive management of fields is the only viable alternative to the current destructive practices associated with communal management. After demarcating land for individual or group management, communities have applied contoured bunds and selective grass planting, transforming severely degraded terrain into productive land within three years. The restoration of grassland has created income-generating livestock grazing services. Once grass is reestablished, trees can be grown, expanding income-generating opportunities to include browse fodder, firewood, and honey. Rehabilitated areas are more resistant to drought and have attracted long-absent birds and insects. The success of this and other pastoralist projects has resulted in their incorporation into Kenya's national poverty reduction strategy.

investments in natural resource assets can free up girls' time to attend school, while increasing women's time for child care and farming and reducing caloric expenditures by pregnant and nursing mothers. Restored ecosystems can enhance natural biodiversity and environmental sustainability, for example, by incorporating wildlife habitat features (McNeely and Scherr 2003).

Experience has established some key principles for ensuring that natural resource investments benefit food-insecure households:

- It is critical to conduct community-based needs identification and planning processes, and to build ownership of investment strategies among all community members, including women and the landless.
- Initiatives should bring both short-term food security improvement and long-term sustainability gains.
- Projects should integrate action on water, forests, soils, and vegetative cover at the watershed or landscape scale.
- Initiatives for ecosystem rehabilitation should be coordinated with those promoting agricultural production, and plant species and management systems selected should contribute to food supply and local livelihoods.
- Community organizations responsible for resource restoration should be technically competent and accountable to their communities, including food-insecure groups.

Many types of resource restoration can be achieved through community action alone

The Task Force on Hunger recommends that district and national governments, as well as NGOs, assist communities in developing natural resource investment plans by providing trained facilitators or advisors, conducting participatory mapping, coordinating cross-community visits to observe innovative approaches, monitoring indicators, and providing financial support. They can also help coordinate larger scale resource restoration plans, and build community and national capacity for natural resource management.

Financial and technical support will be needed to achieve investments in restoring degraded resources at the scale required. One mechanism that has worked well in many places is a matching grant program, in which communities receive assistance to put together a restoration plan, including the commitment of local resources. Most such programs are organized by government agencies, but NGO and private financing may also be used. External contributions can include cash payments, technical services, or food aid, which can be used to employ local workers in community investment projects.

Many types of resource restoration can be achieved through community action alone. But in other cases the scale of the problem or the effectiveness of solutions requires investment programs implemented in a coordinated fashion at a district, watershed, or ecosystem level. To ensure that such initiatives also address local problems effectively, they should be based on integrated cross-sectoral needs assessment. This assessment should include field-based, spatial analysis of the dependence on natural resources for food security and the degree of threat. Such assessments can be used to devise an effective strategy for allocating matching grant resources to local communities, as well as identify interventions that require large-scale, direct public investments.

Public investment priorities should reflect broad poverty reduction strategy priorities, but also the results of direct multistakeholder dialogue and negotiation among local resource users, managers, and off-site beneficiaries. Policymakers can facilitate such investments by providing legislative authorization and an accepted process for action across jurisdictions—and for conflict resolution. District-level natural resource planning should be integrated into broader agriculture and land use planning.

Food aid, ideally from stocks produced by local or national smallholder producers, can be mobilized to pay farmers, herders, and forest dwellers to rehabilitate public resources. Participatory monitoring of resource conditions can provide a mechanism to assess the effectiveness of interventions and ensure accountability. Post-investment responsibility for management must be clearly designated.

There has been widespread decentralization of responsibility for natural resources from central governments to local governments and communities, which can facilitate local needs-based investment in resource restoration. But the process has rarely been accompanied by the necessary capacity building for planning, managing, or monitoring resource-related investments. Resource

Effective incentives often determine the success or failure of resource management programs

restoration on a scale that would contribute to meeting the hunger Goal will require targeted training of professional staff, local governments, technical assistance staff, community facilitators, NGOs, and community groups and their leaders. To be cost-effective, and effective on the ground, farmer and resource-dependent communities, conservation organizations, and public agencies should have joint initiatives for capacity-building.

Secure local ownership, access, and management rights to natural resources

The lack of ownership or access rights to natural resources (including land, forest products, water, fish stocks, or even large game animals in Africa) threatens the livelihoods of millions. The absence of credible, long-term land rights hampers many efforts to improve natural resource conservation and food production by creating a disincentive to invest in the resource base and manage it sustainably. Effective incentives often determine the success or failure of resource management programs. For example, farmers in the Philippines were given legal title to forest land for 25 years, with the stipulation that their rights would be renewed only if the forest was intact at the end of the contract period.

Exchanging information and lessons and accepting technical assistance from outsiders can help guide governments and stakeholders in formulating effective policies. Many countries have laws to enable rural communities and households to obtain such rights. For example, the percentage of locally owned or administered forests in the developing world has doubled in the past 15 years to a current level of 28 percent (box 10.2). This represents significant progress, but high institutional costs have severely hampered effective implementation and enforcement of land rights in many areas. Rural media campaigns should inform poor rural people of their land, forest, and water rights and of the processes they must follow to secure them. Legal support services are needed to enable the poor to bring claims where their rights are denied. Adequate public resources need to be allocated to monitoring large-scale commercial resource exploitation—and, where necessary, the enforcement of regulations that protect the environment and the rights of other resource users. The task force recommends that national governments enact, where needed, pro-poor land tenure and policy reforms to rationalize property rights and ensure effective implementation.

Community management and tenure are being adopted as governments decentralize and social movements assert the rights of indigenous people and other natural resource-dependent groups. An estimated 22 percent of developing country forests are now community owned or managed (White and Martin 2002), a proportion expected to increase significantly between now and 2015. Such arrangements offer local stakeholders greater control over land management and conservation decisions and create opportunities to access markets for environmental goods and services. The task force recommends

Box 10.2

Reducing poverty and hunger by allocating forest rights to communities

Source: White and Martin 2002; White, Martin, and Ellsworth 2003.

Low-income farmers and other rural people depend greatly on forest resources for food, fuel, grazing, construction materials, medicines, and raw materials for household use or sale. Globally, restricted forest access, tenure insecurity, and controls on forest use established by national governments are the most serious constraints to protecting and managing local forest resources to support local livelihoods and develop local forest enterprises. Colonial and post-colonial governments claimed most forests (and even trees on private land) for the state, as well as large deforested areas, degraded forest lands, and farmlands on steeper slopes.

Over the past decade, many countries finally established a legal basis for devolving the management of government-owned forest resources to poor rural and indigenous communities. This has been done under a variety of tenure arrangements, significantly enhancing the assets and food security of the poor.

- In Viet Nam the government has allocated millions of hectares of forest land (much of it with depleted forest cover) to households and cooperatives. Field studies show that the allocation of forest rights to households has led to significant increases in income combined with more sustainable land management practices.
- In the Philippines more than 21 million people living in upland "forest zones" achieved acceptance as legitimate forest managers in 1997.
- In Madhya Pradesh, India, more than 1 million households were granted rights to co-manage more than 600,000 hectares of dry forests, enabling them to earn income from timber sales. This has generated local employment for the landless and restored water tables, wildlife populations, and biodiversity.
- In Sumatra, Indonesia, securing forest rights for forest-dwelling communities has enabled them to keep their indigenous and highly profitable complex agroforests, which support 75 percent of the large mammal and bird diversity found in primary forest.

International support can help countries accelerate the transfer of ownership or use rights to local people. Such transfers protect people's capacity to improve their food and livelihood security, while safeguarding the environmental services that forests provide.

that donors assist national governments in developing and enforcing new regulations or in fully implementing forest tenure reforms by financing mapping, legalization, training, and community capacity building.

Where resources remain legally in public lands, local communities should be engaged in co-management—to ensure their access to critical resources for food security, to share in income generated by the resource, and to secure local support for resource protection.

While initiatives in forestry are most widespread, there are also growing examples of successful community co-management of fisheries in Cambodia, Indonesia, India, the Philippines, and the Shetlands. New models are recognizing and supporting pastoral and mobile people's capacity to manage rangelands sustainably, as in eastern and southern Africa and Mongolia. Aggressive efforts to scale up successful community and comanagement models should be designed as an integrated approach to achieve multiple Goals in resource-dependent communities.

Income-earning opportunities must be developed on a much larger scale

Develop natural resource–based "green enterprises"

For food-insecure communities in rural areas, enterprises based on sustainable management of natural resources—"green enterprises"—can present valuable opportunities to generate income and strengthen livelihoods while also establishing incentives to conserve. There is considerable potential for the small-scale commercialization of natural medicines, nontimber forest products, sustainably grown or certified timber, and other natural products. In southern Mexico, the Project for Conservation and Sustainable Development of Forest Resources in Mexico funded by the World Bank has helped indigenous forest communities establish dozens of market-oriented enterprises. In parts of India, successful enterprises use public forest resources, greatly increasing the income of landless people (Scherr, White, and Kaimowitz 2004).

To be successful, green enterprises require a combination of conservation, business, and management skills. Access to markets—in proximity, information, and contacts—is also key. Experience in Africa over the past decade has demonstrated that enterprises based on harvesting and processing of products from natural resources have the greatest potential for communities that are within 100–150 kilometers of urban markets (USAID and WRI 2002).

In addition to creating income, markets for nontimber forest products can create assets for community forest conservation and better monitoring of controlled extraction (Scherr, White, and Kaimowitz 2004). The returns from nontimber forest products can help sustain community conservation systems. Income-earning opportunities must be developed more comprehensively and on a much larger scale to support these initiatives (Molnar, Scherr, and Khare 2004).

Most critically, communities require access to technical and business support for commercial enterprises for sustainably managed wild raw materials and processed products. Regional and national enterprise support services and capacity building at subsidized cost are critical; business and technical experts in these services must understand the economics and management of community enterprises. Key elements include realistically assessing market opportunities and linking community enterprises and potential wholesale and retail buyers.

Sustainable levels of harvest and "best management practices" for sustainable enterprises must be jointly determined by communities and enterprise managers, with input from conservation professionals. Management plans should be designed to ensure access to the resource for the food-insecure, and to provide employment for workers from food-insecure households. Third-party systems certifying sustainable management of natural resources (such as the Forest Stewardship Council and Marine Stewardship Council) should accelerate the development of simplified modalities for low-income communities (Scherr, White, and Kaimowitz 2004).

Sustainable green enterprises can be obstructed by legal and regulatory frameworks that limit poor producers' access to resources and markets, often

Programs providing payment for environmental services can offer economic benefits for poor rural communities

to protect public or private monopolies or to finance government agencies. The task force recommends that governments work with communities to reform these regulatory frameworks, so that they provide clear local incentives for sustainable use and to encourage green community enterprises. Participatory monitoring strategies should be used to enable more nimble responses to potential environmental threats and assist public agencies to control destructive or illegal harvesting by large-scale, nonlocal business operations.

Pay poor rural communities for environmental services

Protecting and restoring natural resources holds benefits not only for food but also finance as a source of income for the poor and hungry. Private companies, municipal water and electricity utilities, downstream irrigation users, and conservation agencies have become willing to contract with rural communities to conserve, manage, and restore critical natural resources for ecosystem services. Examples include sequestering carbon, conserving biodiversity, and protecting watersheds, public forests, and conservation areas. In many parts of the developing world, international organizations are supporting pilot programs, such as the Global Environment Facility, the International Union for the Conservation of Nature, and the Convention on Biological Diversity.

Programs providing payment for environmental services are generally at an early stage of development. But they hold significant potential for poor and hungry rural communities who reside in areas of high biodiversity value and critical watershed, as well as in degraded areas requiring resource restoration (Landell-Mills and Porrus 2002). Opportunities include:

- Payment for biodiversity protection, including conservation-based land uses or management practices, biodiversity monitoring or stewardship services, species conservation, outsider access for sustainable harvesting or bio-prospecting, and the development of eco-labeled products (Jenkins, Scherr, and Inbar 2004).
- Payment for watershed protection or restoration by downstream water users. These payments can contribute much to local incomes while providing conservation incentives. The benefits of such programs to poor and hungry communities depend, however, on the payment system. Care should be taken to ensure that payments go to the poor (including the landless) or their organizations—and that poor people do not lose rights for land and water use critical to their livelihoods (Rosa, Kandel, and Dimas 2003).
- Future markets for carbon sequestration hold significant potential for poor farmers—with the right rules and protections. Options include reforestation and afforestation funded under the Clean Development Mechanism of the Kyoto Protocol (box 10.3), land use practices funded by investors outside the Kyoto system, and voluntary payments by carbon-emitters to achieve carbon neutrality. Because carbon emis-

Property rights and national legal frameworks need to be strengthened

sion reductions and sequestration anywhere in the world can benefit the global carbon balance, we argue there should be a special effort to direct international carbon finance toward investments that also restore or protect resources critical for food security and poverty reduction.

Since many ecosystem services are public goods, government intervention is usually required to create a functioning market. This may entail paying directly for a service, establishing property rights, or establishing regulations that set caps and govern trading schemes. Government intervention is usually also required to overcome the primary obstacles to ecosystem market development: high transaction costs between buyers and sellers, and the lack of specialized market institutions. To establish effective markets, policymakers also require objective technical advice, useful analytical models, and accurate data. In most developing countries, property rights and national legal frameworks need to be strengthened to allow for effective market development.

If properly designed, the Clean Development Mechanism could offer hundreds of millions of dollars each year for investments with poor rural communities for forest establishment, agroforestry, biomass energy development, and ecosystem restoration (Smith and Scherr 2002). Farmers in humid or subhumid tropical areas will have an advantage, as they can sequester 10 times

Box 10.3

Tapping the Clean Development Mechanism to improve farming systems

Source: Smith and Scherr 2002.

Under the Clean Development Mechanism of the Kyoto Protocol, carbon offset "credits" produced by energy and forestry projects in developing countries can be purchased by businesses to offset their obligations to reduce carbon emissions under the Protocol. Developed countries can only use such deals to offset a limited portion of their carbon obligations, but this still represents a potential private financial flow of $300 million a year. These resources could be used in ways that sharply reduce rural poverty—for example, through community-based carbon trading deals for small-scale forest plantations, regeneration of degraded forests, ecosystem restoration, and agroforestry. Carbon projects could also finance land and forest-improving investments by poor rural producers, and restore ecosystem services on millions of hectares of heavily populated forest and farmland.

Community-friendly forest carbon projects are unlikely to take root without proactive attention in the Clean Development Mechanism rules and in the approaches of developing countries and project designers. It is critical that key steps be taken to:

- Make all types of forestry and agroforestry projects with significant benefits for local communities eligible for the Clean Development Mechanism.
- Reduce risks for local communities by requiring social impact assessments and formalizing community tenure rights.
- Reduce the cost of managing community projects by finding intermediaries to market carbon offsets from multiple producers and by making community-based forestry projects eligible for the low-cost "fast-track" approval process.
- Reduce risks and costs for investors, by developing portfolios that spread risks across projects, and by using insurance approaches that are suitable for poor rural communities.

Payment systems must enable strong community input

more carbon per hectare than those in temperate zones. There are even opportunities in dry areas. Opportunity costs are low, and investments to increase soil organic matter and vegetative cover can catalyze improved agricultural productivity and diversified income sources. At current prices for sequestered carbon, the transfer payments to individual farmers are rather modest—perhaps $30 a year per family. Even so, this is an evolving market. The task force encourages developing country governments to participate actively in Clean Development Mechanism negotiations to gain benefits for their farmers and landscapes. And it recommends that the international community engage in high-level negotiations to ensure that multilateral environmental agreements are integrated closely with strategies to achieve the Millennium Development Goals.

At the same time, it is essential for countries to establish the legal and regulatory framework for ecosystem service markets in ways that are pro-poor. Payment systems must enable strong community input into proposed interventions, to ensure that payments go to the poor (including the landless) or their organizations, and that poor people do not lose rights for land and water use critical to their livelihoods. Ecosystem service payment systems and projects should be designed explicitly to address hunger and poverty reduction (see box 10.3).

Actions needed to implement recommendation seven

Help communities and households restore or enhance natural resources

Assist communities in developing natural resource action and investment plans by providing trained facilitators or advisors, participatory mapping, cross-community visits to observe innovations, and indicators and monitoring. Planning, participation, and ownership of the plans by the community—including women and the landless—are critical. They should be integrated with farming plans and built on local access and control of resources. District governments and NGOs should coordinate planning, with support from state-level ministerial planning groups and local user organizations. By 2008 plans should be in place for 5 million households in 10,000 communities, rising to 10 million households by 2012.

Target natural-resource dependent communities and households, especially those facing hunger and food security threats. Engage in dialogue among resource users, managers, and off-site beneficiaries. Establish legislative authorization and processes for action across jurisdictions. Provide financial and technical support for investments to restore degraded resources. Establish matching grant programs for community plans, using cash, expertise, and food aid. Build these into poverty reduction strategies as "National Sustainability Funds." Mobilize food aid to pay farmers, herders, and forest dwellers to rehabilitate resources.

Secure local ownership, access, and management rights to forests, fisheries, and rangelands	Create new legislation to provide resource tenure or co-management rights, where needed, with attention to land rights for women. Implement devolution of forest or fisheries resource tenure where the legal framework for community rights already exists. Conduct public information campaigns on community resource rights. Build coalitions of national and district governments, legislators, rural and environmental ministries, forest and fisher community organizations, and journalists. Aim for 2006 public campaigns, 2007 legislation and implementation, and 2015 achievement of targets for the devolution of land rights.
Develop natural-resource-based green enterprises	Reduce the regulatory costs and market barriers for low-income producers to commercialize natural resource products and services. Provide technical and business support to community-based commercial enterprises, including experts who understand economics and management of community-based enterprises. Implement community monitoring to assess sustainable levels of harvest and potential markets—and provide local input into identifying "best management practices." Key actors include national legislators, regulatory agencies, community-based enterprises, and the private sector. By 2006 fund green enterprises through poverty reduction strategies and identify necessary regulatory reform through community consultation. By 2007 implement regulatory changes. By 2010 expand green enterprises to benefit 5 million households worldwide, reaching 10 million by 2015.
Pay poor farmers for environmental services	Mobilize pro-poor design of legislation and international agreements on payments for ecosystem services, such as biodiversity conservation and watershed protection. Involve communities in dialogue on developing laws and regulations. Public rural development agencies and NGOs should help implement programs. Use payments to catalyze transitions to improved land-management systems. Use diverse mechanisms to reward good managers. Put in place carbon trading schemes between carbon-emitting industries and low-income farmers and resource-dependent communities, based on the Clean Development Mechanism of the Kyoto Protocol and other carbon trading agreements. In 2006 countries should enact national legislation (as needed) to establish payments for ecosystem services with pro-poor provisions, and develop a strategy for accessing carbon trading finance at preselected sites.

Chapter 11

Implementing the recommendations of the Task Force on Hunger

There have been many plans to end hunger, but few of them have been effectively or efficiently implemented. The reasons for this gap between action and results fall into two broad categories. One is the lack of resources, the second a combination of political, social, technical, or institutional factors. Both reasons are affected by human, technical, or institutional capacity. Previous chapters of this report have addressed many of the constraints to hunger-alleviation efforts that relate to insufficient resources, program, and policy design. This chapter lays out key principles for national and local implementation of the Task Force on Hunger recommendations as well as possible entry points in the fight against hunger.

The centerpiece of the task force's recommended implementation strategy is the creation of national strategies for the elimination of hunger, strategies that should be integrated into existing policy frameworks, such as the poverty reduction strategies. Key elements for effective execution include community-level leadership, active participation of donors and the private sector, and broad capacity building efforts at all levels. Where possible, hunger reduction initiatives should generate multiple benefits, and several examples of such "synergistic" programs are presented at the end of the chapter as suggested starting points for broader national efforts.

Setting priorities for interventions

For seven recommendations in this report, there are 40 proposed interventions. Clearly, not every intervention will be appropriate for every setting. An important first step at the national level will be for governments to work with communities to identify the priority interventions for the conditions that prevail locally. Local participatory problem analysis and planning should form an integral part of identifying the most important interventions. In some

Many interventions will require investments to build capacity at all levels

cases, it will be easier to determine which interventions correspond to certain groups of hungry people—such as expanding nonfarm income opportunities for the urban poor and the rural landless. In other cases, more analysis will be required—particularly at the subnational level—to identify typologies of hunger, identify hotspots more precisely, and work with communities to target them with appropriate interventions.

Typologies of hunger for the different regions will need to be refined, revised, and clarified at the country level (table 11.1). The task force recommends that further work should be carried out to characterize who the hungry are at subnational levels and assist in ranking key interventions for the different groups. Defining typologies of hunger will require reliable, up-to-date information, and donors should be ready to assist countries with the surveys and studies needed. Once the data are available, various participatory decision-making methods can be applied to identify top priorities for action and determine the costs associated with these interventions. The task force sees gender equality, governance, capacity building, and environmental sustainability as cross-cutting issues in all regions, to be fully integrated into all interventions.

Strengthening capacity for scaling up

Past failures in hunger-elimination efforts—and the limited scaling up of successes—are often attributed to the lack of capacity in developing countries. Many of the interventions in this report will require investments to build capacity at all levels, from national to local, in order to scale up. To overcome capacity constraints and achieve rapid progress toward the hunger Goal, donors and country governments will need to make long-term commitments to invest in strengthening human, technical, managerial, and institutional capacity at all levels. Monitoring and evaluation systems need to be built into all capacity building interventions to ensure real-time learning and course correction as needs arise.

Past models of donor assistance have often inadvertently furthered a vicious cycle of dependency and low capacity. Donors have controlled most aspects of their programs, from design and oversight to evaluation. The lack of local participation often led to poorly designed projects that did not fit local priorities or practices and could not be replicated at a larger scale. While local counterparts were trained to participate, they did not have true ownership or participation in most projects. When donors withdrew, local partners lacked the institutional support to lead the projects. This led to a dependency on new projects and sustained ineffectiveness of institutions (Berg 1993; Fukuda-Parr, Lopes, and Malik 2002). This trend is now changing, and many donors now emphasize local ownership of development processes.

National capacities for implementing hunger reduction strategies need to be built very quickly to achieve the Goal by 2015. Capacity strengthening should be based on ensuring the provision of information (including public

Table 11.1
Regional profiles and priorities for investment

	Sub-Saharan Africa	East Asia and the Pacific	South Asia	Latin America and the Caribbean	Central Asia and Eastern Europe	China
Overall trends in status of preschool underweight children	Highest number of countries with increasing rates of malnutrition	Making the best progress of all developing regions	High rates of underweight prevalence, falling slowly. Total number of underweight children extremely high	Moderate levels, increasing in some countries	Moderate levels, increasing in some countries	Rates moderate, falling rapidly. Overall numbers still high
Depth of the problem	About 32 million preschool-age underweight children (23% of the world's total preschool-age underweight population)	About 17 million preschool-age underweight children (13% of the total world's preschool-age underweight population)	About 76 million preschool-age underweight children (57% of the total world's preschool-age underweight population)	About 4 million preschool-age underweight children (3% of the total world's preschool-age underweight population)	About 1.5 million preschool-age underweight children (1% of the total world's preschool-age underweight population)	About 3.1 million preschool-age underweight children (2.3% of the total world's preschool-age underweight population)
Who are the hungry	Smallholder farmers, landless, victims of conflict and extreme climate events victims, resource dependent rural populations	Urban and rural poor	Women and infants in poor households, marginal groups	Urban poor, indigenous populations, marginal groups	Urban and rural poor	Rural poor, especially in western and central provinces
Insufficient agriculture production	Primary reason for hunger	Potential future risk. Productivity increases need to keep pace with growing demand	Potential future risk. Productivity increases need to keep pace with growing demand	Very important reason in the Andean region	Not important: largely food import dependent	Not important. Producing enough food
Poor nutritional status of vulnerable groups	Very important reason	Important reason	Very important reason	Very important reason	Important reason	Important reason
Lack of productive safety nets	Very important reason	Important reason	Very important reason	Very important reason	Less important	Less important
Lack of access to markets and inadequate income levels	Important determinant of hunger, both markets and income	Moderately important determinant of hunger, particularly income	Important determinant of hunger, particularly income	Primary reason for hunger, mainly income	Primary reason for hunger, mainly income	Important determinant of hunger, mainly income
Lack of basic infrastructure	Very important determinant of hunger	Less important	Important	Less important	Less important	Not important anymore
Natural resource degradation	Very important determinant of hunger and poverty, affecting agricultural productivity, water supply, and wild foods and products	Moderately important determinant of rural hunger and poverty	Very important determinant of poverty, affecting agricultural productivity and wild foods for the landless	Moderately important overall; very important determinant of hunger and poverty in mountain and forest communities	Moderately important, through impacts on water quality and agricultural productivity	Very important determinant of poverty and lost agricultural productivity (soils, forests, water)

The lack of a comprehensive and integrated approach has limited the success of many development projects

awareness and exchanges of knowledge among participants in the strategy), the integration of all relevant institutions and players into planning and implementation, and the participation of people, communities, the private sector, and governments (UNDP 2004b). The full participation of a range of actors in the development of national hunger reduction strategies will help to build the capacities needed for effective implementation and scaling up (Dobie 2002).

To scale up hunger reduction strategies, the task force recommends that promising approaches and projects be systematically identified and that major capacity-building efforts be undertaken at all levels. Support for community-based organizations is especially important, due to their capacity for low-cost, high-impact initiatives and the potential for exponential replication of community-based programs, as seen in the rapid spread of women's self-help groups in India. Indeed, the task force views the transformative power of such organizations as one of the most important driving forces in global efforts to meet the hunger Goal. By helping expand the skills, rights, and resources of such groups, governments and donors can enhance their impact.

Refining national hunger strategies

Many development projects aim to improve agricultural production, nutrition, market linkages, clean water, healthcare, or gender equality—but they rarely address all these aspects simultaneously. The lack of a comprehensive and integrated approach has limited the success of many efforts. To mobilize a coordinated and effective effort for eliminating hunger, governments should refine and revise their national strategies, drawing from the recommendations of this report and the FAO's Special Program for Food Security. National poverty reduction strategies, or where applicable, PRSPs, should be built into existing policy processes and reflect a broader need by governments to undertake policy planning for all of the Goals. Key ingredients of such enhanced strategies include the following:

Broad participation. Preparation and implementation of a national strategy to meet the hunger Goal should be undertaken with the full participation of key stakeholders. Consultation is not adequate. The capacities for implementation will be developed only if stakeholders directly contribute to the design of the enhanced strategy and are empowered as partners in its implementation. Key stakeholders include the ministries of agriculture, health, social services, environment, water, transport, commerce, planning, and finance and the government body responsible for food aid. They also include representatives of civil society, the private sector, banks, and other financial institutions, and the donor community, including multilateral and bilateral institutions.

Developing a national MDG-based poverty reduction strategy to meet all the Goals—including the hunger Goal—will require a lead coordinating agency. It will also require considerable investments in capacity building in

Translating global and national commitment and funding into local action remains the greatest challenge

developing and donor countries alike to improve planning and coordination across various sectors. Multilateral organizations, donor agencies, and major NGOs should assist in development of the hunger Goal strategy by providing advice and access to information. The full involvement of all stakeholders—including different government sectors, donors, multilateral organizations, civil society, and the private sector—in developing this strategy will help to ensure their full ownership of the final strategy and its implementation.

Thorough analysis. The strategy should be founded on sound analysis of the scope and typologies of hunger at the national level, on knowledge of lessons learned from existing hunger elimination efforts, particularly in identifying the elements of success in effective programs, and on strategies for scaling up that will be effective in the local context.

Sound policy design and integration into existing processes. Hunger Goal strategies must be fully integrated into the country's national poverty reduction strategy or where applicable, PRSP. The UN Millennium Project recommends that governments undertake a comprehensive needs assessment and costing of the requirements to meet the Millennium Development Goals, to be reflected in the poverty reduction strategy or other national process.

Monitoring and public reporting. Once a national strategy for reducing hunger is incorporated in the poverty reduction strategy or PRSP, and funds are allocated through a related medium-term expenditure framework, the responsibility for implementation will be devolved to line agencies, NGOs, and communities. The Task Force on Hunger recommends a participatory and transparent monitoring process, overseen by a coordinating agency, to track progress toward meeting the Goal.

Securing financing for implementation

Antihunger plans can be financed from a combination of existing public sector resources, official development assistance, private sector investment, and contributions from a variety of private organizations. Governments should work to create dialogue, buy-in, and effective donor coordination in support of their national strategies. Costs and financing strategies will vary significantly depending on the nature and scale of interventions. An initial estimate prepared by the UN Millennium Project outlines the costs of selected agricultural and nutritional interventions related to the hunger Goal for three African countries (table 11.2). The calculations were based on estimated costs of a select array of interventions in agriculture and nutrition (table 11.3).

National hunger reduction strategies should form part of a comprehensive national plan for meeting all the Goals. Though some cost savings can be achieved by designing complementary programs, this will require signifi-

Table 11.2
Estimated costs of hunger interventions for Ghana, Tanzania, and Uganda, 2006–15
Dollars

	Ghana		Tanzania		Uganda	
	Total annual cost (average)	Per capita annual cost	Total annual cost (average)	Per capita annual cost	Total annual cost (average)	Per capita annual cost
Agriculture	66,306,151	2.64	304,668,044	6.89	88,942,219	2.55
Nutrition	29,932,450	1.18	62,159,924	1.43	41,011,968	1.13
Total	96,238,601	3.82	366,827,969	8.31	129,954,187	3.68

Source: UN Millennium Project 2004.

Table 11.3
Proportional costs of select antihunger interventions
Percent

	Ghana	Tanzania	Uganda
Agriculture	69	83	68
Improving soil health	15	18	35
Improved seeds	4	4	8
Small-scale water management	27	46	4
Extension	3	3	5
Research	20	11	16
Nutrition	31	17	32
School meals	17	7	17
Supplementation and fortification	14	10	15
Total	100	100	100

Source: UN Millennium Project 2004.

cant new budget commitments across all sectors. We present here an estimate of average annual costs for achieving the Goals in five countries (table 11.4). The estimates do not include the costs of interventions that are related (and necessary) to achieving the Goals, such as transportation infrastructure, information and communications technology, environmental sustainability, and interventions for slum dwellers.

Implementation at the local level

Translating global and national commitment and funding into local action remains the greatest challenge to achieving the Goals. Without local action, efforts to achieve the Goal will remain top-down, supply-driven, and ineffective. Reaching the target of halving hunger by 2015 will require the engagement of a very large number of affected people. Such an approach requires large investments in retraining experts and politicians in the skills required to become advisors and facilitators of community-led processes. It requires heavy investment for large numbers of facilitators to work with communities in defining locally specific solutions to hunger. It also requires complementing community actions with well targeted safety nets to ensure access to adequate food for those unable to meet their own requirements. These changes require a considerable shift—and may in the initial stages require more time—but investing in them is essential.

Table 11.4

MDG investment needs and MDG financing gaps in Bangladesh, Cambodia, Ghana, Tanzania, and Uganda (2006–15)

2003 US$ per capita

Note: Results describe MDG investment needs without expenditures for capacity building. Due to a lack of data, several groups of interventions have not been included: large infrastructure projects for energy, water management, and transport; interventions to ensure environmental sustainability; and higher education and strengthening of national research systems. It is estimated that at least another $10 per capita (averaged over the full period) will be required to finance these investments, as indicated in the table. Refer to UN Millennium Project (2005) for more details.

a. For MDG interventions not yet included in needs assessment (such as large infrastructure projects, higher education, environmental sustainability).

b. 2002 value calculated as net official development assistance minus technical cooperation, debt relief, aid to NGOs, emergency assistance, food aid using data from OECD–DAC (2002).

Source: UN Millennium Project 2005c.

MDG investment needs	Bangladesh 2006	2010	2015	Cambodia 2006	2010	2015	Ghana 2006	2010	2015	Tanzania 2006	2010	2015	Uganda 2006	2010	2015
Hunger	2	4	8	4	7	13	3	5	12	4	7	14	3	5	10
Education	11	17	25	15	19	22	17	19	22	11	13	17	14	15	17
Gender equality	2	3	3	2	3	3	2	3	3	2	3	3	2	3	3
Health	13	19	30	14	21	32	18	24	34	24	33	48	25	32	44
Water supply and sanitation	4	5	6	3	5	8	6	7	10	4	5	12	2	3	9
Improving the lives of slum dwellers	2	3	4	3	3	4	2	2	3	3	3	4	2	2	3
Energy	20	19	20	9	13	23	13	15	18	14	15	18	6	10	19
Roads	12	21	31	12	21	31	11	10	10	13	21	31	13	20	27
Other[a]	8	9	13	8	9	13	8	9	13	8	9	13	8	9	13
Total	74	100	140	71	101	148	80	94	124	82	111	161	75	100	143
Source of financing															
Household contributions	8	10	14	9	13	18	9	11	15	9	11	17	8	9	14
Government expenditures	23	33	49	22	30	43	19	27	39	24	32	46	27	35	48
MDG financing gap	43	56	77	40	58	87	52	57	70	50	67	98	41	56	80
Shortfall ODA for direct MDG support over 2002 level	42	55	75	22	40	69	36	41	54	35	52	83	29	44	68
For comparison: ODA for direct MDG support 2002[b]		1			18			16			15			12

Box 11.1

The Hunger Project's "epicenters" for grassroots empowerment

Source: The Hunger Project 2004.

The Hunger Project, an international NGO, has implemented a low-cost, people-centered strategy for grassroots mobilization to end hunger in rural African communities with demonstrated success. Its "epicenter" strategy is anchored in community leadership and empowerment at the grassroots level, catalyzed by international staff and implemented by national staff working with local governments and national political leaders.

The Project's process for mobilizing communities starts with selecting a community that is ready to mobilize on a self-reliant basis and that can serve as a catalyst in the region. The Project builds support from local village leaders, and organizes locally led workshops for residents to identify their hunger-free vision for the village and commit to a near-term plan of action toward achieving it. Workshop discussions emphasize overcoming resignation and dependency to build self-reliance. The Project identifies residents with the enthusiasm and commitment to serve as "animators," mobilizing the community toward its goals. It encourages the formation of community-led committees to address basic needs in the village, with equal representation of men and women, and links these to external resources (political, technical, and institutional).

Villages build a community center, which houses a school, health center, food processing and storage facility, rural bank, and meeting room for adult classes in literacy, agricultural techniques, health, and nutrition. The Project emphasizes local resources and income-generating activities rather than external investment to build self-reliance from the start.

Community members, by working together, can devise cost-effective and well targeted strategies to address the underlying causes of hunger through managing natural resources, generating income, reducing vulnerability, and providing critical services (Meizen-Dick and di Gregorio 2004) (box 11.1).

Experience with agricultural improvement programs suggests some key elements in expanding and exchanging local knowledge through hunger reduction programs:

- Participatory rural appraisal is an effective way of engaging the community and harnessing its knowledge to identify community needs, leadership strengths or gaps, and shared productive assets.
- Hands-on field training is an effective technique for transferring knowledge. Knowledge transfer to the community or individuals is critical to success.
- Training local leaders, including women leaders, as facilitators can be highly effective. They understand the local context, are based locally, and have the community's trust.
- "Participatory technology development" allows men and women farmers to experiment with new technologies before applying them broadly, thus reducing risk and increasing understanding.
- Greater gains will be achieved by first disseminating new "entry point" techniques that produce rapid results and are adopted by others. Spreading the idea to others through field trips and knowledge exchange can be highly effective.

Domestic and foreign companies have become more important and influential partners

Village leaders, including both men and women, and other village participants can be assisted in developing meaningful local monitoring methods and trained in appropriate formal and informal monitoring systems. Evaluations should be participatory and transparent, with results made promptly available and program adjustments made accordingly.

Engaging the private sector

Another key component to implementing the recommendations at the local level is the involvement of the private sector. Domestic and foreign companies have become more important and influential partners in many developing countries as a result of privatization and market liberalization, and most organizations have an interest in the future progress of these countries. At the same time there are growing demands for private industry to be more transparent and more accountable for their economic, social, and environmental impacts wherever they operate.

The private sector can address the challenge of halving hunger in the following ways:

Providing affordable products and services. Food and beverage companies can develop new products that combat nutritional deficiencies and are affordable to low-income families. Utility companies can participate in public-private partnerships to increase access to clean water, energy, and telecommunications. Energy companies can support efforts to develop renewable energy sources, particularly for rural communities. Financial services companies can develop banking and insurance services for the poor, including microcredit.

Building local business linkages and employment opportunities. Manufacturing, food and beverage, and consumer goods companies can source raw materials from local suppliers whose business practices benefit the poor or the environment. Agribusiness companies can work with small farmers and their cooperatives along global supply chains to provide credit and improve rural productivity, quality, and food security.

Building local capacity. Companies can help develop integrated community investment initiatives that focus on local institution and capacity building, as well as wider regional approaches. For example, Instituto Ethos—a Brazilian association of more than 900 businesses interested in corporate social responsibility—is working with the government's Zero Hunger program to engage business in the eradication of hunger. Companies can also support social entrepreneurs by volunteering the expertise of their employees for training and assisting with projects.

The combination of three interventions may constitute an effective new approach

Supporting public efforts to build the domestic private sector and attract foreign investment. Companies can build effective business associations and support structures, lobbying governments and helping to build capacity for necessary regulatory and financial reforms—such as providing the poor with access to property rights and increasing market access for small farmers. Financial service, legal, and accounting firms can help to build institutional structures and promote good standards of corporate governance.

Advocating for fairer access to OECD markets and eliminating the OECD's adverse agricultural subsidies. The private sector can help advocate for pro-poor trade policy reform. For example, the World Economic Forum brought together major agribusiness and food companies, NGOs, and UN agencies on a task force to advocate for agricultural policy reform.

Synergistic entry points to overcoming hunger

Presented here are brief profiles of three local-level initiatives that can serve as "entry points" in the battle against hunger, generating synergistic benefits for community hunger alleviation efforts. All three of these programs need to be tailored to local conditions and combined with policy changes, regulatory reforms, and incentives at the national to local levels. They include:

- Community nutrition programs.
- Homegrown school-based feeding programs.
- Investments in soil health and water resources.

In fact, the combination of these three interventions may constitute an effective new approach in rural areas where chronic malnutrition is high and agricultural productivity is low. Community nutrition and homegrown school feeding programs can be initiated in tandem with the basic investments in soil and water, generating increased local production that will have a ready market in the homegrown programs.

Community nutrition programs

An important synergistic approach to combating hunger is the community-led nutrition program. Rather than producing a blueprint for community nutrition programs that can be applied uniformly in all countries and regions, the task force recommends that programs be designed on the basis of local epidemiology, underlying causes of malnutrition, and existing programs. The strategy must first determine the causes of poor nutrition in the program area and define interventions accordingly. Factors include:

- Low food availability—poor nutrition caused by household food insecurity, limited access to food, intrahousehold food allocation, or lack of early breastfeeding and complementary feeding.

It is essential to build local capacity for implementation

- Poor health and sanitation—causing diarrhea and other diseases that "leach" nutrients out of the child's system.
- Poor maternal knowledge and caring practices—where the caregiver has access to some resources—such as breastmilk or access to immunization services—but is not empowered to make the right feeding or healthcare decisions.

The design of community nutrition programs should focus on five principles. First, focus on high-priority target groups, such as pregnant and lactating women and children under five, to concentrate impact in these groups. Second, build community involvement and commitment to get organized and empowered to address malnutrition. Third, allow communities and local governments to choose among a range of interventions and select those most relevant. Fourth, in choosing interventions, address the underlying determinants of malnutrition: household food security, health interventions and a healthy environment, and maternal and caregiver caring capacities. Fifth, use local procurement of food to the greatest possible extent because it provides important economic and social synergies through nutritionally balanced meals, produced locally and suited to local tastes.

The choice of interventions will vary significantly by community, region, and country. Where the health systems are strong, the focus should be on improving household access to food and intrahousehold food allocation patterns. Where rates of breastfeeding are declining, the major focus and intervention should be on infant feeding. Where gender inequalities are a key determinant, equality and empowerment will be the best entry point. Other countries are starting with a focus on micronutrient fortification and supplementation.

To make such programs sustainable, it is essential to build local capacity for implementation. Community-driven approaches require empowering and enhancing village-level capacities to recognize and respond to malnutrition problems—and supporting these efforts through government systems of paraprofessional nutrition extension workers. These approaches have two main elements.

The first is to appoint and train community nutrition extension workers, who complement the work of agricultural extensionists and village-level work on agriculture. Ethiopia is undertaking a large-scale government initiative to invest in training community health and nutrition workers, who will work alongside their agricultural extension counterparts in key areas of the country. Another example is Thailand, which has successfully integrated community actions with national policies and programs to generate sustained nutritional improvements nationwide (box 11.2). The task force recommends that community nutrition extension workers should be trained and deployed in large numbers, closely coordinated with agricultural extension programs.

The second element of the community-driven approach is the promotion of mother- and baby-friendly initiatives to build community awareness

Communities must ensure an enabling environment for mothers to feed and care for their children

and support for breastfeeding, and child and maternal health. This approach empowers communities by training village volunteers who can identify families or individuals most in need of assistance, and enhance their coping strategies through nutrition education, health referral, and the promotion of good practices. The idea is to ensure an enabling environment for mothers to feed and care for their children and to have access to adequate nutrition and care themselves. For women who work outside the home, this requires that their employers be educated and encouraged to support breastfeeding at work—for example, by providing time and space for breastfeeding and other maternity benefits.

To achieve this, village self-help or support groups are trained to offer mothers and fathers nutrition and health education (box 11.3). The subjects covered include a good maternal diet during pregnancy, the benefits of exclusive breastfeeding for six months (including immediate post-natal access to colostrum), the hazards of bottle-feeding, the appropriate forms and uses of complementary foods after the first six months, the importance of good hygiene and environmental health, and the encouragement of greater uptake of government health services (including vaccination, folate distribution, and family planning). Support from paraprofessional health and nutrition extension workers is important, as is regular mother-to-mother support at the home.

There are encouraging signs that the value of these approaches is beginning to be appreciated in government circles. According to a statement endorsed by ministers of health and other government representatives meeting in New Delhi in September 2004, "Mother and child-centered investments are fea-

Box 11.2

A success story from Thailand

Source: Swaminathan 2001.

Thailand has shown remarkable progress in reducing maternal mortality as well as the incidence of low-birthweight children through its Community Volunteer Corps for Household Nutrition Security. Key elements of this program:

- Eliminating severe, moderate, and mild protein-energy malnutrition.
- Monitoring growth among all preschool children and providing food supplements where needed.
- Mainstreaming nutrition in health, education, and agricultural policies.
- Retraining and retooling existing staff and mobilizing community volunteers. One volunteer was chosen for every 10 households.
- Encouraging breastfeeding and organizing school lunch programs.
- Promoting home gardening, consumption of fruits and vegetables, aquaculture, and food safety standards.
- Introducing an integrated food safety net with emphasis on household food and nutrition.

The positive impact of the Nutrition Security Compact is evident from the decline of maternal mortality from 230 per 100,000 live births in 1992 to 17 in 1996 (Philip 2000).

Box 11.3

Mother-friendly and baby-friendly communities

Source: UNICEF 2004.

Innovative activities in The Gambia show that building capacity, knowledge, and motivation at the community level can result in significant and sustainable improvements in nutrition at minimal additional cost.

With a view to improving maternal well being, pregnancy outcomes, and infant feeding practices, the program in The Gambia pursues an integrated approach that builds on widely known baby-friendly hospital initiatives, supported by the United Nations Children's Fund and WHO. The approach is to establish mother-to-mother support groups that become family self-help and support groups, including men.

Five women and two men are identified by each community to be trained as volunteers to implement and monitor the activity. Where available, traditional birth attendants are included in the group. Local problem analysis leads to a 10-step plan, which includes ensuring that families act on nutrition and health advice, that mothers are encouraged and given time and space to pursue exclusive breastfeeding for the first six months, that workplaces in the village and on farms provide shelter for small children accompanying mothers to work, and so on. When all 10 steps have been achieved, it falls to the government to recognize such efforts by awarding mother- and baby-friendly community status to successful villages.

sible and cost-effective and clearly underpin national economic growth. Many policy and program instruments exist for preventing malnutrition, but to implement them it is essential to ensure outreach of services and resources to remote, rural areas where populations prone to malnutrition are concentrated" (Delhi Declaration 2004).

Examples of countries that have used this community-led framework to address malnutrition successfully include:

- In the Iringa project Tanzania focused on growth promotion, reducing women's workloads, and community-driven actions.
- In an integrated nutrition project India's Tamil Nadu focused on monitoring growth and promoting and targeting short-term supplementary feeding for children and pregnant women.
- Bangladesh used growth monitoring and feeding to change maternal behaviors and added a strong focus on micronutrient supplementation and salt iodization.
- Honduras also focuses on behavior change for mothers.

Homegrown school-based feeding programs

A second synergy trigger recommended by the task force is promoting homegrown school-based feeding programs as an effective way of creating agricultural, educational, and market benefits and addressing gender inequality in chronically hungry communities. Nutritious food offered at school will attract hungry children to attend school and improve both attendance and school performance. Providing take-home rations will also offer economic incentives for families to send their children to school.

The task force recommends that interventions for the chronically hungry should be undertaken with locally produced foods

In a recent publication, Ahmed and Caldes (2004) show that governments in some developing countries have used homegrown school feeding programs to stimulate the demand for local produce, increase agricultural growth, and create jobs with impressive results. Some examples:

- China's National Milk Program, launched in 1999 to increase dairy product consumption by school children, creates 233 new jobs in the dairy industry for every 100,000 children who join the program. Participating Chinese dairy farmers earn an additional $400 a year from milk sales for every dairy cow added to their herds.
- Thailand's School Feeding Program, started in 1985, included a national milk scheme. Thailand depended greatly on imported dairy products before 1985. But domestic production then rose from 120,000 liters a day in 1985 to 1,550,000 liters a day in 2001. An estimated 250,000 jobs have been created in the dairy industry.
- When Guatemala shifted its school feeding procurement from central industrial suppliers to local producers and involved local families in the preparation of school meals, markets in the areas covered by the program developed significantly.

The literature indicates, however, that many potential synergies of homegrown feeding programs have either not occurred or been fully documented. The task force, based on the extensive field experience of its members, strongly recommends that such interventions for the chronically hungry be undertaken, as much as possible, with locally produced foods. It is our belief that this will provide major synergies related to multiple Goals, such as the following:

Education. There is substantial evidence that school feeding programs can have a positive effect on students' cognitive functions, increase enrollment and retention, improve attendance, lower repeater and dropout rates, and improve exam performance. In addition, school meals improve students' cognition, short-term memory, verbal fluency, and ability to concentrate (Janke 1996). This measurably improves their educational performance, when compared with students in schools without meal programs. Education, especially for girls, will broaden their options, teach them about nutrition, and offer the best tool for overcoming poverty and hunger (WFP 2001b, Ahmed 2004).

Education gender gap. School meals increase school attendance by girls and help keep them in school. A program in Bangladesh increased girls' enrollment by 44 percent in contrast to 28 percent for boys (Ahmed and del Nimmo 2002). Research shows that educating girls can help delay marriage, reduce family size, create greater spacing between births, boost earning power, and improve the nutritional status of girls' future children. Some 44 percent of the decrease in child malnutrition between 1970 and 1995 is attributable to increased women's education (Smith and Haddad 2000).

School feeding can alleviate short-term hunger, especially in times of crisis

Child mortality. The effects of improved education for girls are reflected in the welfare of the next generation: each added year of schooling for a mother results in a 5–10 percent decrease in child mortality among her children (WFP 2001a). Through nutritional education and school gardens, the programs can provide important knowledge and skills to students, particularly adolescent girls soon to become mothers. Feeding programs can strengthen children's immune systems, reducing their vulnerability to malaria and other widespread diseases.

Nourishment through nutritious foods. School feeding can alleviate short-term hunger, especially in times of crisis. The nourishment these programs provide is significant. In Peru school breakfasts increased children's energy intake by 2 percent, their protein intake by 28 percent, and their iron content by 4 percent (Jacoby, Cueto, and Pollitt 1996). Such programs have also proved effective in delivering micronutrients to children. For example, studies in the Philippines have demonstrated the potential to reduce vitamin A deficiencies among children by providing them with buns made from fortified flour in schools (Solon 2000).

Poverty. Poor, food-insecure families rely on their children to help with farm work, to collect and carry firewood and water, to care for younger siblings, and to help with cooking and food preparation (WFP 2004c). Homegrown feeding programs can help alleviate this burden, and through local sourcing provide farmers with reliable income for their produce, creating opportunities for cottage industries engaged in small-scale processing of added-value products, such as oil, sugar, and fruit drinks. The programs can also become a coping mechanism, providing a reliable source of food that reduces the need for costly risk-mitigation strategies, such as depleting productive assets.

HIV/AIDS. School feeding works as an effective tool and intervention in the HIV/AIDS crisis. Food-assisted literacy and trade-skills training help orphans get some education. Recent studies have also shown that one of the first responses of an HIV/AIDS-affected household is to pull children out of school to help support the family. Foster families and other facilities providing shelter to orphans find their resources stretched thin. Because of family responsibilities and dire poverty, orphans often cannot afford to attend formal school full time. Food assistance and literacy training are two basic investments that can make a significant difference for their futures (WFP 2004c).

Conflict. In times of conflict and crisis, keeping schools open and offering school feeding programs have helped to divert children from child labor or child soldiering. Schools provide children with a sense of normality, unbroken

Homegrown school feeding programs can provide a powerful incentive to local farmers

routine, and friendly and structured environment at a time of turmoil (Ahmed and Caldes 2004).

Agricultural markets. Homegrown school feeding programs can provide a powerful incentive to local farmers to produce and sell more food. A guaranteed price gives farmers greater incentives to obtain credit to make investments in soil health, water management, and higher quality seeds. If scaled up, this approach could generate significant agricultural demand. But there are few examples of school feeding programs designed to benefit local agricultural production.

In a recent study commissioned by the Task Force on Hunger, Ahmed and Sharma (2004) concluded that if school feeding programs with locally produced foods are successful in inducing farmers to adopt modern technology in maize production, then they have the potential to substantially benefit producers and consumers throughout Sub-Saharan Africa. The authors assumed that 50 million primary school–age children (about half the total population) would receive homegrown school feeding. They estimated that in aggregate terms, the supply for maize shifts by 30 percent (translating into a 26.6 percent increase in production from the 2003 baseline), and the demand curve by 20.1 percent.

The greater shift in supply results in a net 7 percent decrease in the unit cost of maize from the 2003 baseline price. But the total cost of production increases by 17.8 percent—mainly due to a 26.6 percent increase in total maize production from the 2003 baseline. The 26.6 percent increase in maize production (9.09 million metric tons) will satisfy the additional maize demand of 7.4 million metric tons for homegrown school feeding.

The total incremental benefits of homegrown school feeding on maize production are potentially worth about $1.6 billion a year in 2003 prices. Of this total, 57 percent would go to consumers, and 43 percent to producers. With the high variability among African countries in development level, market conditions, infrastructure development, political and economic situations, and prices, the authors had to make several assumptions about commodity prices, demand and supply elasticities, maize production market surpluses, and numbers of beneficiaries. But maize or another staple cereal is only part of a balanced homegrown school meals program, so the benefits to local food demand are likely to be higher.

It bears mentioning that there is no single standard for school-meal rations. Normally rations are designed to provide between 400 and 1,200 kilocalories a day. But they vary by gender, age, cultural preference, and location. For example, sorghum is the dominant cereal in Sudan, but depending on the potential for local purchase, other cereals such as millet or wheat are sometimes used. In addition, the number of products used in homegrown school feeding

Homegrown feeding can be fully incorporated into broader community programs

varies widely, and there is no standard share of total calories from the main cereal (Webb 2005).

The local procurement of food in food delivery programs provides important economic and social synergies through nutritionally balanced meals, produced locally and suited to local tastes. Depending on local circumstances, dietary habits and culture, a meal providing approximately 2,000 kilocalories a day could consist of a carbohydrate base (maize, sorghum, sugar), a protein component (chicken, beans, milk, eggs), a fatty acid component (peanut oil and palm oil for frying), a micronutrient component (mango, passion fruit), vegetables and iodized salt, and local foods that provide both carbohydrates and micronutrients (cassava, bananas). Improved soil fertility and water management, along with rural roads, are critical for the success of such a program. They need to be in place so that small farmers can adopt modern agricultural technology.

Such locally produced meals may not always supply the required amounts of vitamins and minerals for school children, so it may be necessary to fortify the fruits and vegetables with premixes of vitamin A, iodine, iron, and zinc. The harvesting and management of wild foods and vegetables and foods from tree gardens, school orchards, and community forests are also good sources of food for these programs.

Components of homegrown feeding can be fully incorporated into broader community programs. School feeding programs should be expanded to ensure that the children are not only fed a meal at school with locally produced food but also given rations of food to bring back home, offering an economic incentive for families to send children to school, especially girls. Due to the importance of education, especially women's education, in contributing to the reduction of malnutrition (Smith and Haddad 2000), these programs should be linked to community nutrition programs described in the previous section to achieve the most synergistic benefits.

Estimates for Ghana suggest that school lunches cost $0.25 a day per child when the food is sourced locally (totaling $50 a year per child) or $0.19 a day per child if sourced from international food assistance. Such assistance is likely to be needed during startup periods, while contracts with local farmers, delivery systems, and financial accountability mechanisms are being set up. Over time and with greater competition and scale, these costs should fall. The future costs and impacts of such programs will need to be monitored at the national level.

Investments in soil health and water resources

The third synergistic trigger recommended by the Task Force on Hunger is increased investment in soil health and water. As already stated, a large percentage of hungry people in Africa and some parts of Asia and Latin America are smallholder farmers with degraded or nutrient-depleted soils, with inadequate soil organic matter, poor physical structure, poor water-holding capacity, lack of soil nutrients, high risk of erosion, and lack of soil biodiversity. Hunger and poverty reduction in such areas will require significant increases in farm production and reduced risk of failed harvests, possible only if water management, soil health, and productivity can be improved or restored.

Soil health investments should include a combination of technical extension and support services, and external support for asset-building farm investments in soil fertility restoration and maintenance, such as agroforestry, green manure and cover crops, conservation tillage, and mineral fertilizers, depending largely on the local economic context. Soil improvements must be linked to access to improved varieties of both staple food crops and of seeds to green manure and cover crops and agroforestry tree species—as well as with associated activities, such as water harvesting and soil and water conservation. These may be also integrated with land management practices outside farm plots to improve watershed functions and the habitat for wildlife.

Investments to improve water resources should include increasing the availability and quality of water—and the associated health benefits for the

Box 11.4

Watershed restoration and management in Orissa, India

Source: Agragamee 2002a,b.

Despite abundant natural resources, Orissa is one of India's hungriest states. During the hungry period (June–September), communities have resorted to eating ground-up mango pits and other normally inedible forest products. In 2001, 200–300 residents died of starvation. A local NGO, Agragamee, which has worked in Orissa's remote tribal areas for 23 years, coordinates community-based programs to increase food security including watershed management projects.

In the Kodikitunda watershed, Agragamee scientists worked with tribal villagers in a "bottom-up planning process" to design a watershed restoration project including:

- Reforestation of degraded ridgelands, formerly used as upland fields.
- Soil and water conservation through construction of earth berms and terraces, boundary planting, stone gullies to channel runoff, check dams, and water ponds for percolation and irrigation.
- Restoration of soil fertility and water absorption capacity through use of nitrogen-fixing trees, including *Simarouba glauca* (a drought-resistant tree that produces oil, processed by the village women's group).
- Crop diversification and intensification, including rice, maize, cashews, spices (turmeric), and fruits (banana, lychee, mango, jackfruit, papaya, and lemon).
- Redevelopment of barren lowlands into rice paddy fields.

By 2002 agricultural production had increased about 70 percent, and cropping intensity 37 percent. Both incomes and health have reportedly improved as a result.

To complement these activities, villagers founded a grain bank to ensure against food shortages. They also created a community savings fund to provide loans and help support the village school. And they lobbied for government funds to establish a road to their village (previously inaccessible by vehicle), helping establish minimal links to agricultural markets. Agragamee managed this project for the first five years (1994–99), after which it was taken over by the Village Watershed Users Association. A model in the region, it continues to show good results.

Water management programs should be based on community action

poor. Water quality will continue to grow in importance with the expansion of periurban livestock, agriculture, and chemical-intensive horticulture production—and with the need to combat waterborne disease to improve health and nutrition, especially for children. Water management programs should be based on community action, but in some cases the scale of the problem or the effectiveness of solutions requires that investment programs be coordinated at district, watershed, or ecosystem level (box 11.4).

The Task Force on Hunger thus recommends kick-starting agriculture-driven rural economic growth by encouraging major and sustained public investment in soil health and water management. Such initiatives are needed in most African countries, as well as in other parts of the world that face similar constraints, until producers overcome this soil infertility-poverty trap. The task force recommends two soil fertility interventions that will assist the food-insecure farmer: voucher systems to reduce input costs and agroforestry fertilizer trees, green manures, and cover crops.

Voucher systems to reduce input costs. There is a tremendous need to reduce the costs of purchased inputs. Various interventions have been shown to have the potential to reduce the costs of inputs that help to improve soil health (Breman and Debrah 2003; IFDC 2003). First, bulk purchases to supply several countries in a region can significantly reduce the unit costs of inputs (as in East Africa). Second, targeted voucher schemes can get subsidized inputs to those most in need without risking the corruption and excesses of earlier subsidy schemes. The schemes would operate as follows:

- Identify poor farmers who qualify for subsidies (say, those who earn less than $1 a day) with NGOs playing a key role, and make sure that sufficient attention is given to women-headed farming families. Farmers in need are then given vouchers for the purchase of inputs, in the form of "smart cards" with picture identification and electronic information, as used successfully in South Africa.
- Use private retailers or agrodealers to redeem the vouchers and deliver the goods. Learn from past experience that direct delivery by government or agencies is detrimental to the private sector, hampering its growth. The retailers exchange the vouchers for money supplied by a government or donor agency.
- Train village-level extension workers to educate farmers to use mineral and organic fertilizers effectively and return crop residues to the soil—and to issue certificates of compliance that subsidized inputs are used in the receiving farmer's fields, to maintain the validity of the smart card for future use.
- Include a sunset clause, so that the subsidies are gradually phased out over a given number of years. In view of the need for long-term commitments if economic development is to take off, this should take about a decade.

Governments and donors, working with the private sector, are the key players in reducing input costs

The key ingredients for the success of voucher schemes thus include the presence of traders and their central role in the scheme, a rigorous targeting and monitoring system, an accountable and transparent system for allocating vouchers, an efficient system for redeeming vouchers, and a sunset clause, typically leading to the reduction of subsidies after 5 years and their total elimination after 10 years. Governments and donors, working closely with the private sector, are the key players in reducing input costs.

Although greater reliance on the private sector for input supply is a step in the right direction, withdrawal by the state from direct trading in such inputs as fertilizers will not ensure that smallholders have access to them, since the private sector may be too weak to step into the vacuum. When state operations are withdrawn, a more gradual scaling down is required than has sometimes been practiced—otherwise a vacuum will almost certainly occur.

At least four conditions must be met to give smallholder farmers access to mineral fertilizers, including highly reactive phosphate rocks:

- The fertilizer sector must have enough competition to keep fertilizer prices low. Governments need to ensure that importers can procure from the lowest priced sources in international markets, and that domestic entrepreneurs and traders have easy entry into the fertilizer distribution business.
- Financial incentives and technical support should be provided to traders operating in remote areas with poor transport links, to persuade them to integrate fertilizer into their operations. If this is not done, fertilizer prices will remain high and supplies will be unreliable.
- Government initiatives are needed to train market entrants in financial transactions and in technical knowledge about the products and how farmers should use them.
- Subsidies need to be strictly time-bound to be fiscally sustainable and well targeted to avoid subsidizing fertilizer use by larger, wealthier cultivators. If properly structured, these can be viewed as investments in restoring productive capacity.

This intervention needs to be linked with interventions that build capacity in logistics and management of these expanded smallholder input delivery systems. It also requires training large numbers of local people to serve as extensionists in their communities, and to facilitate farmers' access to specialized technical information, research findings, and technical knowledge in other communities. Integrated nutrient management strategies (and pest management strategies), combining inorganic and organic nutrient sources and crop rotations, should be pursued.

Agroforestry fertilizer trees, green manures, and cover crops. Agroforestry techniques provide multiple benefits. The main purpose of using agroforestry fertilizer trees (improved leguminous tree fallows) is to capture nitrogen from the

Fertilizer trees also generate benefits related to other Goals

air and incorporate it into the soil where maize or other cereal crops are grown, all at very low cost. This technique can bring an array of benefits to the agricultural productivity of smallholder families:

- A doubling or tripling of maize yields for yields starting from a chronically low base (less than a ton per hectare).
- Recycling other nutrients from the soil, including potassium, calcium, magnesium, sulfur, and micronutrients.
- Reducing weed growth and eliminating the parasitic weed striga.
- Increasing the water-holding capacity of the soil, which reduces vulnerability to drought. During the 2003 drought in Malawi, thousands of farmers who used fertilizer trees obtained low maize yields (about a ton per hectare) while neighbors using mineral or no fertilizer obtained zero yields.

Fertilizer trees also generate benefits related to other Goals, such as:

- Poverty and energy. One-third of a hectare of fertilizer trees provide enough fuelwood for a typical farm household to cook for a year. Farmers can also generate income by selling the fuelwood and crop surpluses from the fertilizer trees.
- Gender. Obtaining fuelwood from their own fields can save women 6–12 hours of hard labor per week, which they can spend caring for family or resting.
- Environment. The fuelwood produced by fertilizer trees reduces wood-gathering in nearby forests and woodlands, reducing deforestation and

Box 11.5

How a smallholder farmer diversified and got out of absolute poverty

Source: Stewart 2004.

Harrison Akumoye farms one hectare of terraced sloping land in Vihiga District in Western Kenya. His maize yields tripled when he restored soil health by using nitrogen-fixing trees, phosphate rock applications, and biomass transfers of the Mexican sunflower that he planted on all his internal farm boundaries.

Realizing that he could feed his family with only a portion of his farm, Akumoye gradually converted his hectare into a diverse enterprise. He grew kale and tomatoes and sold them to the nearby market in Luanda, using mainly biomass transfers. He planted napier grass *(Pennisetum purpureum)* in a field and Calliandra, a nitrogen-fixing tree that produces high-protein fodder and nectar for bees along bunds.

He fed the napier grass and Calliandra leaves to a high-grade milk cow obtained from Heifer International. He now has several cows and sells milk to neighbors. He also planted bananas which he fertilized with Mexican sunflower biomass. He planted *Grevillea robusta* trees for poles and timber and established a small tree nursery to sell fruit, timber, and fertilizer trees to farmers. Fruit trees and passion fruit vines now surround his house. His wife grows grain, legumes, and vegetables for home consumption.

He estimated his income at less than $1 a day in 1997. Six years later it was $10 a day. His house has a zinc roof, also used to harvest rainwater. All his children go to school, wear clean clothes and shoes, and are well nourished. Now a leader in his church, he is building a church for his community.

helping preserve biodiversity. In addition, fertilizer trees sequester considerable amounts of carbon in the soil (1–2 tons of carbon per hectare a year), contributing to the mitigation of climate change.

Much can happen when a poor farmer diversifies through agroforestry and into such high-value products as milk, tomatoes, onions, or kale (box 11.5).

Glossary

Food security

Food security exists when all people, at all times, have physical and economic access to sufficient, safe, and nutritious food to meet their dietary needs and food preferences for an active and healthy life (FAO 1996). This definition is in keeping with the principle that everyone has a right to adequate food, to be free from hunger, and to enjoy general human dignity, enshrined in the International Bill of Human Rights (ECOSOC 1999). The definition also makes it clear that food production does not equal food security.

Food insecurity

Food insecurity is the absence of food security.

Gender

As distinct from biological sex, refers to the socially constructed roles of women and men.

Hunger

A condition in which people lack the basic food intake to provide them with the energy and nutrients for fully productive, active lives. It is an outcome of food insecurity. All hungry people are food-insecure, but not all food-insecure people are hungry.

Low birthweight

Newborn infants who weigh less than 2.5 kilograms at birth.

Macronutrients

The proteins, carbohydrates and fats that are required by the body in large amounts and that are available to be used for energy. Measured in grams.

Malnutrition
Malnutrition results from the interaction of inadequate diet and infection, reflected in poor infant growth and an excess of morbidity and mortality in adults and children alike.

Micronutrients
The vitamins, minerals, and certain other substances required by the body in small amounts. Measured in milligrams or micrograms.

Overnutrition
An excess of certain nutrients such as saturated fats and added sugars in combination with low levels of physical activity.

Overweight and obesity
Body weight that is above normal as a result of an excessive accumulation of fat. It is usually a manifestation of overnourishment. Overweight is defined as a body mass index between 25 and 30 and obesity as a body mass index greater than 30.

Stunting
Low height-for-age, reflecting a sustained past episode or episodes of undernutrition.

Undernourishment
Inadequate consumption of food. Individuals in households consuming less than about 1,900 K calories per capita, depending on age, sex, and height, are considered undernourished, using the FAO's measure based on distribution of household consumption and availability of dietary energy.

Undernutrition
The result of undernourishment, poor absorption, or poor biological use of nutrients consumed.

Underweight
Low weight-for-age in children, and body mass index below 18.5 in adults, reflecting a current condition resulting from inadequate food intake, past episodes of undernutrition, or poor health conditions.

Vulnerability
The presence of factors that place people at risk of becoming food-insecure or malnourished, including factors that affect their ability to cope.

Wasting

Low weight-for-height, generally the result of weight loss associated with a recent period of starvation or disease.

Papers commissioned by the Task Force on Hunger

1. An Assessment of Hunger Hotspots
Deborah Balk, Rafael Flor, Joanne Gaskell, Marc Levy, Manohar Sharma, Adam Storeygard, Center for International Earth Science Information Network

2. Building Political Will to End Hunger
David Beckmann, Emily Byers, Bread for the World

3. The Case for Fertilizer Subsidies for Subsistence Farmers
Jeffrey Sachs, The Earth Institute at Columbia University

4. China's Fight Against Hunger and Poverty: Lessons for Asia
Swarna S. Vepa, Lavanya Ravikanth Anneboina, Ruchita Manghnani, M.S. Swaminathan Research Foundation

5. Climate Variability and the Millennium Development Goal Hunger Target
James W. Hansen, Maxx Dilley, Lisa Goddard, Esther Ebrahimian, Polly Ericksen, International Research Institute for Climate Prediction

6. Costs of Halving Global Hunger: Reducing Micronutrient Deficiencies and Child Underweight Prevalence in Accord with Millennium Development Goals #1 and #4
Joseph Michael Hunt, International Food Policy Research Institute

7. Efficient and Sustainable Water Management in Small-scale Farming

Daniel Hillel, Center for Climate Systems Research, Columbia University

8. Food for Education: A Review of Program Impacts

Natalia Caldes and Akhter U. Ahmed, International Food Policy Research Institute

9. Food-for-Education Programs with Locally Produced Food: Effects on Farmers and Consumers in Sub-Saharan Africa

Akhter U. Ahmed, Manohar Sharma, International Food Policy Research Institute

10. Halving Hunger by 2015: A Framework for Action in the Asia Pacific Region

Swarna S. Vepa, Lavanya Ravikanth Anneboina, Ruchita Manghnani, M.S. Swaminathan Research Foundation

11. HIV/AIDS and Hunger

Stuart Gillespie and Suneetha Kadiyala, International Food Policy Research Institute

12. Increasing Donor Effectiveness in Agricultural Lending

Andrew Goodland and Kevin Cleaver, Agriculture and Rural Development Department, World Bank

13. Micro-level Analysis of Determinants of Underweight Children in Asia

Swarna S. Vepa, Lavanya Ravikanth Anneboina, Ruchita Manghnani, M.S. Swaminathan Research Foundation

14. The Role of Collective Action in Fighting Hunger

Ruth Meinzen-Dick and Monica DiGregorio, International Food Policy Research Institute

15. Towards Achieving the Hunger and Malnutrition Millennium Development Goal: Tailoring Potential Country-Level Solutions to Needs—The "Candidate Actions"

Kavita Sethuraman and Kathleen Kurz, International Center for Research on Women, Meera Shekar, World Bank

Subregional data on underweight prevalence

Table A3.1
Africa

Note: Numbers in bold indicate an underweight prevalence of 20 percent or more; numbers in italics indicate a population of more than 100,000 underweight children. Underweight rates are for the survey year indicated. All populations are approximate.

a. Where year range extends to more than two years, the data used come from one or more unspecified years within the range.

— Not available.

Source: ORC-Macro 2004; African Nutrition Database Initiative; UNICEF 2002, 2003b, 2004; CIESEN 2004; UN Population Division 2002.

Country and subnational region	Under-weight prevalence	Population of underweight children (thousands)	Population density of underweight children (per square kilometer)	Total population 2000 (thousands)	Year of survey[a]
Algeria					
Centre	3.8	45	0.6	10,841	2000
Est	4.6	47	0.5	9,278	2000
Ouest	4.7	32	0.5	6,205	2000
Sud	15.2	41	0.0	2,466	2000
Angola					
Região Capital	**25.0**	*138*	2.1	2,825	2001
Região Centro Sul	**32.0**	93	0.4	1,484	2001
Região Este	**27.6**	44	0.1	815	2001
Região Norte	**32.1**	*149*	0.8	2,361	2001
Região Oeste	**32.9**	*103*	1.1	1,592	2001
Região Sul	**39.9**	*258*	0.8	3,305	2001
Benin					
Atacora	**26.6**	38	1.2	814	2001
Atlantique	18.0	41	13.7	1,289	2001
Borgou	**28.6**	52	1.0	1,036	2001
Mono	**20.0**	31	7.5	869	2001
Oueme	**22.3**	45	10.1	1,141	2001
Zou	**23.3**	43	2.2	1,035	2001
Botswana					
Central, Selebi-Phikwe, Orapa, and Sowa	13.2	8	0.1	449	2000
Gaborone	7.0	2	1.1	153	2000
Ghanzi	**30.6**	0	0.0	1	2000
Kgalagadi	12.7	0	0.0	1	2000
Kgatleng	7.1	1	0.1	62	2000
Kweneng	15.4	4	0.1	201	2000
North West	11.4	1	0.0	63	2000
Northeast (incl. Francistown)	13.0	2	0.4	116	2000

Table A3.1

Africa

(continued)

Country and subnational region	Under-weight prevalence	Population of underweight children (thousands)	Population density of underweight children (per square kilometer)	Total population 2000 (thousands)	Year of survey[a]
South East and Lobatse	10.1	2	0.9	116	2000
Southern and Jwaneng	16.8	3	0.1	117	2000
Burkina Faso					
Central, South	**33.1**	*228*	5.0	3,473	1998–99
East	**32.9**	*193*	2.2	2,965	1998–99
North	**36.8**	*148*	2.6	2,029	1998–99
West	**36.2**	*205*	2.4	2,860	1998–99
Burundi					
East	**44.2**	54	9.6	691	2000
Middle	**54.7**	*140*	28.8	1,445	2000
North	**47.0**	*166*	28.0	1,990	2000
South	**35.9**	50	11.5	782	2000
West	**29.2**	73	18.4	1,421	2000
Cameroon					
Central, south, and east	19.5	*113*	0.5	3,670	1998
North, Extreme north, and Adamaoua	**33.4**	*228*	1.4	4,321	1998
Northwest and southwest	13.6	55	1.3	2,545	1998
West and littoral	10.1	63	1.9	3,977	1998
Central African Republic					
Bamingui-Bangoran	**28.6**	0	0.0	4	2000
Bangui	19.7	14	152.1	423	2000
Basse-Kotto	**32.7**	14	0.8	254	2000
Haute-Kotto	15.6	1	0.0	55	2000
Kemo	19.1	3	0.2	110	2000
Lobaye	**28.2**	10	0.6	222	2000
Mambere-Kadei	**25.5**	13	0.4	301	2000
Mbomou	**28.0**	7	0.1	144	2000
Nana-Grebizi	**24.1**	5	0.3	125	2000
Nana-Mambere	**25.4**	10	0.4	247	2000
Ombella-M'poko	**27.1**	16	0.5	356	2000
Ouaka	**31.0**	14	0.3	270	2000
Ouham	**22.1**	12	0.2	336	2000
Ouham-Pende	**26.9**	17	0.6	392	2000
Sangha-Mbaere	**24.4**	3	0.2	83	2000
Vakaga	**31.2**	0	0.0	4	2000
Comoros					
Mwali	**40.7**	2	10.1	24	2000
Ndzuwani	**36.2**	11	32.1	183	2000
Ngazidja	**22.1**	9	10.1	254	2000
Congo, Dem. Rep.					
Bandundu	**35.5**	*387*	1.3	5,803	2001
Bas-Congo	**37.0**	*215*	4.0	3,090	2001
Equateur	**33.0**	*347*	0.9	5,598	2001
Kasai Occidental	**34.8**	*243*	1.6	3,718	2001
Kasai Oriental	**31.0**	*262*	1.6	4,488	2001
Katanga	**34.3**	*412*	0.9	6,389	2001

Table A3.1

Africa

(continued)

Country and subnational region	Under-weight prevalence	Population of underweight children (thousands)	Population density of underweight children (per square kilometer)	Total population 2000 (thousands)	Year of survey[a]
Kinshasa	19.0	*179*	16.6	5,023	2001
Maniema	**40.0**	94	0.7	1,249	2001
Nord-Kivu	**35.5**	*274*	4.8	4,102	2001
Oriental	**27.9**	*344*	0.7	6,556	2001
Sud-Kivu	**37.5**	*249*	4.3	3,538	2001
Côte d'Ivoire					
Center	**25.5**	40	1.8	1,014	1994
Center East	**28.6**	17	2.5	398	1994
Center North	**21.5**	40	1.2	1,215	1994
Center West	**23.0**	78	2.6	2,218	1994
North	**36.0**	51	1.3	930	1994
North East	**28.1**	31	0.8	726	1994
North West	**30.0**	35	0.7	759	1994
South	18.4	*142*	3.7	5,045	1994
South West	**23.1**	51	2.0	1,451	1994
West	**28.0**	66	2.2	1,537	1994
Egypt					
Alexandria	1.9	7	3.4	3,192	2000
Assuit	10.3	41	21.6	3,257	2000
Aswan	7.8	10	0.8	1,039	2000
Behera	3.5	20	1.7	4,755	2000
Beni Suef	6.1	15	3.2	2,038	2000
Cairo	2.5	24	7.2	7,723	2000
Dakahlia	2.3	14	3.9	4,897	2000
Damietta	6.8	6	10.4	681	2000
Fayoum	3.5	10	1.6	2,244	2000
Gharbia	3.6	16	9.1	3,711	2000
Ismailia	4.8	5	1.0	927	2000
Kafr El-Shei	4.2	14	4.3	2,732	2000
Kalyubia	1.3	5	5.3	3,358	2000
Matroh	1.8	0	0.0	198	2000
Menoufia	1.9	7	4.8	2,958	2000
Menya	5.5	25	1.3	3,720	2000
New Valley	3.4	1	0.0	261	2000
North Sinai	1.8	1	0.0	300	2000
Port Said	2.8	0	1.3	118	2000
Qena	8.7	34	14.8	3,214	2000
Red Sea	4.7	2	0.0	282	2000
Sharkia	2.3	14	2.9	5,066	2000
Souhag	6.3	27	16.0	3,525	2000
South Sinai	1.1	0	0.0	60	2000
Suez	5.0	3	0.3	500	2000
Equatorial Guinea					
Continental	**20.2**	12	0.5	340	2000
Insular	14.7	2	1.3	91	2000
Eritrea					
Anseba	**46.7**	39	1.8	472	2002
Debub	**34.6**	53	5.4	866	2002
Debubawi Keih Bahri	**41.1**	9	0.4	127	2002

Table A3.1

Africa

(continued)

Country and subnational region	Under-weight prevalence	Population of underweight children (thousands)	Population density of underweight children (per square kilometer)	Total population 2000 (thousands)	Year of survey[a]
Gash-Barka	**49.6**	75	2.2	846	2002
Maekel	**23.4**	13	12.4	315	2002
Semenawi Keih Bahri	**51.2**	87	2.5	951	2002
Ethiopia					
Addis	13.9	58	107.4	2,333	2000
Affar	**50.7**	*250*	2.0	2,737	2000
Amhara	**51.5**	*1,503*	9.8	16,218	2000
Ben-Gumz	**42.9**	44	0.9	573	2000
Dire Dawa	**30.9**	16	12.6	289	2000
Gambela	**38.3**	10	0.4	142	2000
Harari	**27.0**	7	17.8	135	2000
Oromiya	**42.9**	*1,698*	4.8	21,993	2000
SNNP	**52.5**	*1,139*	10.4	12,057	2000
Somali	**43.4**	*169*	0.7	2,168	2000
Tigray	**48.3**	*317*	6.5	3,651	2000
Gabon					
Est	14.5	4	0.1	170	2000
Nord	16.0	4	0.0	165	2000
Ouest	9.1	8	0.1	561	2000
Sud	17.7	3	0.1	130	2000
Ghana					
Ashanti Region	**24.7**	*135*	5.5	3,750	1998
Brong Ahafo Region	**24.1**	63	1.7	1,799	1998
Central Region	**26.3**	61	6.3	1,587	1998
Eastern Region	**22.3**	73	4.3	2,228	1998
Greater Accra Region	12.2	49	16.4	2,745	1998
Northern Region	**38.2**	*104*	1.5	1,862	1998
Upper East Region	**34.0**	45	5.2	910	1998
Upper West Region	**28.4**	24	1.3	572	1998
Volta Region	**24.7**	62	3.5	1,729	1998
Western Region	**25.6**	70	2.9	1,877	1998
Guinea					
Central Guinea	**26.2**	89	1.6	1,908	1999
Conakry	19.1	0	0.6	5	1999
Lower Guinea	**23.3**	88	2.0	2,114	1999
Upper Guinea	**24.4**	75	0.7	1,723	1999
Guinea-Bissau					
Autonomous Sector of Bissau (SAB)	13.9	5	64.1	167	2000
Bafata	**29.9**	11	1.9	191	2000
Biombo	18.0	3	4.6	94	2000
Bolama, Bijagos	16.8	1	0.7	23	2000
Cacheu	**23.4**	9	1.9	192	2000
Gabu	**38.9**	11	1.2	148	2000
Oio	**33.5**	12	2.3	191	2000
Quinara	**26.3**	2	0.9	46	2000
Tombali	**23.9**	4	1.1	77	2000
Kenya					
Central	15.4	*104*	8.1	4,509	2000

Table A3.1
Africa
(continued)

Country and subnational region	Underweight prevalence	Population of underweight children (thousands)	Population density of underweight children (per square kilometer)	Total population 2000 (thousands)	Year of survey[a]
Coast	**21.1**	78	1.0	2,467	2000
Eastern	**29.6**	*228*	1.5	5,132	2000
Nairobi	12.4	30	42.0	1,594	2000
North Eastern (Urban only)	—	—	—	452	2000
Nyanza	19.9	*157*	13.1	5,252	2000
Rift Valley	**24.9**	*267*	1.6	7,152	2000
Western	**21.5**	*119*	14.1	3,684	2000
Lesotho					
Berea	13.3	5	2.5	279	2000
Butha-Buthe	**20.6**	3	1.7	110	2000
Leribe	17.4	7	2.6	308	2000
Mafeteng	15.9	5	2.2	237	2000
Maseru	13.1	7	1.8	412	2000
Mohale's Hoek	**25.4**	7	2.0	200	2000
Mokhotlong	**23.4**	3	0.7	92	2000
Qacha's Nek	**28.8**	3	1.3	76	2000
Quthing	18.5	3	1.2	136	2000
Thaba-Tseka	**22.9**	5	0.9	147	2000
Libyan Arab Jamahiriya					
Bengasi	3.8	3	0.1	834	1995
El-Zawia	3.5	2	0.2	559	1995
Gulf of Serte	6.7	7	0.0	936	1995
Jabel El-Achder	4.0	2	0.0	407	1995
Jabel El-Gharbi	6.7	2	0.0	212	1995
Sebha	6.7	1	0.0	90	1995
Tripoli	3.8	6	1.6	1,528	1995
Madagascar					
Antananarivo	**43.8**	*363*	6.2	4,628	1997
Antsiranana	**31.8**	65	1.5	1,149	1997
Fianarantsoa	**44.1**	*259*	2.6	3,277	1997
Mahajanga	**34.2**	*102*	0.7	1,674	1997
Toamasina	**40.2**	*184*	2.6	2,563	1997
Toliary	**34.3**	*132*	0.8	2,157	1997
Malawi					
Central	**27.9**	*247*	6.8	4,627	2000
North	17.4	47	1.7	1,408	2000
South	**25.0**	*244*	7.5	5,112	2000
Mali					
Gao	**36.2**	77	0.1	1,079	2001
Kayes	**32.0**	71	0.6	1,132	2001
Koulikoro	**25.8**	*131*	1.4	2,584	2001
Mopti	**33.7**	95	1.1	1,433	2001
Segou	**36.5**	*118*	1.9	1,638	2001
Sikasso	**40.7**	*233*	3.3	2,902	2001
Mauritania					
Nouakchott	**24.8**	23	17.0	537	2000–01
Zone Centre	**34.9**	28	0.2	459	2000–01
Zone Fleuve	**37.1**	55	0.4	857	2000–01

Table A3.1

Africa

(continued)

Country and subnational region	Under-weight prevalence	Population of underweight children (thousands)	Population density of underweight children (per square kilometer)	Total population 2000 (thousands)	Year of survey[a]
Zone Sud	**34.5**	24	0.1	394	2000–01
Morocco					
Centre	10.1	84	2.0	7,575	1992
Centre Nord	8.0	31	0.7	3,495	1992
Centre Sud	6.2	14	0.3	2,085	1992
Nord Ouest	7.3	48	1.6	5,916	1992
Oriental	3.9	9	0.2	2,078	1992
Sud	17.1	62	0.2	3,279	1992
Tensift	9.9	44	1.1	4,058	1992
Mozambique					
Cabo Delgado	**49.8**	*124*	1.6	1,479	1997
Cidade de Maputo	9.0	2	33.2	120	1997
Gaza	15.7	32	0.4	1,225	1997
Inhambane	17.8	38	0.6	1,275	1997
Manica	**33.6**	70	1.1	1,245	1997
Maputo	5.7	19	0.8	1,987	1997
Nampula	**29.1**	*159*	2.0	3,256	1997
Niassa	**38.1**	56	0.5	875	1997
Sofala	**25.4**	62	0.9	1,457	1997
Tete	**41.4**	100	1.0	1,437	1997
Zambezia	**33.2**	*180*	1.7	3,234	1997
Namibia					
Caprivi	18.2	2	0.1	60	2000
Erongo	8.9	1	0.0	51	2000
Hardap	**22.2**	1	0.0	27	2000
Karas	13.7	1	0.0	31	2000
Kavango	**28.3**	7	0.1	145	2000
Khomas	19.1	7	0.2	213	2000
Kunene	17.3	0	0.0	2	2000
Ohangwena	**35.6**	12	1.1	201	2000
Omaheke	**25.7**	0	0.0	8	2000
Omusati	**28.3**	9	0.3	193	2000
Oshana	**22.8**	5	0.7	145	2000
Oshikoto	**26.7**	6	0.2	128	2000
Otjozondjupa	15.9	2	0.0	61	2000
Niger					
Agadez	**35.7**	13	0.0	166	2000
Dosso	**37.7**	*119*	4.2	1,495	2000
Maradi	**46.0**	*201*	5.2	2,068	2000
Tahoua	**33.2**	*131*	1.3	1,870	2000
Tillaberi (incl. Niamey)	**33.6**	*181*	2.0	2,546	2000
Zinder Diffa	**51.0**	*247*	0.9	2,292	2000
Nigeria					
Central	**23.9**	*849*	2.7	20,540	1999
North East	**38.0**	*1,438*	6.5	21,870	1999
North West	**45.2**	*1,418*	8.2	18,137	1999
South East	18.3	*760*	10.3	24,009	1999
South West	**25.1**	*1,237*	11.2	28,497	1999

Table A3.1
Africa
(continued)

Country and subnational region	Under-weight prevalence	Population of underweight children (thousands)	Population density of underweight children (per square kilometer)	Total population 2000 (thousands)	Year of survey[a]
Rwanda					
Butare	**27.0**	40	21.9	823	2000
Byumba	**30.4**	33	19.1	605	2000
Cyangugu	**29.4**	26	15.2	502	2000
Gikongoro	**31.4**	29	14.6	511	2000
Gisenyi	**20.0**	27	17.5	763	2000
Gitarama	**30.9**	51	23.7	914	2000
Kibungo	**36.6**	40	13.9	615	2000
Kibuye	**31.1**	28	20.7	510	2000
Kigali-Rural	**25.0**	47	15.4	1,047	2000
Kigali-ville	**21.8**	7	151.9	177	2000
Ruhengeri	**28.2**	41	25.6	813	2000
Umutura	**28.7**	15	3.6	283	2000
Senegal					
Diourbel	**24.6**	33	7.6	820	2000
Fatick	**24.5**	28	3.4	689	2000
Kaolack	**35.8**	60	3.9	1,023	2000
Kolda	**33.2**	42	2.0	774	2000
Louga	**20.9**	23	0.8	676	2000
Saint Louis	**21.5**	29	0.7	831	2000
Tambacounda	**32.5**	26	0.4	479	2000
Thies	16.0	32	4.8	1,222	2000
Ziguinchor	18.2	15	2.2	511	2000
Sierra Leone					
East	**34.6**	70	4.4	1,125	2000
North	**30.5**	76	2.2	1,392	2000
South	**24.7**	38	1.9	854	2000
West	**21.3**	34	60.1	879	2000
Somalia					
Central, South	**27.5**	*247*	1.2	4,467	2000
Northeast	**26.8**	*132*	0.5	2,450	2000
Northwest	**21.0**	55	0.3	1,305	2000
South Africa					
Eastern Cape	11.4	83	0.5	6,588	1995
Free State	13.0	39	0.3	2,718	1995
Gauteng	5.9	51	2.8	7,839	1995
KwaZulu Natal	3.8	37	0.4	8,706	1995
Mpumalanga	7.4	27	0.3	3,228	1995
North West	13.4	51	0.4	3,444	1995
Northern Cape	15.9	14	0.0	766	1995
Northern Province	12.6	72	0.6	5,114	1995
Prince Edwards Islands	—	—	—	—	1995
Western Cape	6.5	28	0.2	3,916	1995
Sudan					
Al-Gadarif	**51.3**	67	1.0	854	2000
Al-Gazira	**43.8**	*149*	6.1	2,244	2000
Blue Nile	**45.3**	38	1.0	555	2000
Kassala	**35.2**	72	1.6	1,353	2000
Khartoum	**37.1**	*220*	10.2	3,903	2000

Table A3.1

Africa

(continued)

Country and subnational region	Underweight prevalence	Population of underweight children (thousands)	Population density of underweight children (per square kilometer)	Total population 2000 (thousands)	Year of survey[a]
Northern	**36.6**	26	0.1	469	2000
Northern Darfur	**48.9**	*103*	0.3	1,392	2000
Northern Kordufan	**51.2**	*125*	0.7	1,604	2000
Red Sea	**43.4**	70	0.4	1,068	2000
River Nile	**39.9**	61	0.5	1,008	2000
Sinnar	**46.4**	99	2.4	1,404	2000
Southern Darfur	**41.2**	*127*	1.0	2,024	2000
Southern Kordufan	**34.2**	63	0.8	1,218	2000
Southern Sudan	—	—	—	5,786	2000
Western Darfur	**40.0**	97	1.5	1,602	2000
Western Kordufan	**47.5**	87	0.8	1,205	2000
White Nile	**45.2**	*129*	3.2	1,878	2000
Swaziland					
Hhohho	11.1	4	1.2	241	2000
Lubombo	10.3	3	0.5	195	2000
Manzini	9.4	4	1.0	270	2000
Shiselweni	13.3	4	1.1	196	2000
Tanzania, United Republic					
Arusha	**35.1**	*143*	1.8	2,338	1996
Coast	**34.3**	92	2.9	1,546	1996
Dar es Salaam	**22.2**	62	62.1	1,594	1996
Dodoma	**34.2**	*103*	2.5	1,724	1996
Iringa	**48.2**	*130*	2.3	1,555	1996
Kigoma	**43.1**	*125*	3.2	1,660	1996
Kilimanjaro	**21.0**	53	4.1	1,442	1996
Lindi	**41.4**	57	0.9	795	1996
Mara	18.9	44	2.2	1,339	1996
Mbeya	**20.8**	75	1.2	2,059	1996
Morogoro	**25.5**	79	1.1	1,775	1996
Mtwara	**35.6**	69	4.0	1,107	1996
Mwanza	**27.0**	*136*	7.5	2,903	1996
Pemba	**42.7**	23	29.1	312	1996
Rest of Zanzibar	**26.0**	21	15.7	474	1996
Rukwa	**30.5**	58	0.9	1,093	1996
Ruvuma	**29.4**	58	0.9	1,134	1996
Shinyanga	**27.8**	*134*	2.7	2,761	1996
Singida	**28.4**	54	1.1	1,097	1996
Tabora	14.2	42	0.6	1,683	1996
Tanga	**36.2**	*103*	3.9	1,642	1996
Gambia, The					
Banjul	7.8	0	50.9	19	2000
Basse	**26.7**	8	3.6	176	2000
Brikama	13.3	7	4.0	335	2000
Janjabureh	**31.2**	4	3.2	87	2000
Kanifing	11.6	4	67.3	205	2000
Kerewan	**22.5**	6	2.9	175	2000
Kuntaur	**27.1**	4	2.3	90	2000
Mansakonko	18.6	2	1.4	69	2000

Table A3.1
Africa
(continued)

Country and subnational region	Under-weight prevalence	Population of underweight children (thousands)	Population density of underweight children (per square kilometer)	Total population 2000 (thousands)	Year of survey[a]
Togo					
Centrale	**24.5**	22	1.7	522	1998
Kara	**24.2**	25	2.1	614	1998
Marities	**20.2**	58	9.5	1,708	1998
Plateaux	**24.2**	43	2.5	1,041	1998
Savanes	**38.8**	34	3.9	523	1998
Tunisia					
Centre Est	3.4	6	0.4	1,981	2000
Centre Ouest	6.5	8	0.4	1,353	2000
Grand Tunis	2.3	4	1.5	1,919	2000
Nord Est	3.1	4	0.4	1,284	2000
Nord Ouest	4.5	5	0.3	1,266	2000
Sud Est	3.3	2	0.0	830	2000
Sud Ouest	5.5	3	0.1	542	2000
Uganda					
Central	**21.1**	*301*	7.6	6,950	2000–01
Eastern	**27.3**	*317*	10.6	5,669	2000–01
Kitgum	—	—	—	1,301	2000–01
Northern	**31.6**	*219*	3.5	3,377	2000–01
Western	**23.8**	*285*	6.3	5,840	2000–01
Zambia					
Central	**26.6**	48	0.5	1,000	2000–01
Copperbelt	**29.0**	84	2.7	1,605	2000–01
Eastern	**32.1**	77	1.1	1,336	2000–01
Luapula	**33.0**	47	1.0	797	2000–01
Lusaka	**21.7**	57	2.5	1,456	2000–01
Northern	**33.8**	77	0.5	1,263	2000–01
Northwestern	**27.1**	27	0.2	549	2000–01
Southern	**23.6**	52	0.6	1,213	2000–01
Western	**23.7**	33	0.3	763	2000–01
Zimbabwe					
Bulawayo	8.1	8	16.6	614	1999
Harare	5.8	13	15.2	1,517	1999
Manicaland	16.3	45	1.3	1,796	1999
Mashonaland Central	17.4	25	0.9	949	1999
Mashonaland East	15.2	37	1.2	1,610	1999
Masvingo	11.3	22	0.4	1,289	1999
Matabeleland North	18.9	24	0.3	834	1999
Matabeleland South	15.3	17	0.3	710	1999
Midlands	9.9	24	0.5	1,565	1999
Countries without subnational data					
Cape Verde	14.0	7	2.0	352	—
Chad	**38.8**	*553*	0.4	7,501	1996–97
Congo	—	—	—	2,959	—
Djibouti	—	—	—	585	—
Liberia	—	—	—	2,810	—
Mauritius	16.0	15	8.1	1,114	1995–00
São Tomé and Principe	16.0	3	3.5	127	1995–00
Seychelles	6.0	-	-	54	-

Table A3.2

Asia

Note: Numbers in bold indicate an underweight prevalence of 20 percent or more; numbers in italics indicate a population of more than 100,000 underweight children. Underweight rates are for the survey year indicated. All populations are approximate.

a. Where year range extends to more than two years, the data used come from one or more unspecified years within the range.

— Not available.

Source: ORC-Macro 2004; UNICEF 2002, 2003b, 2004; CIESEN 2004; UN Population Division 2002.

Country and subnational region	Underweight prevalence	Population of underweight children (thousands)	Population density of underweight children (per square kilometer)	Total population 2000 (thousands)	Year of survey[a]
Armenia					
Aragatsotn	2.0	0	0.1	197	2000
Ararat	3.3	1	0.4	443	2000
Armavir	1.4	0	0.0	42	2000
Gegharkunik	3.6	1	0.1	306	2000
Kotayk	9.3	2	1.2	496	2000
Lori	0.0	0	0.0	396	2000
Shirak	5.9	1	0.4	361	2000
Syunik	5.2	0	0.1	177	2000
Tavush	1.4	0	0.0	179	2000
Vayots Dzor	4.3	0	0.1	76	2000
Yerevan	0.7	0	1.8	1,086	2000
Bangladesh					
Barisal	**50.7**	*573*	69.9	8,071	1999–00
Chittagong	**46.1**	*1,636*	56.6	25,348	1999–00
Dhaka	**47.4**	*2,760*	93.9	41,592	1999–00
Khulna	**41.8**	*952*	45.0	16,270	1999–00
Rajshahi	**48.6**	*2,257*	66.2	33,177	1999–00
Sylhet	**56.8**	*697*	58.4	8,763	1999–00
Cambodia					
Banteay Mean Chey	**39.5**	41	6.3	671	2000
Bat Dambang, Krong Pailin	**36.4**	51	4.1	903	2000
Kampong Chaam	**47.7**	*140*	14.7	1,883	2000
Kampong Chhnang	**46.5**	35	6.7	488	2000
Kampong Speu	**44.0**	46	6.6	670	2000
Kampong Thum	**48.5**	51	4.1	673	2000
Kampot, Krong Kaeb, Sihanoukville	**39.8**	47	7.8	759	2000
Kandaal	**47.8**	95	27.2	1,280	2000
Kaoh Kong	**41.7**	8	0.7	124	2000
Mondol Kiri, Rotanak Kiri	**54.0**	13	0.5	150	2000
Phnom Penh	**34.9**	65	174.5	1,198	2000
Pousaat	**46.7**	28	2.4	384	2000
Preah Vihear, Stueng Traeng, Kracheh	**47.0**	39	1.0	534	2000
Prey Veaeng	**55.8**	96	19.9	1,103	2000
Siem Reab, Otdar Mean Chey	**49.9**	67	3.9	864	2000
Svaay Rieng	**46.2**	41	14.4	574	2000
Taakaev	**39.9**	60	17.1	964	2000
China					
Anhui	2.8	*129*	0.9	60,762	2002
Beijing	0.5	5	0.3	13,932	2002
Fujian	2.7	71	0.6	34,424	2002
Gansu	5.7	*111*	0.3	25,541	2002
Guangdong	2.3	*150*	0.9	85,992	2002
Guangxi	5.0	*170*	0.7	44,711	2002
Guizhou	6.1	*168*	1.0	36,202	2002

Table A3.2
Asia
(continued)

Country and subnational region	Under-weight prevalence	Population of underweight children (thousands)	Population density of underweight children (per square kilometer)	Total population 2000 (thousands)	Year of survey[a]
Hainan	4.7	27	0.8	7,514	2002
Hebei	3.7	*221*	1.1	78,499	2002
Heilongjiang	1.4	39	0.1	36,792	2002
Henan	5.2	*370*	2.2	93,685	2002
Hong Kong	—	—	—	135	2002
Hubei	2.6	*119*	0.7	60,475	2002
Hunan	2.7	*135*	0.6	65,619	2002
Inner Mongolia	2.6	46	0.0	23,380	2002
Jiangsu	1.5	77	0.9	67,672	2002
Jiangxi	5.2	*164*	1.0	41,442	2002
Jilin	4.6	96	0.5	27,356	2002
Liaoning	1.9	61	0.4	42,519	2002
Nanjin	0.8	3	1.1	4,314	2002
Ningxia	12.6	53	1.0	5,583	2002
Qinghai	5.8	20	0.0	4,500	2002
Shaanxi	3.2	88	0.4	36,286	2002
Shandong	1.8	*126*	0.9	92,109	2002
Shanghai	0.2	3	0.5	16,689	2002
Shanxi	4.1	*104*	0.7	33,341	2002
Sichuan	2.7	*237*	0.4	115,729	2002
Taiwan	—	—	—	20,942	2002
Tibet	6.3	10	0.0	2,166	2002
Xinjiang	2.8	38	0.0	18,040	2002
Yunnan	8.0	*262*	0.7	43,174	2002
Zhejiang	1.6	55	0.6	45,596	2002
Abkhaxia, South Osetia	—	—	—	289	1999
Georgia					
Ajara	3.3	1	0.2	370	1999
Guria, Samegrelo	4.1	2	0.2	-	1999
Kakheti	5.9	2	0.1	465	1999
Kvemo Kartli, Samtskhe-Javakheti	4.2	2	0.1	977	1999
Mtskheta-Mtianeti, Shida Kartli	3.8	1	0.1	576	1999
Racha-Lechkhumi, Imereti	3.2	1	0.1	781	1999
Tbilisi	0.8	0	0.9	1,013	1999
India					
Andaman and Nicobar Islands	—	—	—	—	—
Andhra Pradesh	**37.7**	*3,619*	13.2	80,672	1998–99
Arunachal Pradesh	**24.2**	37	0.5	1,282	1998–99
Assam	**36.1**	*1,077*	13.7	25,065	1998–99
Bihar	**54.3**	*7,506*	43.3	116,156	1998–99
Chandigarh	—	—	—	—	—
Dadra and Nagar Haveli	—	—	—	—	—
Daman and Diu	—	—	—	—	—
Goa	**28.6**	46	10.9	1,342	1998–99
Gujarat	**45.1**	*2,805*	17.2	52,256	1998–99

Table A3.2

Asia

(continued)

Country and subnational region	Under-weight prevalence	Population of underweight children (thousands)	Population density of underweight children (per square kilometer)	Total population 2000 (thousands)	Year of survey[a]
Haryana	**34.6**	*925*	20.8	22,461	1998–99
Himachal Pradesh	**43.7**	*375*	7.3	7,210	1998–99
Jammu	**34.6**	*424*	4.4	10,288	1998–99
Karnataka	**43.8**	*2,599*	13.6	49,859	1998–99
Kerala	**26.9**	*776*	20.7	24,249	1998–99
Lakshadweep	—	—	—	—	—
Madhya Pradesh	**55.2**	*5689*	12.7	86,612	1998–99
Maharashtra	**49.6**	*5,977*	19.3	101,259	1998–99
Manipur	**27.6**	82	3.8	2,490	1998–99
Meghalaya	**37.9**	*122*	5.6	2,716	1998–99
Mizoram	**27.7**	32	1.5	958	1998–99
Nagaland	**23.6**	49	3.0	1,739	1998–99
New Delhi	**34.6**	*402*	312.6	9,773	1998–99
Orissa	**54.5**	*2,404*	16.3	37,061	1998–99
Pondicherry	—	—	—	—	—
Punjab	**28.7**	*900*	17.7	26,348	1998–99
Rajasthan	**50.7**	*3,636*	10.7	60,273	1998–99
Sikkim	**20.7**	15	3.0	601	1998–99
Tamil Nadu	**36.6**	*2,130*	16.5	48,894	1998–99
Tripura	**42.6**	*157*	15.0	3,093	1998–99
Uttar Pradesh	**51.4**	*9,295*	32.1	151,971	1998–99
West Bengal	**49.1**	*3,938*	47.3	67,400	1998-99
Jordan					
Central	4.7	21	1.4	3,139	1997
North	5.2	10	0.3	1,303	1997
South	7.9	4	0.1	382	1997
Kazakhstan					
Almaty city	4.5	3	15.0	775	1999
Central region	3.4	4	0.0	1,584	1999
East region	0.8	1	0.0	1,489	1999
North region	5.7	16	0.0	3,749	1999
South region	3.9	15	0.0	4,929	1999
Western region	6.7	8	0.0	1,581	1999
Bishkek	4.3	2	15.9	524	1997
East	12.3	4	0.1	279	1997
North	6.0	11	0.2	1,700	1997
South	14.0	37	0.6	2,492	1997
Lao PDR					
Central	2.3	8	0.1	2,112	2000
North	2.6	8	0.1	2,048	2000
South	4.2	7	0.2	1,081	2000
Lebanon					
Beirut	2.2	1	32.3	274	2002
Bekaa	4.2	2	0.4	436	2002
Mount Lebanon	1.0	1	0.6	1,249	2002
Nabatieh	9.8	2	2.1	184	2002
North Lebanon	2.3	1	0.7	644	2002
South Lebanon	4.1	1	1.2	349	2002

Table A3.2

Asia

(continued)

Country and subnational region	Under-weight prevalence	Population of underweight children (thousands)	Population density of underweight children (per square kilometer)	Total population 2000 (thousands)	Year of survey[a]
Myanmar					
Ayeyarwady	**36.8**	*281*	8.6	6,748	2000
Bago	**37.4**	*219*	5.8	5,187	2000
Chin	**41.3**	24	0.6	514	2000
Kachin	**27.3**	35	0.4	1,139	2000
Kayah	**35.9**	11	1.0	271	2000
Kayin	**40.1**	38	1.3	842	2000
Magway	**36.5**	*191*	4.3	4,619	2000
Mandalay	**31.2**	*233*	6.4	6,603	2000
Mon	**33.5**	88	8.3	2,315	2000
Rakhine	**48.1**	*140*	4.3	2,577	2000
Sagaing	**31.5**	*196*	2.0	5,499	2000
Shan	**32.1**	*156*	1.0	4,303	2000
Tanintharyi	**40.1**	57	1.4	1,259	2000
Yangon	**33.4**	*206*	21.9	5,462	2000
Nepal					
Central	**52.0**	*645*	23.9	8,211	2001
Eastern	**41.2**	*348*	13.7	5,596	2001
Far-western	**54.7**	*181*	9.3	2,189	2001
Mid-western	**52.3**	*239*	5.9	3,031	2001
Western	**44.2**	*309*	11.1	4,627	2001
Pakistan					
Azad Kashmir Province	—	—	—	1,129	1990–91
Balochistan	**56.4**	*627*	1.8	7,131	1990–91
Federally Administered Tribal Areas	—	—	—	3,399	1990–91
Northern Areas	—	—	—	3,709	1990–91
NW Frontier	**38.0**	*1,110*	15.3	18,724	1990–91
Punjab	**37.2**	*4,574*	22.2	78,815	1990–91
Sindh	**47.6**	*2,300*	16.9	30,978	1990–91
Turkey					
Central	5.4	*123*	0.5	21,822	1998
East	17.1	*382*	1.4	21,471	1998
North	4.8	25	0.4	5,002	1998
South	8.9	73	0.8	7,929	1998
West	3.8	24	0.2	6,061	1998
Turkmenistan					
Akhal	7.6	6	0.1	725	2000
Ashgabad city	11.7	0	0.0	0	2000
Balkan	11.6	6	0.1	444	2000
Dashoguz	16.0	18	0.3	1,028	2000
Lebap	12.1	14	0.1	1,051	2000
Mary	11.2	14	0.2	1,174	2000
Uzbekistan					
Region 1	14.5	43	0.3	2,634	1996
Region 2	**24.5**	*156*	0.8	5,687	1996
Region 3	16.3	*135*	2.5	7,414	1996
Region 4	**21.4**	*155*	8.7	6,469	1996
Tashkent	4.2	10	35.3	2,082	1996

Table A3.2
Asia
(continued)

Country and subnational region	Under-weight prevalence	Population of underweight children (thousands)	Population density of underweight children (per square kilometer)	Total population 2000 (thousands)	Year of survey[a]
Yemen					
North and West	**29.0**	*829*	6.2	14,891	1991–92
South and East	**29.0**	*168*	0.6	3,026	1991–92
Countries without subnational data					
Afghanistan	**48.0**	*1,802*	2.8	21,457	1995–01
Azerbaijan	17.0	*117*	1.4	7,921	1995–00
Bahrain	9.0	4	7.6	401	1995–00
Bhutan	19.0	63	1.7	2,130	1995–00
Brunei Darussalam	—	—	—	289	—
Cyprus	—	—	—	714	—
Indonesia	**26.0**	*5,443*	3.0	203,236	1995–00
Iran, Islamic Rep.	11.0	60	0.0	6,108	1995–00
Iraq	15.9	*562*	1.3	22,648	2000
Israel	—	—	—	6,676	—
Japan	—	—	—	120,698	—
Kuwait	10.0	18	1.1	1,758	1995–00
Malaysia	18.0	*449*	1.4	20,949	1995–00
Maldives	43.0	1	168.3	7	1995–00
Mongolia	13.0	19	0.0	1,339	1995–00
Korea, Rep.	**27.9**	*528*	4.4	21,771	2000
Oman	**24.0**	*145*	0.5	4,303	1995–00
Philippines	**28.0**	*2,548*	9.2	70,000	1995–00
Qatar	6.0	3	0.3	504	1995–00
Saudi Arabia	14.0	*402*	0.2	19,278	1995–00
Singapore	—	—	—	3,149	—
Korea, Dem. Rep.	—	—	—	43,569	—
Sri Lanka	**33.0**	*487*	7.7	18,217	1995–00
Syrian Arab Republic	13.0	*283*	1.5	16,116	1995–00
Tajikistan	—	—	—	5,930	—
Thailand	—	—	—	61,722	—
United Arab Emirates	14.0	30	0.4	2,434	1995–00
Viet Nam	**33.0**	*2,451*	7.6	75,026	1995–00

Table A3.3

Latin America

Note: Numbers in bold indicate an underweight prevalence of 20 percent or more; numbers in italics indicate a population of more than 100,000 underweight children. Underweight rates are for the survey year indicated. All populations are approximate.

a. Where year range extends to more than two years, the data used come from one or more unspecified years within the range.

— Not available.

Source: ORC-Macro 2004; UNICEF 2002, 2003b, 2004; CIESEN 2004; UN Population Division 2002.

Country and subnational region	Underweight prevalence	Population of underweight children (thousands)	Population density of underweight children (per square kilometer)	Total population 2000 (thousands)	Year of survey[a]
Bolivia					
Beni, Pando	9.5	6	0.0	421	1998
Chuquisaca	10.5	11	0.2	701	1998
Cochabamba	8.8	24	0.4	1,908	1998
La Paz	6.9	32	0.2	3,196	1998
Oruro	6.3	4	0.1	487	1998
Potosi	13.4	18	0.2	940	1998
Santa Cruz	4.8	17	0.0	2,424	1998
Tarija	3.5	3	0.1	512	1998
Brazil					
Centro Leste	5.5	*108*	0.2	20,492	1996
Centro Oeste	3.0	31	0.0	10,591	1996
Nordeste	8.3	*355*	0.2	44,584	1996
Norte	7.7	71	0.0	9,594	1996
Rio de Janeiro	3.8	49	1.1	13,420	1996
Sao Paulo	4.7	*165*	0.7	36,629	1996
Sul	2.0	47	0.1	24,286	1996
Colombia					
Atlantica	7.4	71	0.5	8,432	2000
Bogota	5.4	35	18.6	5,706	2000
Central	7.6	94	0.5	10,906	2000
Oriental	5.8	53	0.3	8,127	2000
Pacifica	6.5	55	0.4	7,458	2000
Territorios Nacionales	—	—	—	680	2000
Dominican Republic					
Cibao Central	3.8	8	0.9	1,871	1996
Cibao Occidental	5.3	1	0.3	243	1996
Cibao Oriental	8.9	8	1.5	768	1996
Distrito Nacional	3.0	8	6.2	2,472	1996
El Valle	16.5	10	1.4	558	1996
Enriquillo	10.7	5	0.8	427	1996
Peravia, San Cristobal, Monte Plata	6.1	7	1.4	1,076	1996
Yuma	6.0	6	0.7	822	1996
El Salvador					
Ahuachapan	17.2	7	5.5	307	2001
Cabanas	12.1	2	2.2	149	2001
Chalatenango	18.0	4	2.4	190	2001
Cuscatlan	12.7	3	5.0	207	2001
La Libertad	10.0	9	5.9	720	2001
La Paz	7.6	3	2.3	273	2001
La Union	17.0	6	3.0	259	2001
Morazan	12.3	3	2.2	185	2001
San Miguel	3.2	2	0.9	467	2001
San Salvador	9.8	24	26.2	1,907	2001
San Vicente	12.6	3	2.2	169	2001
Santa Ana	13.9	10	4.6	545	2001
Sonsonate	11.2	7	5.4	481	2001
Usulutan	11.3	5	2.5	339	2001

Table A3.3

Latin America

(continued)

Country and subnational region	Under-weight prevalence	Population of underweight children (thousands)	Population density of underweight children (per square kilometer)	Total population 2000 (thousands)	Year of survey[a]
Guatemala					
Central	**21.7**	47	6.5	1,343	1995
Metropolitan	18.9	72	33.5	2,354	1995
North	19.4	30	2.3	961	1995
Northeast	**29.1**	47	3.2	1,001	1995
Northwest	**33.4**	76	5.2	1,401	1995
Peten	—	—	—	291	1995
Southeast	**21.4**	36	4.2	1,027	1995
Southwest	**29.4**	*138*	11.3	2,897	1995
Haiti					
Artibonite	**20.6**	32	7.2	1,134	2000
Centre	14.5	13	3.4	635	2000
Grand-Anse	19.9	18	6.5	662	2000
North	18.9	21	10.0	791	2000
Northeast	16.2	6	3.8	284	2000
Northwest	17.3	11	5.6	477	2000
Ouest (incl. Port-au-Prince)	—	—	—	2,376	2000
South	**24.6**	23	9.5	674	2000
Southeast	19.3	18	8.0	673	2000
Nicaragua					
Boaco	13.9	3	0.8	155	1997–98
Carazo	7.8	2	2.2	182	1997–98
Chinandega	14.7	9	2.0	398	1997–98
Chontales	9.6	2	0.4	163	1997–98
Estelí	8.6	3	1.2	204	1997–98
Granada	10.2	3	3.4	182	1997–98
Jinotega	18.6	8	0.8	263	1997–98
Leon	13.2	8	1.7	397	1997–98
Madriz	**21.1**	4	2.4	117	1997–98
Managua	10.5	21	5.9	1,260	1997–98
Masaya	8.1	4	6.5	294	1997–98
Matagalpa	12.7	9	1.0	437	1997–98
Nueva Segovia	12.3	4	1.1	182	1997–98
RAAN	14.0	4	0.1	187	1997–98
RAAS	11.5	5	0.2	249	1997–98
Río San Juan	9.2	1	0.2	85	1997–98
Rivas	9.2	2	1.3	155	1997–98
Paraguay					
Asuncion and Metropolitan Area	3.4	9	3.9	1,910	1990
Center-South	3.3	5	0.1	989	1990
Chaco	—	—	—	119	1990
East	2.9	6	0.1	1,566	1990
North	6.5	6	0.1	669	1990
Peru					
Amazonas	10.5	5	0.1	381	2000
Ancash	6.0	7	0.2	989	2000
Apurimac	12.3	6	0.3	382	2000

Table A3.3

Latin America

(continued)

Country and subnational region	Under-weight prevalence	Population of underweight children (thousands)	Population density of underweight children (per square kilometer)	Total population 2000 (thousands)	Year of survey[a]
Arequipa	4.0	5	0.1	1,078	2000
Ayacucho	10.1	5	0.1	454	2000
Cajamarca	12.0	20	0.6	1,409	2000
Cusco	13.0	18	0.2	1,176	2000
Huancavelica	17.5	8	0.4	402	2000
Huanuco	11.6	10	0.3	718	2000
Ica	1.2	1	0.0	591	2000
Junin	10.0	13	0.3	1,116	2000
La Libertad	7.2	12	0.5	1,373	2000
Lambayeque	3.8	5	0.4	1,054	2000
Lima	0.8	7	0.2	7,385	2000
Loreto	17.3	15	0.0	714	2000
Madre de Dios	4.8	1	0.0	218	2000
Moquegua	0.4	0	0.0	113	2000
Pasco	12.2	3	0.1	228	2000
Piura	8.2	14	0.4	1,406	2000
Puno	6.1	10	0.1	1,388	2000
San Martin	8.2	8	0.1	796	2000
Tacna	0.8	0	0.0	263	2000
Tumbes	4.4	1	0.2	194	2000
Ucayali	11.0	6	0.1	428	2000
Countries without subnational data					
Anguilla	—	—	—	6	—
Antigua and Barbuda	—	—	—	56	—
Argentina	5.0	*165*	0.1	35,143	1995–01
Aruba	—	—	—	74	—
Barbados	—	—	—	224	—
Belize	—	—	—	210	—
British Virgin Islands	—	—	—	10	—
Cayman Is.	—	—	—	21	—
Chile	1.0	14	0.0	14,436	1995–00
Costa Rica	5.0	20	0.4	3,960	1995–00
Cuba	3.9	26	0.2	10,571	2000
Dominica	—	—	—	62	—
Ecuador	15.0	*212*	0.9	12,183	1995–00
French Guiana	—	—	—	135	—
Greenland	—	—	—	35	—
Grenada	—	—	—	78	—
Guadeloupe	—	—	—	340	—
Guyana	12.0	8	0.0	659	1995–00
Honduras	**25.0**	*232*	2.1	6,195	1995–00
Jamaica	—	—	—	2,462	—
Martinique	—	—	—	328	—
Mexico	8.0	*887*	0.5	97,277	1995–00
Montserrat	—	—	—	3	—
Netherlands Antilles	—	—	—	141	—
Panama	7.0	21	0.3	2,728	1995–00
Puerto Rico	—	—	—	3,735	—

Table A3.3

Latin America

(continued)

Country and subnational region	Under-weight prevalence	Population of underweight children (thousands)	Population density of underweight children (per square kilometer)	Total population 2000 (thousands)	Year of survey[a]
St. Kitts and Nevis	—	—	—	23	—
St. Lucia	—	—	—	130	—
St. Vincent and the Grenadines	—	—	—	73	—
Suriname	—	—	—	339	—
The Bahamas	—	—	—	184	—
Trinidad and Tobago	—	—	—	1,158	—
Turks and Caicos Is.	—	—	—	5	—
Uruguay	5.0	13	0.1	3,147	1995–00
Venezuela	5.0	*135*	0.2	23,356	1995–00
Virgin Islands	—	—	—	72	—

Notes

Chapter 2

1. Baseline and trend data for stunting exist for very few countries, and malnourishment is generally calculated at the national level.

2. Geo-referenced data means data that have been associated with longitudinal and latitudinal coordinates.

3. Halving the prevalence of underweight between 1990 and 2015 means that all countries have to achieve a minimum annual rate of decrease of 2.7 percent. For more information, see Chhabra and Rokx (2004).

Chapter 4

1. The heads of state or government of the major developed democracies, including Canada, France, Germany, Italy, Japan, the Russian Federation, the United Kingdom, and the United States, meet annually to deal with the major economic and political issues facing their domestic societies and the international community as a whole. The G8 Summit has consistently dealt with macroeconomic management, international trade, and relations with developing countries.

Chapter 7

1. The Task Force on Child Health and Maternal Health, and the Task Force on HIV/AIDS, Malaria, Tuberculosis, and Access to Essential Medicines address some of these interventions in greater depth. They are mentioned here because they are essential in the fight against hunger.

2. The Task Force on Child Health and Maternal Health addresses the issues raised by child and maternal health systems, sexual and reproductive health and rights, and neonatal mortality (UN Millennium Project 2005b). The Task Force on Hunger's recommendations therefore focus on other aspects of nutrition throughout the lifecycle.

3. The analysis in chapter 3 shows that low birthweight is strongly and significantly correlated with child malnutrition within defined hunger hotspots.

4. Each of these factors is a significant correlate of child malnutrition (chapter 3).

Chapter 8

1. Acute undernutrition of the kind that typically occurs in major humanitarian crises may or may not overlap with the hunger hotspots defined in our earlier analysis. Indeed, the largest numbers of underweight children are to be found in countries like India, Indonesia, China, Bangladesh, Pakistan, and Nigeria—which do not these days feature on the lists of countries most affected by famines or acute food crises. Nor, indeed, are they countries recently disrupted by armed conflict. In other words, shock-spots need to be better defined on a country-by-country basis, with a view to improving the design of tailored early warning systems and related contingency plans.

2. The Sphere Initiative was launched in 1997 by a group of humanitarian NGOs and the Red Cross and Red Crescent movement, which framed a humanitarian charter and identified minimum standards to be attained in disaster assistance in five key sectors (water supply and sanitation, nutrition, food aid, shelter, and health services). These contribute to an operational framework for accountability in disaster assistance efforts.

3. The Consolidated Appeals Process is an emergency response program cycle used by agencies working with relevant authorities at field level, coordinated by the UN, and supported by donors, to give people in need the best available protection and assistance when they need it most.

Chapter 9

1. The report of the Task Force on Science, Technology, and Innovation addresses the need to create the appropriate enabling environments for using information and communication technologies (UN Millennium Project 2005a).

References

Adesina, A. 2004. "Making Markets Work for the Poor in Africa." Address to the Presidential-Level Seminar on Innovative Approaches to Meeting the Millennium Hunger Development Goal for Africa, July 5, Addis Ababa.

African Union Assembly. 2003. "Declaration on Agriculture and Food Security in Africa." July 10–12, Maputo.

Agragamee. 2002a. *Annual Report 2001–2002.* Orissa, India.

———. 2002b. "Report of Post-Project Status of Kodikitunda Watershed." Orissa, India.

Ahmed, A.U. 2004. "Impacts of Feeding Children in School: Evidence from Bangladesh." Draft report commissioned by the United Nations University. International Food Policy Research Institute, Washington, D.C.

Ahmed, A., and N. Caldes. 2004. "Food for Education: A Review of Program Impacts." Background paper for *Report of the Task Force on Hunger.* UN Millennium Project, New York.

Ahmed, A., and C. del Nimmo. 2002. "The Food for Education Programme in Bangladesh: An Evaluation of Its Impacts on Educational Attainment and Food Security." FCN Discussion Paper 138. International Food Research Policy Institute, Food Consumption and Nutrition Division, Washington, D.C.

Ahmed, A., and M. Sharma. 2004. "Food-for-Education Programs with Locally Produced Food: Effects on Farmers and Consumers in Sub-Saharan Africa." Background paper for the Report of the Task Force on Hunger. International Food Policy Research Institute, Washington, D.C.

Allen, L.H., and S.R. Gillespie. 2001. *What Works? A Review of the Efficacy and Effectiveness of Nutrition Interventions.* Geneva: United Nations Administrative Committee on Coordination/Sub-Committee on Nutrition and Manila: Asian Development Bank.

Alleyne, E.P, A. Kapungwe, and R. Kamona. 2001. *The Impact of HIV/AIDS on Agricultural Extension Organization and Field Operations in Zambia.* Lusaka.

Anand, S., and M. Ravallion. 1993. "Human Development in Poor Countries: On the Role of Private Incomes and Public Services." *Journal of Economic Perspectives* 7(1):133–50.

Arcand, J.L. 2001. "Undernourishment and Economic Growth. The Efficiency Cost of Hunger." Economic and Social Development Paper 147. Food and Agriculture Organization, Rome.

Barrett, C.B., and D.G. Maxwell. 2004. "Recasting Food Aid's Role." Policy Brief. Cornell University, Ithaca, N.Y.

———. Forthcoming. *Food Aid after Fifty Years: Recasting Its Role.* London: Routledge.

Barrett, C.B., T. Reardon, and P. Webb. 2001. "Nonfarm Income Diversification and Household Livelihood Strategies in Rural Africa: Concepts, Dynamics, and Policy Implications." *Food Policy* 26(4):315–31.

Beckmann, David. 2004. Personal communication with President of Bread for the World Institute.

Beckmann, David, and E. Byers. 2004. "Building Political Will to End Hunger." Background paper for *Report of the Task Force on Hunger.* UN Millennium Project, New York.

Behrman, J.R., H. Alderman, and J. Hoddinott. 2004. *Hunger and Malnutrition.* Copenhagen Consensus Challenge Paper. Environmental Assessment Institute, Copenhagen.

Benson, Todd. 2004. "Africa's Food and Nutrition Security Situation—Where Are We and How Did We Get Here?" 2020 Discussion Paper 37. International Food Policy Research Institute, Washington, D.C.

Berg, E.J. 1993. *Rethinking Technical Assistance: Reforms for Capacity Building in Africa.* New York: United Nations Development Programme.

Block, Stephen, and Patrick Webb. 2004. "Nutrition Information and Formal Schooling as Inputs to Child Nutrition." *Economic Development and Cultural Change* 52(4):801–21.

Bojö, J., and R.C. Reddy. 2003. "Status and Evolution of Environmental Priorities in the Poverty Reduction Strategies." Environmental Economics Paper 93. World Bank, Washington, D.C.

Borlaug, N. E. 2001. "Feed the World in the 21st Century: The Role of Agricultural Science and Technology." Speech given at Tuskegee University, Alabama.

BPNI (Breastfeeding Promotion Network of India). 2004. "Faulty Feeding Practices and Malnutrition." New Delhi. [Retrieved on November 14, 2004, from www.bpni.org/cgi/faultyfeeding.asp].

Brazil. 2002. "Projeto fome zero (The Zero Hunger Project)." White Paper. Brasilia.

Breman, H., K. Debrah. 2003. "Improving Africa Food Security." *SAS Review* 23(1):153–70.

Bridges, M., I. Hannam, R. Oldeman, F. Penning de Vries, S.J. Scherr, and S. Sombatpanit, eds. 2001. *Response to Land Degradation.* New Delhi: Oxford University Press and IBH Publishers.

Buchanan-Smith, M., and S. Davies. 1995. *Famine Early Warning and Response: The Missing Link.* London: Intermediate Technology Group.

Bunch, Roland. 2001a. "A Proven Technology for Intensifying Shifting Agriculture, Green Manure/Cover Crop Experience around the World." Paper presented at the International Institute for Rural Reconstruction Conference on Best Practices in Shifting Agriculture and the Conservation of Natural Resources in Asia, August 14–26, Silang, Cavite, Philippines.

———. 2001b. "Achieving the Adoption of Green Manure/Cover Crops." Paper presented at the International Institute for Rural Reconstruction Conference on Best Practices in Shifting Agriculture and the Conservation of Natural Resources in Asia, August 14–26, Silang, Cavite, Philippines.

Candler, W., and N. Kumar. 1998. "India: The Dairy Revolution. The Impact of Dairy Development in India and the World Bank's Contribution." World Bank, Operations Evaluation Department, Washington, D.C.

Caulfield, L.E., and R.E. Black. Forthcoming. "Malnutrition and the Global Burden of Disease: Underweight and Cause-Specific Mortality." In *World Health Organization, Comparative Quantification of Health Risks: The Global and Regional Burden of Disease Due to 25 Selected Major Risk Factors.* Cambridge, Mass.: Harvard University Press.

Caulfield, L.E., M. de Onis, M. Blössner, and R. E. Black. 2004. "Undernutrition as an Underlying Cause of Child Deaths Associated with Diarrhea, Pneumonia, Malaria and Measles." *American Journal of Clinical Nutrition* 80(1): 193–98.

CESCR (Committee on Economic, Social, and Cultural Rights). 1999. "Substantive Issues Arising in the Implementation of the International Covenant on Economic, Social and Cultural Rights." General Comment 12: The Right to Adequate Food (Article 11). United Nations Economic and Social Council, 20th session, E/C.12/1999/5 (General Comments) May 12, Geneva.

CGD (Center for Global Development) and Foreign Policy. 2004. "Ranking the Rich." *Foreign Policy* 142(May/June):46–56.

CGIAR (Consultative Group on International Agricultural Research). 2000. "A Food-Secure World for All. Toward a New Vision and Strategy for the CGIAR." Food and Agricultural Organization of the United Nations, Technical Advisory Committee Secretariat, Rome.

———. 2002. "Biofortified Crops for Improved Human Nutrition." Challenge program proposal presented by the International Center for Tropical Agriculture and the International Food Policy Research Institute on behalf of an international consortium of collaborative partners, September, Rome.

Chambers, R., A. Pacey, and L.A. Thrupp. 1989. *Farmer First: Farmer Innovation and Agricultural Research.* London: ITDG Publishing.

Chhabra, R., and C. Rokx. 2004. "The Nutrition MDG Indicator: Interpreting Progress." World Bank, Health, Nutrition and Population Division, Washington, D.C.

China. 2004. "Report on the Work of the Government." Beijing.

CIESIN (Center for International Earth Science Information Network). 2004. "Gridded Population of the World (GPW)." Version 3. Palisades, N.Y. [http://sedac.ciesin.columbia.edu/gpw].

Collier, P., L. Elliott, H. Hegre, A. Hoeffler, M. Reynal-Querol, and S. Nicholas. 2003. *Breaking the Conflict Trap: Civil War and Development Policy.* World Bank Policy Research Report. New York: Oxford University Press.

Copenhagen Consensus. 2004. "Copenhagen Consensus: The Results." Press Release. May 29, Copenhagen.

Coutsoudis, A., and N. Rollins. 2003. "Breast-feeding and HIV-transmission: The Jury Is Still Out." *Journal of Pediatrics, Gastroenterology, and Nutrition* 36: 434–42.

Cramer, C. 2003. "Does Inequality Cause Conflict?" *Journal of International Development* 15(4):397–412.

De Soto, H. 2000. *The Mystery of Capital: Why Capitalism Triumphs in the West and Fails Everywhere Else.* New York: Basic Books.

De Wall, A., and A. Whiteside. 2003. "New Variant Famine: AIDS and Food Crisis in Southern Africa." *Lancet* 362(9391):1234–37.

Delhi Declaration. 2004. "The 'Delhi Declaration' on Maternal and Child Nutrition in Asia." [www.foodsecurity.gov.kh/otherdocs/Delhi-Declaration.pdf].

Del Rosso, J.M., and T. Marek. 1996. *Class Action: Improving School Performance in the Developing World through Better Health and Nutrition.* Washington, D.C.: World Bank.

Devereux, S. 1993. "Goats before Ploughs: Dilemmas of Household Response Sequencing during Food Shortages." *IDS Bulletin* 24(4):52–59.

DFID (U.K. Department for International Development), EC (European Commission), UNDP (United Nations Development Programme), and World Bank. 2002. "Linking Poverty Reduction and Environmental Management: Policy Challenges and Opportunities." Background paper for the World Summit on Sustainable Development, August 26–September 4, Johannesburg.

Dobie, Philip. 2001. *Poverty and the Drylands.* Nairobi: United Nations Development Programme, Drylands Development Centre.

———. 2002. "Models for National Strategies: Building Capacity for Sustainable Development." *Development Policy Journal* 1:1–18.

Drimie, S. 2003. "HIV/AIDS and Land: Case Studies from Kenya, Lesotho, and South Africa." *Development Southern Africa* 20(5):647–58.

Earth Institute. 2004. "Field Visit to Bar Sauri: Town Meeting." Bar Sauri, Kenya.

ECLAC (Economic Commission for Latin America and the Caribbean). 2004. "Hunger in Latin America and the Caribbean: Its Scale, Characteristics and Likelihood of Eradication." In *Social Panorama of Latin America 2002–2003.* Santiago.

ECOSOC (United Nations Economic and Social Council). 1996. "ECOSOC Resolution 1996/31." New York.

———. 1999. "International Bill of Human Rights." New York.

———. 2004. "Resolutions and Decisions Adopted by the Economic and Social Council at Its Organizational Session for 2004." New York.

ECOSOC, Committee on Economic, Social and Cultural Rights. 1996. "Draft Optional Protocol to the International Covenant on Economic, Social and Cultural Rights." Geneva.

Engh, I.E., L. Stouklal, and J. du Guerny. 2000. *HIV/AIDS in Namibia: The Impact on the Livestock Sector.* Rome: Food and Agricultural Organization.

Engle, P. 1993. "Influences of Mother's and Father's Income on Children's Nutritional Status in Guatemala." *Social Science Medicine* 37(11):1303–12.

Engle, P., P. Menon, and L. Haddad. 1999. "Care and Nutrition: Concepts and Measurement." *World Development* 27(8):1309–37.

Esty, Daniel C., Jack Goldstone, Ted Robert Gurr, Barbara Harff, Pamela T. Surko, Alan N. Unger, and Robert Chen. 1998. "The State Failure Project: Early Warning Research for U.S. Foreign Policy Planning." Paper presented at the Conference for Failed States and International Security: Causes, Prospects, and Consequences, February 25–27, West Lafayette, Ind.

Ezzati, M., A. Lopez, A. Rodgers, S. Vander Hoorn, C. Murray, and the Cooperative Risk Assessment Collaborating Group. 2002. "Selected Major Risk Factors and Global and Regional Burden of Disease." *Lancet* 360(9343):1–14.

Fan, S., L. Zhang, and X. Zhang. 2002. *Growth, Inequality, and Poverty in Rural China: The Role of Public Investments.* Research Report 125. International Food Policy Research Institute, Washington, D.C.

FAO (Food and Agricultural Organization of the United Nations). 1996. "Rome Declaration on World Food Security and World Food Summit Plan of Action." Adopted at the World Food Summit, November 13–17, Rome.

———. 1997. *Women: The Key to Food Security.* Rome.

———. 2000. *The State of Food and Agriculture 2000: Lessons from the Past 50 Years.* Rome.

———. 2001a. *The State of Food Insecurity in the World: 2001.* Rome.

———. 2001b. *World Food Summit: Five Years Later.* Report of the High-Level Panel on Resources Mobilization for Food Security and for Agricultural and Rural Development, Rome.

———. 2001c. *From Farmer Field Schools to Community IPM: Ten Years of IPM Training in Asia.* Rome.

———. 2002a. "FAO Unveils Global Anti-Hunger Programme." News Story. June 4. [Retrieved on November 12, 2004 from www.fao.org/english/newsroom/news/2002/5500-en.html].

———. 2002b. *Mobilizing the Political Will and Resources to Banish World Hunger.* Technical background documents for *World Food Summit: Five Years Later.* Rome.

———. 2002c. *State of Food Insecurity in the World: 2002.* Rome.

———. 2003. *The State of Food Insecurity in the World 2003: Monitoring Progress towards the World Food Summit and Millennium Development Goals.* Rome.

———. 2004a. "Final Report of the Chair." Report of the Council Hundred and Twenty-Seventh Session. September 23, Rome.

———. 2004b. *The State of Food and Agriculture 2003–2004: Agricultural Biotechnology: Meeting the Needs of the Poor?* Rome.

———. 2004c. *The State of Food Insecurity in the World: 2004.* Rome.

———. 2004d. "Report of the Thirtieth Session of the Committee on World Food Security (CFS)." November 22–27, Rome.

———. 2004e. "Supplement to the Final Report to the Chair." Report of the Council Hundred and Twenty-Seventh Session. September 20–23, Rome.

FAO (Food and Agriculture Organization of the United Nations) and WHO (World Health Organization). 1992. *Promoting Appropriate Diets and Healthy Lifestyles.* Major Issues for Nutrition Strategies Theme Paper 5. Rome.

Fawzi, W.W. 2003. "Micronutrients and Human Immunodeficiency Virus Type 1 Disease Progression among Adults and Children." *Clinical Infectious Diseases* 37(suppl. 2):S112–116.

Fawzi, W.W, R. Mbise, D. Spiegelman, M. Fataki, E. Hertzmark, and G. Ndossi. 2000. "Vitamin A Supplements and Diarrheal and Respiratory Tract Infections among Children in Dar es Salaam, Tanzania." *Journal of Pediatrics* 137(5):660–67.

Fawzi, W.W., G.I. Msamanga, D. Spiegelman, E.J. Urassa, N. McGrath, D. Mwakagile, G. Antelman, R. Mbise, G. Herrera, S. Kapiga, W. Willett, and D.J. Hunter. 1998. "Randomised Trial of Effects of Vitamin Supplements on Pregnancy Outcomes and T Cell Counts in HIV-1-Infected Women in Tanzania." *Lancet* 351(9114):1477–82.

FIVIMS (Food Insecurity and Vulnerability Information and Mapping Systems). 2004. "The FIVIMS Programme." Rome. [www.fivims.net].

Frongillo, E.A., Jr, M. de Onis, M. Blössner, K.M.P. Hanson, and M.G. Cavanaugh, "Factors Associated with Nations' Progress in Reducing Child Malnutrition." *FASEB Journal* 13(4, part 1 suppl.):A543.

Fukuda-Parr, S., C. Lopes, and K. Malik. 2002. *Capacity for Development: New Solutions to Old Problems.* London: Earthscan Publications and United Nations Development Programme.

Gallardo, Carmello. 2001. "Guatemala: Inequality and Food Security." In *Action against Hunger, The Geopolitics of Hunger, 2000–2001: Hunger and Power.* Boulder, Colo.: Lynne Rienner Publishers.

Garrett, James L. 2000. "Overview: Achieving Urban Food and Nutrition Security in the Developing World." 2020 Focus 3, Brief 1. International Food Policy Research Institute, Washington, D.C.

Gladwin, C.H., A.M. Thomson, J. Peterson, and A.S. Anderson. 2001. "Addressing Food Security in Africa via Multiple Livelihood Strategies of Women Farmers." *Food Policy* 26(2):177–207.

Goodlund, Andrew, and Kevin Cleaver. 2002. "Increasing Donor Effectiveness in Agricultural Lending." Background report for *Report of the Task Force on Hunger.* UN Millennium Project, New York.

Grantham-McGregor, S., and C. Ani. 2001. "A Review of Studies on the Effect of Iron Deficiency on Cognitive Development in Children." *Journal of Nutrition* 131(suppl.):649S–68S.

Grantham-McGregor, S., L. Fernald, and K. Sethuraman. 1999a. "Effects of Health and Nutrition on Cognitive and Behavioral Development of Children in the First Three Years of Life. Part 1: Low Birthweight, Breastfeeding, and Protein-Energy Malnutrition." *Food and Nutrition Bulletin* 20(1):53–75.

———. 1999b. "Effects of Health and Nutrition on Cognitive and Behavioral Development of Children in the First Three Years of Life. Part 2: Infections and Micronutrient Deficiencies: Iodine, Iron, and Zinc." *Food and Nutrition Bulletin* 20(1):76–99.

Grobler-Tanner, Caroline, and Steve Collins. 2004. "Community Therapeutic Care (CTC): A New Approach to Managing Acute Malnutrition in Emergencies and Beyond." Technical Note 8. Food and Nutrition Technical Assistance, Washington, D.C.

Hack, M. 1998. "Effects of Intrauterine Growth Retardation on Mental Performance and Behavior, Outcomes during Adolescence and Adulthood." *European Journal of Clinical Nutrition* 52(suppl. 1):S65–71.

Haddad, L. 1999. "Women's Status: Levels, Determinants, Consequences for Malnutrition, Interventions, and Policy." *Asian Development Review* 17(1–2):96–131.

Haddad, L., and L. Smith. 1999. *Explaining Child Malnutrition in Developing Countries: A Cross-Country Analysis.* Research Report 111. Washington, D.C: International Food Policy Research Institute.

Haddad, L., P. Webb, and A. Slach. 1997. *Intrahousehold Resource Allocation in Developing Countries: Models, Methods and Policy.* Baltimore: Johns Hopkins University Press.

Haddad, L., M. D. Westbrook, D. Driscoll, E. Payongayong, J. Rozen, and M. Weeks. 1995. *Strengthening Policy Analysis: Econometric Tests Using Microcomputer Software.* Microcomputers in Policy Research 2. Washington, D.C.: International Food Policy Research Institute.

Hansen, J.W., M. Dilley, L. Goddard, E. Ebrahimian, and P. Ericksen. 2004. "Climate Variability and the Millennium Development Goal on Hunger." Technical Report 04-04. Columbia University, Earth Institute, International Research Institute on Climate Prediction, Palisades, N.Y.

Haslwimmer, M., and D. Chupin, eds. 1994. "Is HIV/AIDS a Threat to Livestock Production? The Example of Rakai, Uganda." *World Animal Review* 80/81(3–4).

Hayzer, N. 2003. "Priorities of Rural Women for the Achievement of the Millennium Development Goals." A presentation to the informal ECOSOC dialogue session, March, 24, New York.

Hazell, Peter. 2001. *Strategies for the Sustainable Development of Dryland Areas.* Washington, D.C.: International Food Policy Research Institute.

Heifer International. 2004. "Inside Heifer: Mission and History." Little Rock, Ark. [Retrieved on December 1, 2004 from www.heifer.org/Inside_Heifer/Mission_and_History/Index.shtml].

Hillel, D. 2004. "Efficient and Sustainable Water Management in Small-Scale Farming." Background paper for *Report of the Task Force on Hunger.* UN Millennium Project, New York.

HKI (Helen Keller International) and IPHN (Institute of Public Health Nutrition). 2001. "Undernutrition in Mothers in Rural Bangladesh: Findings from the Nutritional Surveillance Project Indicate 'Critical' Food Insecurity." Nutritional Surveillance Project Bulletin 7. Dhaka.

Holmgren, P., E.J. Masakha, and H. Sjoholm. 1994. "Not All African Land is Being Degraded: A Recent Survey of Trees on Farms in Kenya Reveals Rapidly Increasing Forest Resources." *Ambio* 23(7):390–95.

Homer-Dixon, T. 1999. *Environment, Scarcity, and Violence.* Princeton, N.J.: Princeton University Press.

Horton, S. 1999. "Opportunities for Investments in Nutrition in Low-Income Asia." *Asian Development Review* 17(1–2):246–73.

Horton, S., and J. Ross. 2003. "The Economics of Iron Deficiency." *Food Policy* 28(1):51–75.

Houghton, J.T., Y. Ding, D.J. Griggs, M. Noguer. P.J. van der Linden, X. Dai, K. Maskell, and C.A. Johnson, eds. 2001. *Climate Change 2001: The Scientific Basis.* New York: Cambridge University Press.

Huddleston, B., E. Ataman, L. d'Ostiani, P. Salvo, M. Zanetti, M. Bloise, J. Bel, and G. Franceschini. 2003. "Towards a GIS-Based Analysis of Mountain Environments and Populations." Environment and Natural Resources Working Paper 10. Food and Agriculture Organization, Sustainable Development Department, Rome.

The Hunger Project. 2004. "Ending Hunger in Africa. The People-Centered Perspective." Background paper for *Halving Hunger: It Can Be Done.* Report of the Task Force on Hunger. New York.

IAAST (International Assessment of Agricultural Science and Technology for Development). 2003. "An Assessment of Agricultural Science and Technology for Development." Final report of the Steering Committee for the Consultative Process on Agricultural Science and Technology, August 12. Nairobi.

IAC (InterAcademy Council). 2004. "Realizing the Promise and Potential of African Agriculture: Science and Technology Strategies for Improving Agricultural Productivity and Food Security in Africa." Amsterdam.

IFDC (International Fertilizer Development Center). 2003. "Input Subsidies and Agricultural Development: Issues and Options for Developing and Transitional Economies." Muscle Shoals, Ala.

IFPRI (International Food Policy Research Institute). 2002a. "Food for Education." Washington, D.C.

———. 2002b. "Sound Choices for Development: The Impact of Public Investments in Rural India and China." Issue Brief 7. Washington, D.C.

ISDR (International Strategy for Disaster Reduction). 2003. "Living with Risk: An Integrated Approach to Reducing Societal Vulnerability to Drought." Ad Hoc Discussion Group on Drought, Geneva.

Jacoby, E., S. Cueto, and E. Pollitt. 1996. "Benefits of a School Breakfast Programme among Andean Children in Huaraz, Peru." *Food and Nutrition Bulletin* 17(1):54–64.

Jama, B., R.A. Swinkels, and R.J. Buresh. 1997. "Agronomic and Economic Evaluation of Organic and Inorganic Sources of Phosphorus in Western Kenya." *Agronomy Journal* 89(4):597–604.

Janke, C. 1996. "Food and Education: Background Considerations for Policy and Programming." Catholic Relief Services, Baltimore, Md.

Jenkins, M., S. Scherr, and M. Inbar. 2004. "Markets for Biodiversity Services: Potential Roles and Challenges." *Environment* 46(6):32–42.

Johns Hopkins University, Bloomberg School of Public Health. 2002. "Birth spacing: Three to Five Saves Lives." Population Reports Series L, number 13. Baltimore, Md. [www.infoforhealth.org/pr/l3edsum.shtml].

Johnson, N., T.A. White, and D. Merrot-Maitre. 2001. "Developing Markets for Water Services from Forests: Issues and Lesson for Innovators." Forest Trends, World Resources Institute, and the Katoomba Group, Washington, D.C.

Kadiyala, S., and S. Gillespie. 2003. "Rethinking Food Aid to Fight HIV/AIDS." FCN Discussion Paper 159. International Food Policy Research Institute, Food Consumption and Nutrition Division, Washington, D.C.

Katon, Brenda M., Anna Knox, and Ruth Meinzen-Dick. 2001. "Collective Action, Property Rights, and Devolution of Natural Resource Management." CAPRi Working Paper 7. Consultative Group on International Agricultural Research, System-wide Program on Property Rights and Collective Action, Washington, D.C.

Kherallah, M., C. Delgado, E. Gabre-Madhin, N. Minot, and M. Johnson. 2000. "The Road Half Traveled: Agricultural Market Reform in Africa." Food Policy Report. International Food Policy Research Institute, Washington, D.C.

Krishna, Anirud. 2002. "Enhancing Political Participation in Democracies. What is the Role of Social Capital?" *Comparative Political Studies* 35(4):437–60.

Kumwenda, N., P.G. Miotti, E. Taha, R. Broadhead, R.J. Biggar, J.B. Jackson, G. Melikian, and R. D. Semba. 2002. "Antenatal Vitamin A Supplementation Increases Birth Weight and Decreases Anemia among Infants Born to Human Immunodeficiency Virus-Infected Women in Malawi." *Clinical Infectious Diseases* 35(5):618–24.

Kwesiga, F.R., S. Franzel, F. Place, D. Phiri, and C.P. Simwanza. 1999. "Sesbania sesban Improved Fallows in Eastern Zambia: Their Inception, Development, and Farmer Enthusiasm." *Agroforestry Systems* 47: 49–66.

Lal, Rattan, and C. Dowswell. 2004. Personal communication.

Landell-Mills, Natasha, and Ina Porras. 2002. "Markets for Forest Environmental Services: Silver Bullet or Fool's Gold?" International Institute for Environment and Development, London.

Lanjouw, P. 1999. "Rural Non-Agricultural Employment and Poverty in Ecuador," *Economic Development and Cultural Change* 48(1):91–122.

Lanjouw, Peter, and Nicholas Stern. 1998. *Economic Development in Palanpur over Five Decades.* New York: Oxford University Press.

Lefort, P. 2001. "Sierra Leone: Food at the Heart of the Conflict." In *Action against Hunger, The Geopolitics of Hunger, 2000–2001: Hunger and Power.* Boulder, Colo.: Lynne Rienner Publishers.

Lele, U., ed. 2002. "Managing a Global Resource: Challenges of Forest Conservation and Development." World Bank Series on Evaluation and Development Vol. 5. New Brunswick, N.J.: Transaction Publishers.

LoPriore, C., P. Webb, and C. Van Nieuwenhuyse. 2004. "Best Practices in the Use of Food for Maternal and Child Nutrition Interventions." Draft. Rome.

Majid, N. 2004. "Reaching Millennium Goals: How Well Does Agricultural Productivity Growth Reduce Poverty?" Employment Strategy Papers. International Labour Organization, Employment Analysis Unit: Employment Strategy Department, Geneva.

Marshall, M., and T.R. Gurr. 2003. *Peace and Conflict 2003: A Global Survey of Armed Conflicts, Self-Determination Movements, and Democracy.* College Park, Md.: University of Maryland Center for International Development and Conflict Management.

Maxwell, S., and Tim Frankenburger. 1992. *Household Food Security: Concepts, Indicators, Measurements.* New York and Rome: United Nations Children's Fund and International Fund for Agricultural Development.

McCulloch, N., L. A. Winters, and X. Cirera. 2001. *Trade Liberalization and Poverty: A Handbook.* London: Centre for Economic Policy Research.

McNeely, J.A., and S.J. Scherr. 2003. *Ecoagriculture: Strategies to Feed the World and Save Wild Biodiversity.* Washington, D.C.: Island Press.

Meinzen-Dick, Ruth, and Monica di Gregorio. 2004. "The Role of Collective Action in Fighting Hunger." Background paper for the UN Millennium Project, *Report of the Task Force on Hunger.* CGIAR System-wide Program on Collective Action and Property Rights, Washington, D.C.

Messer, E., M.J. Cohen, and J. D'Costa. 1998. "Food from Peace: Breaking the Links between Hunger and Conflict. Food, Agriculture, and the Environment Discussion Paper 24. International Food Policy Research Institute, Washington, D.C.

Messer, E., M.J. Cohen, and T. Marchione. 2001. "Conflict: A Cause and Effect of Hunger." Environmental Change and Security Project Report 7. Smithsonian Institution Woodrow Wilson Center, Washington, D.C.

Meyerhoff, Elizabeth. 1991. *Taking Stock: Changing Livelihoods in an Agropastoral Community.* Nairobi: ACTS Press.

Mihrshahi, Seema, Wendy Oddy, and Jennifer K. Peat. "Promoting Human Rights and Social Policies for Women: Monitoring and Achieving the Millennium Development Goals." Draft paper. New School for Social Research, New York.

MI (Micronutrient Initiative) and UNICEF (United Nations Children's Fund). 2004. *Vitamin and Mineral Deficiency: A Global Progress Report.* New York.

Molnar, A., S. Scherr, and A. Khare. 2004. *Who Conserves the World's Forests? Community-Driven Strategies to Protect Forests and Respect Rights.* Washington, D.C.: Forest Trends.

Montresor, A, D.W.T. Crompton, T.W. Gyorkos, and L. Savioli. 2002. *Helminth Control in School-Age Children: A Guide for Managers of Control Programmes.* Geneva: World Health Organization.

Morduch, J. 1999. "The Microfinance Promise." *Journal of Economic Literature* 35:1569–1614.

Nafziger, E. Wayne, and J. Auvinen. 2000. "The Economic Causes of Humanitarian Emergencies." In E. Wayne Nafziger, Frances Stewart, and Raimo Väyrynen, eds., *War, Hunger, and Displacement: The Origins of Humanitarian Emergencies.* Vol. 1. Oxford, U.K.: Oxford University Press.

Nelson, M., R. Dudal, H. Gregersen, N. Jodha, D. Nyamai, J.P. Groenewold, F. Torres, and A. Kassam. 1997. "Report of the Study on CGIAR Research Priorities for Marginal Lands." Technical Advisory Committee Secretariat Working Document. Food and Agricultural Organization, Rome.

Nestel, P. 2000. "Strategies, Policies and Programs to Improve the Nutrition of Women and Girls." Food and Nutrition Technical Assistance Project, Washington, D.C.

Omamo, S.W. 2002. "Fertilizer Trade and Pricing in Uganda." Paper prepared for the workshop on the Assessment of the Fertilizer Sub-Sector in Eastern Africa and Strategic Planning of a Regional Project to Improve Fertilizer Availability, Access, and Utilization, July 15–17, Nairobi.

ORC-Macro. 1996. *DHS Sampling Manual.* Calverton, Md.

———. 2004. Demographic and Health Surveys (DHS) Database. Data for various years. [www.measuredhs.com].

Osami, S.R. 2001. *Participatory Governance and Poverty Reduction in Choices for the Poor.* New York: United Nations Development Programme.

Oxfam. 2002. "Stop the Dumping! How EU Agricultural Subsidies Are Damaging Livelihoods in the Developing World." Briefing Paper 31. Oxfam, Oxford, U.K.

Paarlberg, R. 2000. "The Weak Link between World Food Markets and World Food Security." *Food Policy* 25(3):317–35.

———. 2002. "Governance and Food Security in an Age of Globalization." Vision Discussion Paper 36. International Food Policy Research Institute, Washington, D.C.

Palm, C.A., R.J.K. Myers, and S.M. Nandwa. 1997. "Combined Use of Organic and Inorganic Nutrient Sources for Soil Fertility Maintenance and Replenishment." In R. J. Buresh, and P. A. Sanchez, eds., *Replenishing Soil Fertility in Africa.* Madison, Wis.: Soil Science Society of America and American Society of Agronomy.

Pelletier, D.L., E.A. Frongillo, D.G. Schroeder, and J.P. Habicht. 1995. "The Effects of Malnutrition on Child Mortality in Developing Countries." *Bulletin of the World Health Organization* 73(4):443–48.

Penning de Vries, F.W.T, H. Acquay, D. Molden, S.J. Scherr, C. Valentin, and O. Cofie. 2003. *Integrated Land and Water Management for Food and Environmental Security.* Comprehensive Assessment of Water Management in Agriculture Research Report 1. Colombo: International Water Management Institute.

People's Union for Civil Liberties. 2001. "'PUCL Has Done Pioneering Work in Human Rights' Says India Centre." *PUCL Bulletin.* [Retrieved on December 1, 2004 from www.pucl.org/reports/National/2001/india_center.htm].

———. 2001. "Written Petition (Civil) No. 196 of 2001." *(People's Union of Civil Liberties v. Union of India and Ors.).* Dehli.

Philip, J. 2000. "Ending Malnutrition by 2020: An Agenda for Change in the Millennium." *Food and Nutrition Bulletin* 21(3s):70–73.

Pinstrup-Anderson, P. 2001. "Achieving Sustainable Food Security for All: Required Policy Action." Paper presented at the Mansholt Lecture, November 14, Wageningen University, Netherlands.

Powell, I., A. White, and N. Landell-Mills. 2001. *Developing Markets for Ecosystem Services of Forests.* Washington, D.C.: Forest Trends.

Ramalingaswami, Vulimiri, Urban Jonsson, and Jon Rohde. 1996. "Commentary: The Asian Enigma." In United Nations Children's Fund, *Progress of Nations 1996.* New York.

Rahman, A., M. Wahmed, M. Alam, T. Ahmed, F. Ahmed, M. Quaiyum, and D. Sack. 2002. "Randomized, Double-Blind Controlled Trial of Wheat Flour (Chapatti) Fortified with Vitamin A and Iron in Improving Vitamin A and Iron Status in Healthy, School Aged Children in Rural Bangladesh." Report to the MOST Project. United States Agency for International Development, Washington, D.C.

Ravallion, M. and Datt, G. 1999. "When is Growth Pro-Poor? Evidence from the Diverse Experience of India's States." Policy Research Paper 2263. World Bank, Washington, D.C.

Reardon, Thomas, and J.A. Berdegué. 2002. "The Rapid Rise of Supermarkets in Latin America: Challenges and Opportunities for Development." *Development Policy Review* 20(4):371–88.

Rosa, Herman, Susan Kandel, and Leopoldo Dimas. 2003. "Compensation for Environmental Services and Communities: Lessons from the Americas and Key Issues for Strengthening Community Opportunities." Fundación PRISMA, San Salvador.

Rosegrant, Mark W., X. Cai, S.A. Cline, and N. Nakagawa. 2002. "The Role of Rainfed Agriculture in the Future of Global Food Production." Environment and Protection Technology Department Discussion Paper 90. International Food Policy Research Institute, Washington, D.C.

Runge, C.F., B. Senauer, P.G. Pardey, and M.W. Rosegrant. 2003. *Ending Hunger in Our Lifetime.* Baltimore: International Food Policy Research Institute and Johns Hopkins University Press.

Sanchez, P.A. 2002. "Soil Fertility and Hunger in Africa." *Science* 295: 2019–20.

———. Personal communication with Director of Tropical Agriculture, The Earth Institute at Columbia University.

Sanchez, P.A., and B.A. Jama. 2002. "Soil Fertility Replenishment Takes Off in East and Southern Africa." In D.B. Vanlauwe, J. Diels, N. Sanginga, and R. Merckx, eds., *Integrated Nutrient Management in Sub-Saharan Africa.* Wallingford, U.K.: CAB International.

Scherr, S. 2003. "Background paper for the Report of the Task Force on Hunger." UN Millennium Project, New York.

Scherr, S., A. White, and D. Kaimowitz. 2004. *A New Agenda for Forest Conservation and Poverty Reduction: Making Markets Work for Low-Income Producers.* Washington, D.C.: Forest Trends.

Semba, R. D., N. Shah, R. S. Klein, K. H. Mayer, P. Schuman, L. I. Gardner, D. Vlahov, and HER (Human Immunodeficiency Virus Epidemiology Research) Study Group. 2001. "Highly Active Antiretroviral Therapy Associated with Improved Anemia among HIV-Infected Women." *AIDS Patient Care STDS* 15(9):473–80.

Semega-Janneh, I.J., E. Bohler, H. Holm, I. Matheson, and G. Holmboe-Ottesen. 2001. "Promoting Breastfeeding in Rural Gambia: Combining Traditional and Modern Knowledge." *Health Policy and Planning* 16(2):199–205.

Sethuraman, K., M. Shekar, and K. Kurz. 2003. "Towards Achieving the Hunger and Malnutrition Millennium Development Goal: Tailoring Potential Country-Level Solutions to Needs—The 'Candidate Actions' Approach." Background paper for *Report of the Task Force on Hunger.* UN Millennium Project, New York.

Shrimpton, R. "Preventing Low Birthweight and Reduction of Child Mortality." *Transactions of the Royal Society of Tropical Medicine and Hygiene* 97(1):39–42.

Shrimpton, R., K. Tripp, and A. Thorne-Lyman. 2002. "Refugee Nutrition and Low Birthweight in Nepal." Report to United Nations High Commissioner for Refugees and World Food Programme, London.

Smith, Joyotee, and Sara J. Scherr. 2002. "Forest Carbon and Local Livelihoods: Assessment of Opportunities and Policy Recommendations." Occasional Paper 37. Centre for International Forestry Research and Forest Trends, Bogor, Indonesia.

Smith, L., and L. Haddad. 2000. "Overcoming Child Malnutrition in Developing Countries: Past Achievements and Future Choices." Food, Agriculture and the Environment Discussion Paper 30. International Food Policy Research Institute, Washington, D.C.

———. 2002. "How Potent Is Economic Growth in Reducing Undernutrition? What Are the Pathways of Influence? New Cross-Country Evidence." *Economic Development and Cultural Change* 51(1):55–76.

Solon, F.S. 2000. "Efficacy of a Vitamin A-Fortified Wheat Flour Bun on the Vitamin A Status of Filipino Schoolchildren." *American Journal of Clinical Nutrition* 72(3):733–44.

Sommer, F. 1998. "Pastoralism and Drought Early Warning and Response." Overseas Development Institute, London.

Spencer, Dunstan. 1994. "Infrastracture and Technology Constraints to Agricultural Development in the Humid and Subhumid Tropics of Africa." Discussion Paper 3. International Food Policy Research Institute, Environment and Protection Technology Department, Washington, D.C.

Sphere Project. 2004. "Minimum Standards in Food Security, Nutrition and Food Aid." In *Humanitarian Charter and Minimum Standards in Disaster Response.* Geneva. [www.sphereproject.org/handbook/hdbkpdf/hdbk_full.pdf].

Staal, S.J., C. Delgado, and C. Nicholson. 1997. "Small-Holder Dairying under Transactions Costs in East Africa." *World Development* 25: 779–94.

Stewart, F. 2002. "Horizontal Inequalities: A Neglected Dimension of Development." WIDER Working Paper 81. United Nations University, World Institute for Development Economics Research, Helsinki.

Stewart, Janet. 2004. "Report on a Visit to Kenya and Uganda, 5–23 June 2004." Oxford Forestry Institute, University of Oxford. [www.frp.uk.com/dissemination_documents/R6549_-_trip_report_Africa_-_June_04.pdf].

Stoltzfus, R.J., M.L. Dreyfuss, H.M. Chwaya, and M. Albonico. 1997. "Hookworm Control as a Strategy to Prevent Iron Deficiency." *Nutrition Review* 55(6):223–32.

Swaminathan, M.S. 2001. "Bridging the Nutritional Divide." *The Little Magazine* 2(6) [www.littlemag.com/hunger/swami.html].

———. 2004. Personal communication with UNESCO Chair of Ecotechnology and President of the M.S. Swaminathan Research Foundation.

Templeton, Scott R., and Sara J. Scherr. 1999. "Effects of Demographic and Related Microeconomic Change on Land Quality in Hills and Mountains of Developing Countries." *World Development* 27(6):903–18.

Tiffen, M., M. Mortimore, and F. Gichuki. 1995. *More People Less Erosion: Environmental Recovery in Kenya.* Chichester, U.K.: Wiley.

Toulmin, C. 1995. "Tracking Through Drought: Options for Destocking and Restocking in Living with Uncertainty." In Ian Schoones, ed., *Living with Uncertainty: New Directions in Pastoral Development in Africa.* London: Intermediate Technology Publications.

UN (United Nations). 2004. "Millennium Development Goals: China's Progress 2003." Assessment by the United Nations Country Team in China, Office of the United Nations Resident Coordinator in China, Beijing.

UN ACC/SCN (United Nations Administrative Committee on Coordination/Sub-Committee on Nutrition). 1993. *Second Report on the World Nutrition Situation.* Volume II: Country Trends, Methods, and Statistics. Geneva.

———. 1994a. "Controlling Vitamin A Deficiency." Nutrition Policy Discussion Paper 14. Geneva.

———. 1994b. "Update on the Nutrition Situation." Geneva.

———. 2000. *Fourth Report on the World Nutrition Situation: Nutrition Throughout the Life Cycle.* Geneva.

UNDESA (United Nations Department of Economic and Social Affairs). 2004. "Progress towards the Millennium Development Goals, 1990–2004." Working Paper. Statistics Division. New York.

UNDP (United Nations Development Programme). 2003. *Human Development Report 2003. Millennium Development Goals: A Compact among Nations to End Human Poverty.* New York.

———. 2004a. "Drylands Development Centre." [Retrieved on November 29, 2004 from www.undp.org/drylands/].

———. 2004b. "What Is Capacity 21?" [Retrieved on December 1, 2004 from www.undp.org/seed/cap21/whatis.html].

UNDP (United Nations Development Programme) Office to Combat Desertification and Drought and WRI (World Resources Institute). 1997. "Aridity Zones and Drylands Populations." Nairobi.

UNICEF (United Nations Children's Fund). 1990. "Strategy for Improved Nutrition of Children and Women in Developing Countries." New York.

———. 2001. *Progress since the World Summit for Children: A Statistical Review.* New York.

———. 2002. *State of the World's Children 2002.* New York.
———. 2003a. *Orphans and Other Children Affected by HIV/AIDS.* New York.
———. 2003b. *State of the World's Children 2003.* New York.
———. 2004a. *State of the World's Children 2004.* New York.
———. 2004b. MICS (Multiple Indicator Cluster Survey). Data for various years. [www.childinfo.org/MICS2/MICSDataSet.htm].
UNICEF (United Nations Children's Fund) and WHO (World Health Organization). "2003 Global Strategy for Infant and Young Child Feeding." Geneva.
Unilever. 2003. "Health Institute Symposium." April 21–22, Vlaardingen, Netherlands.
United Nations General Assembly. 2000. "United Nations Millennium Declaration." New York.
UN Millennium Project. 2003a. "Background paper for *Report of the Task Force on Water and Sanitation.*" New York.
———. 2003b. "Background paper for *Report of the Task Force on Trade.*" New York.
———. 2003c. Field Visit to Malawi. Task Force on Hunger. New York.
———. 2003d. "Promises to Keep: Achieving Gender Equality and the Empowerment of Women." Background paper for *Taking Action: Achieving Gender Equality and Empowering Women.* Task Force on Education and Gender Equality. New York.
———. 2004. "Millennium Development Goals Needs Assessment: Background Paper to 'Ending Africa's Poverty Trap.'" Working paper. New York.
———. 2005a. *Innovation: Applying Knowledge in Development.* Report of the Task Force on Science, Technology, and Innovation. New York.
———. 2005b. *Who's Got the Power? Transforming Health Systems for Women and Children.* Report of the Task Force on Child Health and Maternal Health. New York.
———. 2005c. *Investing in Development: A Practical Plan to Achieve the Millennium Development Goals.* New York.
UN Population Division. 2000. *World Population Prospects: 2000 Revision.* New York.
———. 2002. "World Population Prospects: The 2002 Revision" database. [http://esa.un.org/unpp].
UN SCN (United Nations Standing Committee on Nutrition). 2004. *5th Report on the World Nutrition Situation: Nutrition for Improved Development Outcomes.* Geneva.
USAID (United States Agency for International Development). 2003. "Ethiopia–Drought. Fact Sheet #17. (FY 2003)." Bureau for Democracy, Conflict, and Humanitarian Assistance, Office of U.S. Foreign Disaster Assistance, Washington, D.C.
——— 2004. "Ethiopia: Complex Health/Food Insecurity Emergency Situation Report #1 (FY 2004)." Washington, D.C.
USAID (United States Agency for International Development) and MOST (The MOST Project). 2003. "Food for Work." Part II: Module 2 of *Food for Peace, Commodities Reference Guide.* [www.usaid.gov/our_work/humanitarian_assistance/ffp/crg/module2.html].
USAID (United States Agency for International Development) and WRI (World Resources Institute). 2002. *Nature, Wealth, and Power: Emerging Best Practice for Revitalizing Rural Africa.* Washington, D.C.
Vedeld, Paul, Arild Angelsen, Espen Sjaastad, and Gertrude Kobugabe Berg. 2004. "Counting on the Environment: Forest Incomes and the Rural Poor." Environmental Economics Paper 98. World Bank, Washington, D.C.
Vepa, S.S., L.R. Anneboina, and R. Manghnani. 2004. "China's Fight against Hunger and Poverty: Lessons for Asia." Background paper for the Report of the Task Force on Hunger. M. S. Swaminathan Research Foundation, Chennai, India.
Verweel, G., A.M. van Rossum, N.G. Hartwig, T.F. Wolfs, H.J. Scherpbier, and R. de Groot. 2002. "Treatment with Highly Active Antiretroviral Therapy in Human

Immunodeficiency Virus Type-1 Infected Children Is Associated with a Sustained Effect on Growth." *Pediatrics* 109(2):E25.

Villamor, E., R. Mbise, D. Spiegelman, E. Hertzmark, M. Fataki, K.E. Peterson, G. Ndossi, and W.W. Fawzi. 2002. "Vitamin A Supplements Ameliorate the Adverse Effect of HIV-1, Malaria, and Diarrhoeal Infections on Child Growth." *Pediatrics* 109(1):6.

Webb, P. 1998. "Isolating Hunger: Reaching People in Need Beyond the Mainstream." In *World Food Programme, Time for Change: Food Aid and Development.* Rome.

———. 2005. "Famine." In Griffiths, M., ed., *Encyclopedia of International Relations and Global Politics.* London: Routledge.

Webb, P., and A. Harinarayan. 1999. "A Measure of Uncertainty: The Nature of Vulnerability and Its Relationship to Malnutrition." *Disasters* 23(4):292–305.

Webb, P., and B. Rogers. 2003. *Putting the "In" Back into Food Insecurity.* Occasional Paper 1. United States Agency for International Development, Office of Food for Peace, Washington, D.C.

WFP (World Food Programme). 2001a. "School Feeding Works: An Annotated Biography." Rome.

———. 2001b. "Checklist for Meeting the WFP Commitments to Women, 1996–2001." [Retrieved on December 1, 2004 from www.wfp.org/operations/vam/docs/wfp_gender_checklist.htm].

———. 2002. "VAM (Vulnerability Analysis & Mapping) Standard Analytical Framework Guideline: Role and Objectives of VAM Activities to Support WFP Food-Oriented Interventions." Rome.

———. 2004a. "Flooding Fails to Drown Hope." Newsroom. Rome

———. 2004b. *Global School Feeding Report 2004.* Rome.

———. 2004c. "School Feeding Programs: Why They Should Be Scaled Up Now." Rome.

White, T.A., and A. Martin. 2002. *Who Owns the World's Forests?* Washington, D.C.: Forest Trends.

White, Andy, and Alejandra Martin, and Lynn Ellsworth. 2003. *Strategies for Strengthening Community Property Rights over Forests: Lessons and Opportunities for Practitioners.* Washington, D.C.: Forest Trends.

Wood, S., K. Sebastian, and S.J. Scherr. 2000. *Agroecosystems: Pilot Analysis of Global Ecosystems.* Washington, D.C.: International Food Policy Research Institute and World Resources Institute.

World Commission on Environment and Development. 1987. *Our Common Future.* ["The Brundtland Report"]. Oxford, U.K.: Oxford University Press.

World Bank. 2002. *World Development Report 2003: Sustainable Development in a Dynamic World: Transforming Institutions, Growth, and Quality of Life.* New York: Oxford University Press.

World Health Organization. 1997. *Health And Environment In Sustainable Development—Five Years After The Earth Summit.* Geneva.

———. 2001. "Expert Consultation on the Optimal Duration of Exclusive Breastfeeding." Geneva.

———. 2002. "Prevention and Control of Schistosomiasis and Soil-Transmitted Helminthiasis." Report of a WHO Expert Committee. Technical Report Series 912. Geneva.

———. 2003a. "Nutrient Requirements for People Living with HIV/AIDS: Report of a Technical Consultation." Geneva.

———. 2003b. "WHO Global Database on Child Growth and Malnutrition." Geneva.

Zeller, M., and R. L. Meyer. 2002. "The Triangle of Microfinance: Financial Sustainability, Outreach, and Impact." Food Policy Statement 40. International Food Policy Research Institute, Washington, D.C.

Ziegler, Jean. 2002 "Report of the Special Rapporteur of the Commission on Human Rights on the Right to Food." Fifty-seventh Session of the United Nations General Assembly, New York.

DATE DUE

APR 1 3 2009			
JAN 3 1 2010			